SQUARE EYES

SQUARE EYES

Children, Screen Time and Fun

EMILY BOOKER

Square Eyes: Children, Screen Time and Fun

© Copyright 2018 Emily Booker
All rights reserved. Apart from any uses permitted by Australia's Copyright Act 1968, no part of this book may be reproduced by any process without prior written permission from the copyright owners. Inquiries should be directed to the publisher.

Monash University Publishing
Matheson Library and Information Services Building
40 Exhibition Walk
Monash University
Clayton, Victoria 3800, Australia
www.publishing.monash.edu

Monash University Publishing brings to the world publications which advance the best traditions of humane and enlightened thought.

Monash University Publishing titles pass through a rigorous process of independent peer review.

www.publishing.monash.edu/books/se-9781925523584.html

ISBN: 9781925523584 (paperback)
ISBN: 9781925523591 (pdf)
ISBN: 9781925523607 (epub)

Series: Cultural Studies

Design: Les Thomas

Cover image: courtesy Shutterstock

A catalogue record for this book is available from the National Library of Australia

Printed in Australia by Griffin Press an Accredited ISO AS/NZS 14001:2004 Environmental Management System printer.

The paper this book is printed on is certified against the Forest Stewardship Council ® Standards. Griffin Press holds FSC chain of custody certification SGS-COC-005088. FSC promotes environmentally responsible, socially beneficial and economically viable management of the world's forests.

CONTENTS

Preface and Acknowledgments ix

Introduction xiii

1 Television Terrors: Psychopaths, Couch Potatoes and Panics 1
   Unpopular 'Popular' Culture 3
   Moral Panics 9
   The Fear of TV Violence 14
   Couch Potatoes 26
   Creativity and Imagination: Reading versus Television 33

2 Innocence or Ignorance? How We Safeguard Children
   in Our Own Interest.. 43
   Education and Work versus Pleasure................................. 50
   The Threat of Popular Culture – and Bad Taste 55
   Education and Popular Culture 58
   Parents as Police and Adult Secrets 65
   Powerful 'Myths' and the Sexualisation of the Child 72
   Beyond the Myths 75
   Play – Is It Fun? 80

3 Let's Just Have Fun: Entertainment and Why It Matters 93
   Where is Fun in the Picture? 96
   Fandom and Its Pleasures 108
   'It's fun and interesting': Children Negotiating the
   Negative Public Discourses..111

	'Do you think television is good?'	118
	Favourites: 'What do you like about these programs?'	121
	Children's Views about Television Being Bad for You	125
4	'The funnest thing in the world'	135
	Fun with TV: A Physical and Imaginative Experience	137
	Joining a Crowd, and Solitary Pleasures, around Television	150
	The Fun of Sharing: TV in Children's Social and Cultural Lives	159
	Sharing Talk with Friends: Competitive Critics or Partners in Pleasure?	164
	Television, Friends and Games	177
	Talking about TV to Adults	182
5	Sharing Pleasure, Humour and the 'Feel' of Utopia	195
	Parents and Children: Conspiring for Pleasure	197
	Humour	218
	Passing the Time with Television	233
	'Learning' from Television	237
	The 'Feel' of Utopia	249
Conclusion		267
Appendix		277
Bibliography		291
Index		305

CONTENTS

Drawings

Drawing 1: 10-year-old girl's drawing of a room centred on the television 156

Drawing 2: 7-year-old girl's front and back covers 171

Drawing 3: 8-year-old girl's front and back covers 172

Drawing 4: 10-year-old girl's cover sheet for story about Ja'mie ... 241

Drawing 5: 8-year-old boy's drawing based on *Adventure Time* 254

Drawing 6: 8-year-old boy's picture with The Barn 259

Stories

Story 1: 10-year-old boy's story of the underworld 148

Story 2: 10-year-old girl's story about Ja'mie 242

Story 3: 8-year-old boy's story of television sucking in viewer 250

To Richard and Jane

PREFACE AND ACKNOWLEDGMENTS

In the day of the anxious child and the even more anxious 'helicopter' parent wouldn't it be wonderful to be able to offer children a secret place to goof off – one that was safe and easily reachable? A place they could laugh, relax and imagine – without necessarily improving their minds, their bodies or their morals?

Well, this place is right here – literally in front of our eyes – on the screen nearest to you.

Television, according to children themselves, is 'the funnest thing in the world'; it presents an opportunity to 'have a little world of monsters or anything'. It is a rich and special place to explore relationships, to dream, to laugh at crass and revolting slapstick or simply to sit quietly and fill in spare and idle moments. And now it is available on a range of screens at any time of the day.

But that pleasure – and particularly that apparent idleness – is anathema to the adults who supervise children's lives. The picture of a child flopped in front of a screen seems to drive adult minders to distraction.

Just look at the headlines and you'll get the picture. *The New York Post* declared in March 2017 that 'Kids TV shows push cultural limits – but they're damaging kids' (Riley 2017), while at home *The Australian Financial Review* offers the advice: 'Kids addicted to screens? Here's how to unplug them' (Maher 2016). No-one is saying how delightful it is that our young ones are sitting quietly in front of their favourite TV show, on whatever screen they chose, happily absorbed in their own 'little world of monsters' or whatever.

The curious thing about the panicked headlines and the articles full of advice to the fearful and guilt-ridden parent is that the voices of children are absent. The news largely presents the view of experts, who are always adults, telling parents how to regulate, control and police their children. Television is always bad.

This book looks at television through children's own eyes – by listening to what they say about it. I have some fascinating comments, drawings and stories from children about their take on television. Talking to me for my PhD research, 'fun' and 'funny' were the words they used most often to describe TV. I explore what they say about why it is so much fun, and I look also at why we feel compelled to judge such fun so harshly.

This approach to children's engagement with television is controversial, as I have found from many dinner table conversations with fellow parents and adults. Many of them feel that television at best is a surrogate babysitter, or might perhaps be acceptable if the child watches something 'educational'. But having a laugh at some mindless cartoon or enjoying 'crap' American television is almost universally condemned: much better that the child should fill her free hours with music lessons, playing sport or reading a book.

So how have we come to this place – where we feel compelled to regulate our children's lives for their own good and against their own pleasures? How has the demon screen come to represent such a threat to a successfully ordered existence for our young ones?

My book explores this tension but from an entirely different angle to that shared widely in the media. Rather than a focus on the dangers of the screens that are 'taking over' our children's lives, it looks at the

PREFACE AND ACKNOWLEDGMENTS

'fun' these screens offer children – and how this is both an important and a valuable part of their lives.

***

The value of television to children, and indeed of television to all of us, has been discussed by many researchers and scholars in a number of academic fields including cultural studies. I am indebted to many of these writers for their extensive and imaginative insights: in particular, David Buckingham, John Hartley and Patricia Palmer. Alan McKee generously shared his ideas with me on the value of fun for its own sake – confirming what was evident from my interviews with the children in my research. Richard Dyer's and Terence Hawkes's insights into entertainment were invaluable also to my research. And I would like to thank Fiona Giles, Sue Turnbull and Rebekah Willett for their thoughtful and thought-provoking comments on my thesis. A particular thanks to Sue for the title of this book!

Above all I would like to thank Catharine Lumby for her inspiring guidance and advice throughout the writing of the doctoral thesis on which this book is based. I am grateful too for the support of the Media, Music, Communication and Cultural Studies Department at Macquarie University and the University's award to me of an Australian Postgraduate Award scholarship. Thanks are due also to Nathan Hollier and Monash University Publishing for guiding the publication of this book.

Of course the book wouldn't exist without the ideas, drawings and stories of the children who took part in my research and I am truly indebted to them, in particular for sharing their enthusiasm and delight in a wide range of TV shows.

Finally, thanks to my TV sofa-buddies, my husband Richard Spencer and my daughter Jane, for hours of shared pleasure in front of the screen.

INTRODUCTION

My daughter was a *Teletubbies* baby. Born six months after the launch in March 1997 of the British preschool children's television series, she watched many episodes during her first and second years of life. She had her own favourite bits: the smiling baby face in the middle of the sun (an image which I myself found slightly creepy); the magical carousel that arrived spinning from the sky and unloaded a dancing bear; and the short segments that featured real children involved in various activities. Another program that captivated her attention was a live action Australian–Chinese production called *Magic Mountain* that used full-body animal puppets. In this program it was the musical introduction over the opening credits that most delighted her; she would immediately interrupt anything she was doing when she heard the music start, run to the television and stand fixed to the floor immediately in front of the screen jigging along to the tune.

My reactions to her fascination with these scenes on the television were mixed. I couldn't help smiling at her obvious delight and I was also grateful for the diversion, for something that would give me a break from having to respond to her needs; I welcomed the television's role as a 'babysitter'. But even though I had myself worked in television, as a current affairs reporter and producer, and was an advocate of its social value, I still felt guilty. Should my toddler be watching television at such a young age? At this point I would ring a friend of mine who also worked in the television industry and had a child the same age, and we would both say to each other, 'Thank God for *Teletubbies*'. Sharing the guilt helped to assuage it.

But why didn't we share the joy and delight that our children displayed? We were condoning each other's parenting, acknowledging that we were taking advantage of a dubious babysitter, admitting to guilty pleasures. We were certainly not up to seeing anything positive in our babies' fascination with the screen beyond allowing us a few moments to ourselves. This had, we suspected, been stolen at the expense of corrupting our tender-aged children. If our toddlers had been outside playing in the 'fresh air', speaking words precociously or giggling with delight at something 'real', we would have happily celebrated this behaviour. But we weren't about to admit that our children were excited about television. Being happy about our children watching the 'idiot box' was not something we could admit to. We were as much trapped in the dominant negative discourse around children and television as other parents.

So even though I had seen utter delight on my child's face as she watched her favourite shows, I felt that I had to make sure that she would get something more than pleasure out of the screen. I did what many parents do and sought out the educational; I turned to *Sesame Street*. Despite being one of the most popular and widely-viewed children's television series ever produced, my daughter unfortunately did not like it. And despite my persistence, she never liked it. The inanely grinning baby inside the sun on *Teletubbies* did it for her every time.

Looking back on my own reactions and experiences I can see that I too was caught up in the prevailing view of television as a largely negative, and ubiquitous, influence on children's lives. Television was okay if you were desperate for some time to yourself, or if you could

INTRODUCTION

get your child to watch the 'quality' programs that might teach them something. But there was never any suggestion of being guided by your child's own choices, especially when such choices were based simply on what they enjoyed.

Decades of public debate and academic research appear to have strengthened this negative perception of children and television and contributed to the ways parents view their children's engagement with it. Many of the questions that are debated in the public and the academic spheres ask why television is bad for children, and then consider the ways in which we can mitigate its harm. Even when the question is about what 'good' television can deliver, the focus is on how can we take advantage of the child's engagement to educate them, stimulate their imagination, develop their understanding of the world: to 'do' anything except allow them simply to enjoy the fun of it. It seems that rarely do we ask what it is that delights children and attempt to appreciate and understand this aspect of their TV watching, let alone celebrate it. Yet this delight in the fun and entertainment that television provides appears to be at the core of why children watch it. From an early age, they have quite particular likes and dislikes, and they seek to watch their own favourites: not the ones provided by anxious parents.

If you ask children themselves about their favourite television programs, and you manage to convince them that you are really interested in their own views and are not going to judge their responses, they do share their excitement and delight. I have found that it can be quite a conversation-starter with children, even those who are shy, taciturn or simply uninterested in talking to adults. This anecdotal evidence of their pleasure in favourite shows is also supported by existing research with children, as I show in this book. It was certainly apparent in my own research and interviews with children.

Listening more carefully to children themselves led me to believe that the public discourse focuses largely on the wrong questions and that this focus in turn produces an intangible but nevertheless widespread anxiety among parents and others involved in the care of children. Instead of considering the television as a threat, trying to understand it from the child's point of view seemed to me a more fruitful way of understanding its place in our lives. What if we were to ask children themselves to explain, talk about, and share what it is that they enjoy about television? Why and how do they find it fun? Wouldn't this information provide us with greater insight into the role television plays in their lives? There is little doubt that parents do see the fun and joy that television provides their children. But why is it that we don't allow ourselves to celebrate this aspect of children's engagement with the screen?

At this point the critic might ask why it matters that we should seek answers to such a question. Surely it is clear that children are simply addicted to the ubiquitous screens. Surely it is only important to make certain they don't watch too much and that, if they must watch it at all, they watch the 'right' kind of programs. But this seems to me to be coming at the question from the wrong angle. It denies the value of fun and entertainment in children's lives and fails to recognise the value of a leisure pursuit that makes them, from their own accounts, happy. As one 9-year-old girl said in my research about why she enjoyed her favourite programs, 'they are funny and make you feel good'.

In considering these questions I have looked at the academic research conducted over the past couple of decades in the field of children

INTRODUCTION

and television. In many of these studies there has been considerable research into what children themselves say about television which reveals the pleasure they get out of the medium. And I have also drawn on academic research into the nature and value of entertainment. Although this research does not focus particularly on children, the insights of these writers showed the significance and value of entertainment to the lives of not only children but also adults.

In writing this book I tried to get at what it is that children are saying themselves about what they like and enjoy about television – and what this means to them. In doing so, I had to try to distance myself from the concerns of a guilty parent and from a culture that is nervous about children's uninhibited pleasure in the 'wrong' things. I also found that I had to distance myself from judgments of taste. I thought back to my own reaction to my daughter's fascination with *Teletubbies*. I had to get over that unsettling question: How could my child really enjoy that creepy image of a baby's disembodied head inside a sun? I realised that her view of the program was completely different to mine. She liked the freaky baby-face-sun. I, on the other hand, liked the rolling green grass of the hills – which appeared to stimulate in me a mild nostalgia for the never-never land of childhood.

I realised that trying to keep an open mind about different responses to television shows was essential in order to try to understand the endless variety of ways children enjoy television. This questioning approach led me one day recently to ask my 19-year-old daughter why she had never liked *Sesame Street*. I had never thought to ask her before and I guess in part I didn't really expect her to be able to remember her reactions or to be able to articulate the reasons for her disinterest so long ago. So I was quite surprised when she responded immediately with: 'The puppets were ugly'. It was the aesthetics of the show she hated! That reason for a preschooler's dislike of a television show like *Sesame Street* would never have entered my mind. It was a clear reminder of the importance of trying to enable children themselves to share their own feelings about TV – not to prejudge their reactions – and to believe that they are capable of articulating their own likes and dislikes. Hopefully this is what I have done in this book.

Chapter 1

TELEVISION TERRORS: PSYCHOPATHS, COUCH POTATOES AND PANICS

It's a common theme today: screens are threatening our children's lives and wellbeing. The mantra is the same as that directed against television from its early days. The damaging 'effects' of television on the young, particularly its capacity to make children violent, have been a common thread of complaint against the 'idiot box'. The curious part of this discussion, both in the last century and today, is that it focuses on the screen itself – whether it's a television, a computer, a tablet or a smartphone – as though this screen were some kind of disembodied threat to our children's wellbeing.

In the 1970s and 1980s, academics and authors such as George Gerbner (1988) and Marie Winn (1985) condemned television as an hypnotic, potentially evil, device: the title of Winn's famous and widely popular book, *The Plug-in Drug*, captures these fears. The anxieties that swirled around television in the 20th century are today being focused more commonly on the newer screens. News headlines warn us of the danger: 'Screen junkies: kids addicted to technology' (Machell 2017); 'Screen violence changing young brains: researchers' (Browne 2013); 'Too much screen time is harmful for children; what can parents do?' (Barker 2014); 'Kids addicted to screens? Here's how to unplug them' (Maher 2016). This fear appears in part to replace the earlier demonisation of the television screen as an 'idiot box' and a 'boob tube' (Murray 1969, 1), though criticism of TV still remains steady in headlines: 'Children addicted to television at age of two' (Markham 2015).

What is entirely missing from these fearful and panicky headlines, and the public discourse on children and television in general, is a consideration of what the children themselves say about television. We rarely seem to explore the question of what children are actually watching and why, and focus instead on their apparently obsessive addiction to the 'screen'. But if you talk to children themselves – and this is supported by both my own and others' research (Buckingham 1993a; Palmer 1986) – they are watching because they enjoy the *content* and above all they are having fun. It is the content that absorbs their interest and provides them with pleasure. They may look to the prejudiced observer to be hypnotically in thrall to the screen but in fact they are happily and excitedly engrossed in its stories. That this pleasure itself seems also to unsettle us, and has an impact on our reactions to children and television, I will consider in depth in the next two chapters. But first I want to explore the reasons why television has been viewed with such suspicion ever since its arrival in our living rooms last century.

Despite a shift in focus from the threats inherent in television to the dangers of tablet and smartphone screens, parents, teachers and social commentators are still concerned today about television's negative impact. Fears abound that TV viewing makes children fat, stupid and, in the worse cases, violent. The UK's *Independent* declares in a headline that 'Watching lots of TV makes you stupid' (Henderson 2015) while one popular parenting website offers this 'expertise': 'Three reasons why television violence affects kids' (Fonseca 2017). This discourse is reflected in the direction that much academic research takes too: a current scan of 'children and television viewing' in Google Scholar brings up on the first page nine out of 10 items that address television's potential to promote violence or obesity.

These items all address negative 'effects' of television on children. Such a focus is not new either in the media or in academia. The academic tradition of looking for the negative effects of television in particular, and of popular media in general, has a long history (Barker and Petley 2001; Hartley 1999). So does the media discourse on the 'threat' to our children and other vulnerable groups of popular entertainment, television and the screens of the latest technological inventions (Barker and Petley 2001; Hartley 1999, 2008). While arguments on both sides of this debate have been extensively covered elsewhere, I wanted to consider some of the key points that help to explain our preoccupation with television's potential to harm our children.

Unpopular 'Popular' Culture

To understand how the negative effects discourse on television has come to have such a hold on our imaginations, and why it creates such anxiety, it is useful to look at our attitudes to popular culture over the past two centuries. These are dominated in particular by a fear that such culture is a potentially corrupting influence on the weak and the vulnerable members of society. Children are always included in this group. Women and the working classes have also been identified as weak and vulnerable, and therefore corruptible. Importantly these groups are always identified as 'other'; they are in need of protection from the media whereas those in power consider themselves to be immune to such negative effects (Buckingham 2000, 170; Petley 2001). According to Buckingham (1996, 60), this negative view of television has developed into a 'popular mythology'. It is something we believe without question.

Negative attitudes to new forms of media, and to the popular culture that they bring into our societies, go back a long way. The Greek philosopher Plato (1948, 73) warned in *The Republic* that young minds could be corrupted by the poets and by their stories of the exploits of the gods. He warned that the Greek youth must be protected from such pernicious influence: 'We must stop such stories lest they breed in our young men a ready disposition to evil' (Plato 1948, 73). Comics and 'dime novels' were blamed for rising crime and amorality in late 19th century Britain and America (Gauntlett 2005, 5; Murdock 2001, 151) and 'music halls in Victorian Britain … were said to promote lawlessness, immorality and violence' (Gauntlett 2005, 125).

There appears in these attitudes to be a powerful need to explain social ills, to find a cause for such ills, and to attack it. Media effects provide this 'cause' and the fear generated by our perceptions of the threat posed by popular culture has resulted in a 'moral panic firmly rooted in both history and class fears' (Gauntlett 2005, 125). Graham Murdock (2001, 151) notes that this notion of negative effects:

> draws its power from a deep reservoir of social fear and dogma which first formed in the mid-nineteenth century as commentators began to link the social costs of modernity with the proliferation of new forms of popular entertainment.

As Buckingham (2000, 144) points out, this same purpose has continued to be served today. We can blame media violence for a multitude of social ills:

CHAPTER 1

the decline of the family and of organized religion, … the changing nature of literacy and contemporary culture, and … the pace of technological change.

We could add to that the obesity 'epidemic' facing today's children and young people. Despite some evidence that watching television doesn't appear to affect childhood obesity, we continue to blame TV viewing for making our children fat (Sanghavi 2012). Television appears to be a handy scapegoat for our anxieties and fears. But as Buckingham (2001a, 75) goes on to argue, the debate is:

> about other things, many of which have very little to do with the media. It is a debate that involved deep-seated moral and political convictions, and it is rooted in people's unsettling experiences of social change and their genuine fears for the future.

As mentioned above, fears about the negative effects of popular culture are almost always fears about effects on 'other people'. A large part of the focus of the media discourse today is on the negative effects on children and young people but the 'other' has often also included the 'lower' and 'uneducated' classes. Julian Petley (2001, 170) has observed: 'lurking behind these fears about the "corruption of innocent minds" [is] a potent strain of class dislike and fear'. He quotes a study by Geoffrey Pearson (1983, 208) of the history of middle-class disapproval of working-class culture:

> Popular entertainments of all kinds have been blamed for dragging down public morals in a gathering pattern of accusation which remains essentially the same even though it is attached to radically different forms of amusement: pre-modern feasts and festivals; eighteenth-century theatres and bawdy houses; mid-nineteenth-century penny gaffs; … the Hollywood picture palaces between the wars; and then television viewing in our own historical times. Each, in its own time, has been accused of

encouraging a moral debauch; each has been said to encourage imitative crime among the young.

Petley (2001, 171) traces these attitudes towards the working class, drawing on media sources across the last two centuries, to illustrate his argument that the debate about the negative effects of popular culture is largely class-based. It is never the upper and middle classes that will behave badly after watching the latest film, hearing the newest form of 'wild' music, or watching the latest soapie on TV: it is the working classes, and their young.

The same sort of distaste for the lower classes shown in these criticisms of their attraction to popular culture appears to attach itself to popular culture itself (Gauntlett 2005, 129). Popular culture is looked down on by those who believe they have 'superior taste'. Petley (2001, 171) notes that Herbert Gans (1974) 'has argued that dislike of popular culture frequently stems from "a marked disdain for ordinary people and their aesthetic capacities"'. John Hartley (2008, 7) argues persuasively that this view of popular entertainment is driven by a need to 'create' an opposite to the 'highly-valued' elements of culture:

> Media and methods need to be placed at one end of a value hierarchy in order to sustain culturally preferred values at the other. Popular entertainment is easily consigned to the opposite pole from truth-seeking philosophy in a print-literate, science-based intellectual universe.

In this scheme, books, science and 'high art' are at the top of the pole; popular television is at the bottom.

The weight of these negative views of popular culture according to Hartley (1999, 65) had the effect of predetermining the view that would be taken of television – even before it actually appeared:

CHAPTER 1

> This powerful rhetoric of denunciation was in place, complete with a full repertoire of concepts, theories, even phrases, ready to be applied to television before it was invented, since the small screen was simply assumed to be an extension (perhaps even more pernicious) of previously despised popular media from newspapers to Hollywood … It follows that the critical onslaught which television has faced throughout its existence has its roots not in the medium itself, but in a pre-existing discourse of anxiety about popularization and modernity; a quite straightforward fear of and hostility to the democratization of taste.

Interestingly, this hostility to taste – more explicitly the 'bad' taste of the socially and intellectually inferior (Davies, Buckingham and Kelley 2000) – manifests itself today in the disparagement of children's taste as I explore in the next chapter.

It seems that from the moment television arrived in our living rooms, we already knew what to fear; this latest provider of popular culture was bound to have a damaging effect on the 'masses' and on our vulnerable children. Not only was this reflected in media coverage of the day (Murdock 2001) and in the advice of 1950s parenting manuals (Spigel 1998, 122) (Jenkins 1998b; Spigel 1998; Wolfenstein 1998), it informed the focus of academic research: 'The dominant research tradition adopted the definition of the "problem" already established in popular and political commentary' (Murdock 2001, 152). This is a pattern that has continued through to today. Buckingham (1993a, 10) argues that:

> the deep-seated assumptions and anxieties which underlie much of the public debate about children and television have largely set the agenda for academic research. What 'the public' wants … is proof of the negative effects of television, and this is largely what researchers have sought to provide.

As is apparent from these comments, a number of scholars have criticised the extensive academic body of broadly labelled 'media effects' research. It is clearly a hotly debated field. Its supporters of course believe that their findings make a significant contribution to the study of television, and they have defended their approach (Bushman and Anderson 2001; Comstock and Scharrer 2007; Gentile 2003; Gerbner 1988; Gerbner et al. 1969). Both sides of the debate believe television is a major part of our lives and needs to be understood; but the approaches to understanding its influence are significantly different. In this book I argue that the focus of the effects tradition is limiting and its approaches do not allow for a meaningful investigation of the diverse and complex ways in which viewers, including children, engage with the medium. As Buckingham (1996, 8) states: 'the narrow concern with imitative behavioural effects ... has proven to be profoundly unproductive ... it seeks for simplistic explanations for extremely complex phenomena'. Elsewhere Buckingham (1998b, 42-3) observes that:

> Both in research and in public debate, the argument about the effects of television has repeatedly come down to a set of either/or choices: either television is bad for children, or it is good for them. Yet it is precisely these narrow, either/or choices that we need to move beyond.

I too believe the media effects tradition does not have the capacity to investigate in a meaningful way the role of pleasure in children's media consumption and I would suggest that the dominant effects discourse has in fact stymied the development of a comprehensive body of research into what television means to them and how it potentially enhances their lives. It has also fed a public debate that encourages parents to feel concern and guilt over their children's

CHAPTER 1

enjoyment of television. And it has fuelled the moral panics that regularly crop up on the media, directed against television and other popular media.

Moral Panics

The moral panics aroused by fear of the effects of the media are particularly apparent in news coverage of tragic, often aberrant violence. Seeking a cause for the murder of 2-year-old James Bulger by two 10-year-old boys in February 1993 in Liverpool, England, it wasn't long before the media turned to the screen for a cause: watching the slasher horror film *Child's Play 3* must have turned the boys into monstrous murderers (Buckingham 1996, 22-3). Martin Barker (2001, 28) points out that even though 'there was not a scrap of evidence that the boys had watched the film', none of the media, nor the anti-media campaigners who touted the story, ever retracted their statements or admitted they were wrong. In Australia, when Martin Bryant shot dead 35 people at Port Arthur in Tasmania in April 1996, 'within days, media speculation about Bryant's motives began to include references to his taste for violent videos' (Turnbull 2001, 117). When academic researcher Sue Turnbull (2001, 118) spoke to the forensic psychiatrist who had interviewed Bryant, she discovered that in fact Bryant had three copies of *The Sound of Music* in his collection and that 'he had cited Disney's *The Lion King* as his favourite film'. David Buckingham (1996, 60) argues that cases such as James Bulger, where the media 'causes' of the tragedy are debated not only in the media 'but also in everyday discussion', come to form:

> a 'popular mythology' of media effects. It is this mythology, perhaps to a greater extent than the more equivocal evidence provided by academic research, that informs the dominant

discourses about media effects, and hence the dominant arguments for regulating and intervening in children's viewing.

In Barthes's notion of a myth, this belief in negative media effects has come to be understood largely as 'common sense' (Barthes 1973). As Barker (2001, 29) observes:

> In the Bulger case, it seemed to 'make sense' to explain their behaviour by saying they had been 'corrupted' by watching videos – and never mind that they hadn't actually watched them at all. They could have, might have; it could all make sense if they had.

What is interesting in the media debates about the dangerous effects of screen violence, that escalate into moral panics, is that children's voices are seldom, if ever, included. We don't really want to know whether the young boys in the Bulger case had actually watched violent videos. This is perhaps the nature of such moral panics over children and the media; they are sites – rather than individual human beings – where the protectors of the innocent fight over the best ways to keep them safe.

Kenneth Thompson's (1998, 8) broad definition of the historical representation of moral panics illustrates this point:

> Implicit in the use of the two words 'moral panic' is the suggestion that the threat is to something held sacred by or fundamental to the society. The reason for calling it a moral panic is precisely to indicate that the perceived threat is not to something mundane…but a threat to the social order itself or an idealised (ideological) conception of some part of it. The threat and its perpetrators are regarded as evil 'folk devils' (S. Cohen 1972), and excite strong feelings of righteousness … The response to such threats is likely to be a demand for greater social regulation or control.

CHAPTER 1

Thompson's description here suggests a possible reason for the frequent public calls to control children's television viewing. Allowing their corruption by the evil 'folk devil' of television might possibly unleash a fundamental threat to society. This is surely what happened to the young murderers of James Bulger.

Joanne Faulkner's (2011) account of the way in which our culture holds sacred the notion of the 'innocence' of childhood would certainly indicate that perceived threats to children provide a fertile ground for moral panics. The drive to protect this innocence fuels the panic, but more dangerously, Faulkner argues, it has come to threaten the wellbeing of our real children. 'Real' children have dangerous tendencies lurking below the surface and these need to be carefully handled. Because of this, we need even more assiduously to guard the 'innocence of childhood', and, as Faulkner (2011. 67) contends, this has resulted in 'a political prison for children … children … must be controlled and carefully handled, lest humanity lose its way'.

There appears to be no place for the voice of real, individual children within the debates generated by their 'sacred' place in our culture. The moral panics that circulate around the threats to childhood innocence posed by the media are singularly lacking in the voices of real children. Charles Krinsky (2008, 1) writes that it is adults who participate in the debates generated by moral panic: 'members of the media, politicians, clergy, "experts", and activists unite to do battle with an exaggerated or imagined social menace'.

Researchers including Gauntlett (2005), Murdock (2001) and Barker (2001) have traced the history of moral panics connected in particular with new communication technologies and popular entertainment. These scholars argue that moral panics crop up around new communication technologies in every era and then fade as the next threat emerges; the implication from this argument is that these fears are therefore largely unfounded and present no basis for real concern. The effects researchers refute this position (Bushman and Anderson 2001) and continue to search for evidence of direct effects, in particular, of violence on the behaviour of children (Warburton and Braunstein 2012). But these direct effects appear particularly hard to pin down as I discuss later in this chapter.

The debates generated by these panics are often polarised with the effects researchers on one side and the cultural studies researchers on the other (Kline 2005). Recently scholars have criticised this dynamic and called for a different approach to both the arguments and to the view taken by scholars, such as those mentioned above, to moral panics themselves (Buckingham and Jensen 2012; Lumby and Funnell 2011).

Stephen Kline (2005) has argued that we should not dismiss the underlying concerns about television's influence in our haste to condemn the hyperbole of the moral panic. He suggests these panics at least serve to bring an important issue into the public sphere for discussion (2005, 94).

Buckingham and Jensen (2012) too have criticised the polarisation of the debates about children and the media that emerges from the moral panics. They argue that:

> merely rejecting disproportionate and alarmist claims about the harmful influence of the media leaves us trapped in a tiresome and binary debate about whether media are good or bad for children. (2012, 423)

Buckingham and Jensen (2012, 426-7) advocate an approach that goes further than Kline and seeks not just to avoid 'pathologizing' the arguments of the effects theorists but aims to promote a more useful

CHAPTER 1

discussion. This is an argument put forward by Lumby and Funnell (2011, 279) who explore the possibility of how we can 'use our longstanding critical analyses of historical and current moral panics to reframe contemporary media discourses, public perceptions, and political and public policy responses'.

Enabling the views of children to enter the largely negative public debates over children and the media could provide just such benefits as are suggested by these researchers. The diversity of the picture that emerges from research with children might plausibly be of enough interest in its novelty to be taken up by the media. Perhaps it is worth looking for 'an opportunity for finding a shared language at moments when there is an intense media and community focus on a controversial subject' (Lumby and Funnell 2011, 282) and present an alternative view.

Certainly in my research and that of other researchers who have sought the views on television of children themselves (Buckingham 1993a, 1996, 2000; Gauntlett 2007; Götz et al. 2005), the picture of children's engagement with television is far richer and more diverse than the thin sketch drawn in the media discourse of the moral panic. In fact, it is not easy to recognise the pictures created by these different perspectives as being on the same topic.

Because the effects discourse has long dominated the way we talk about children and television, I would argue that it has hindered us from fully exploring the diverse ways that children actually enjoy and get pleasure from watching television. This aspect of their viewing has certainly largely failed to be covered in the media, and is not something that parents are likely to celebrate when asked about their children's viewing habits. More immediate reactions from parents focus on discussions of how much television should be allowed and what type of programs should be permitted (Australian Communications and Media Authority 2015b, 12-13). And of course, if television makes you fat, stupid and violent, you would want to regulate it.

There is another element of TV viewing that seems also to disconcert parents – the fact that children might actually be enjoying it. One news article was particularly concerned at the risk posed by the popularity of the animated cartoon *Peppa Pig* and feared 'The wildly popular little brat leading our kids astray' (Campbell 2013a). When 'pleasure' is raised in the public discourse on media effects it is tainted with the negative and is often perceived as having a questionable moral base. The very suggestion that killers such as Martin Bryant, and Robert Thompson and Jon Venables (Bulger's murderers), supposedly found violent videos 'pleasurable' implies the suspect nature of such enjoyment of popular media. This perception of pleasure as undesirable and even dangerous is a powerful undercurrent in our western notion of childhood. As I discuss in the next chapter, the drive to maintain the vulnerable innocence of the child in the face of corruption from both adult secrets and the child's own unruly passions has developed steadily over the past two hundred years. But first I would like to consider further the impact of the effects debate on our attitudes to children's TV viewing.

The Fear of TV Violence

Hartley (1999, 132) has characterised the two sides of the debate over the effects of television in a way that I find useful in understanding why we have been reluctant to acknowledge the pleasure children get from television. He has separated different approaches to the study of television into two schools of thought – 'desire' and 'fear' – arguing

CHAPTER 1

that 'the most familiar to the public is the "fear" school'. The 'fear' school includes:

> all those from behavioural psychologists to moral entrepreneurs ('clean-up-TV' campaigners) who believe that television affects its audiences for the worse. They generate the rhetoric of sex, violence and bad language that has heckled television since it started. (1999, 132-3)

A large body of research suggests that this 'fear' school has driven the attitude to children and television which prevails in the public discourse today and has resulted in the extensive academic body of research that investigates television's negative effects. I would argue too that this dominance of the 'fear' tradition has inhibited the development of a richer and deeper picture of children's imaginative and pleasurable engagement with the medium, both in the public discourse and in the academic research tradition. As Buckingham (1996, 7) has pointed out, there has been 'little research on the emotional dimensions of children's relationship with television'.

To get an idea of what has informed this 'fear' discourse around children and television, I think it is useful to look at three particular areas in the media effects tradition. The first and most extensive of these areas is the research conducted into the effects of television violence on the audience, and its potential to produce aggressive behaviour in individuals, particularly children. The other two areas that I would like to consider are the research that presents television viewers as undiscerning and indiscriminate (as passive 'couch potatoes') and the studies that argue that watching television stifles creativity and imagination, particularly in children.

The search for evidence of the negative effects of television dominated research in the 1950s in the United States in the 'mass communication' tradition that coincided with television's ascendancy (Hartley 1999, 131). Among the influential researchers in this tradition were Hilda Himmelweit (1958) and George Gerbner (1988) and it is a tradition that continues today; some of the latest research is turning to neuroscience to search for the potentially damaging 'effects' on children's brains, and thus on their behaviour, of television and other screens (Anderson et al. 2006; Carnagey, Anderson and Bartholow 2007; Warburton and Braunstein 2012). The 1950s tradition was informed by the discipline of psychology, and, according to one of its critics, 'was interested not in television but in finding scientific ways to describe observable behaviour in individuals, and in finding ways of doing replicable scientific experiments using "subjects" from rats to students' (Hartley 1999, 131). Buckingham (1993a, 10-11) argues that this tradition has continued through the remainder of the century and has sought to deliver 'proof of the negative effects of television … Using behaviourist models researchers have attempted to identify the various ways in which a violent stimulus would produce an aggressive response'.

The voluminous results of this research have been both widely commended and soundly criticised. But the findings continue to be disputed, and the value of this approach to research into children and television has also been questioned because of its limited capacity to illuminate the complexity of audience engagement with television (Buckingham 1993a; Gauntlett 2005; Hartley 2008; Hodge and Tripp 1986). One particular criticism focuses on the effects tradition's reliance on the method of content analysis in interpreting the effects of screen violence on the audience. Content analysis seeks to objectively itemise and count scenes of violence in films and television programs and quote this as evidence of its capacity to inflict harm on the viewer. It is a method that has been criticised by many working in the media and cultural studies framework for failing to take account of the subjective and diverse reactions of widely different audiences. It assumes that:

> effects can simply be 'read off' from the analysis of content … statistical studies of the representation of particular social groups on television, for example, are often implicitly taken as evidence of its influence on children's beliefs about those groups. (Buckingham 1998a, 135-6)

As Buckingham (1993a, 12) argues, it also fails to:

> address the meaning of violence, both on television and in everyday life … By isolating 'violence' from other aspects of television, and 'aggressions' from other aspects of social life, researchers have effectively failed to explain either phenomenon.

One of the strengths of the effects tradition in the view of its proponents is its pursuit of empirical scientific approaches. Enormous amounts of data have been collected by researchers analysing everything from how often children watch television and with whom, to where they access the screens that they watch, to how many violent scenes are contained in particular genres of television programs, to how watching television in a laboratory increases aggressive responses in children. Experiment designs are studied and refined and the 'data' are extensively analysed (Comstock and Scharrer 2007). This 'scientific' analysis is highly regarded; it sits at the top of Hartley's (2008, 7) hierarchy in the 'science-based intellectual universe'. As Murdock (2001, 152) argues, this approach was widely respected from the start 'because its investigative procedures corresponded to common-sense notions of what "proper" science was

– the image of controlled experimentation being particularly central'. Because of this, 'its "findings" seemed to offer strong confirmation of popular assumptions and anxieties' (Murdock 2001, 152). Here again the academic research tradition is feeding the public sphere the answers that are being sought: the 'proof' that Buckingham (1993a) argues some commentators from both right- and left-leaning positions are seeking. That is, the 'empirical facts' that television is bad for you.

But while this scientific approach might be highly placed in the cultural hierarchy and sought after in the public discourse, it has been heavily criticised over the past three decades by researchers seeking a broader and deeper understanding of children's engagement with television. Does it really tell us anything about how children actively engage with television? David Gauntlett (2005, 14) has argued that the traditional method of scientific experiment is simply not suited to studying:

> such complex systems as human psychology, behaviour and social life. Whilst natural scientists can generally hope to observe stable and verifiable effects of one object on another, similarly straightforward predictions about social action obviously cannot be made.

Buckingham (1993a) too points to the inadequacies of this approach in trying to measure the complex ways in which audiences engage with television. He points out that the behaviourist model measures the process of stimulus and response and assumes that children simply react to a fixed meaning in the stimulus. In this scenario, 'television is seen as an extremely powerful influence, which moulds children's consciousness and behaviour, and which they are largely powerless to resist' (1993a, 10). Children here are simply the receptacle of the

CHAPTER 1

message and once filled they respond in predictable ways to the content. Gauntlett (2005, 16) also points up the flaws in this approach:

> The question 'what effect does all the violence on screen have upon its viewers?', for example, is asked as if it were just as clear-cut as any other scientific problem about the response of a liquid to heat, or the role of a component in an electrical circuit. And yet throughout this review we will be dogged by the unavoidable demands of exactitude and authenticity: What effects? Which viewers? Whose violence? … movies and television can suggest meanings and values, but the influence of these has to be far removed from the usual definitions of cause and effect.

There has been a long and intense debate about whether the scientific experiments which attempt to measure the impact of violence on children's aggressive behaviour have been fruitful. Proponents argue that the vast amount of research into this question itself shows that there is 'sufficient evidence of the toxic effects of a diet rich in violence and sexualised material' (Hayes and Jean 2012, 233). Critics argue that not only has the connection failed to be demonstrated unequivocally, but that the method is flawed in that it does not allow for understanding the complexity of the audience's relationship with television (Gauntlett 2005).

The effects researchers themselves have often acknowledged that a causal relationship between television viewing and behaviour has not been conclusively proven. One of the largest-scale studies in this tradition, conducted by Himmelweit, Oppenheim and Vince (1958, 220), found no 'causal relationships between seeing these programmes (crime, westerns, detective series) and behaving undesirably'. Despite this finding, Himmelweit, Oppenheim and Vince (1958, 220) go on to argue: 'but what relationship exists we have shown to be *more likely* to be harmful than desirable' (italics mine). Using an assumed correlation as a basis for judging television to be harmful to children is a pattern that appears in other studies that continue to pursue evidence of harmful 'effects' today. In reviewing whether the latest neuroscience findings into the operations of the brain indicate a direct causal effect of television violence on children, John P. Murray (2012, 50) writes:

> It is possible that repeated exposure to media violence *may* lead to changes in both the prefrontal cortex and limbic system interactions, and that these *may* disrupt the processing of aggressive, emotion-laden information. The result *may* be an increase in aggressive behaviour and/or the triggering of excessive aggression in response to provocation ... Hence ... the *clear threat* to the social and intellectual development of children and youth. (italics mine)

There is no evidence of direct causal effect, as indicated even in the language Murray himself uses and that I have highlighted in italics, and yet there is still a 'clear threat' indicated here to children from watching television.

It is not that the researchers in the media effects tradition have not considered broader questions, but that the tradition overall has come to operate persistently and predominantly within the 'fear' discourse – focusing on trying to prove that television does indeed harm children and cause them to become aggressive. In fact, at the start of this tradition, researchers such as Himmelweit, Oppenheim and Vince (1958) had a broader approach, taking care 'to emphasize the influence of "intervening variables" such as the family and social class, and to caution against the more alarmist views which were already circulating in public debate' (Buckingham 1993a, 11). Interestingly, Himmelweit, Oppenheim and Vince (1958) found a wide range of ways in which children enjoy and engage with television. This was based on their extensive research, which was conducted, significantly, with a large sample of children (4,500) and which included the children's own comments. The researchers' findings went far beyond the focus on violence and found that children actually enjoy television: 'For younger children especially, one of television's biggest pleasures lies in the excitement of action and constant change' (1958, 159). Himmelweit, Oppenheim and Vince (1958, 155-9) list the attractions of viewing for children as including: 'emotional appeal' (romantic heroes), 'the appeal of security and familiarity' (companionship and comfort), 'the appeal of satisfied curiosity', and 'the appeal of action and constant change'. This is a list which would seem to indicate a wide and varied response to television programs and in fact points to many of the themes that appeared in my own research.

This broader view, however, wasn't sustained as the effects research tradition gathered momentum in the 1960s and 1970s. Instead it began to focus systematically on elaborately designed and executed laboratory studies that aimed to show that watching violence did have direct – and negative – effects on viewers (Hodge and Tripp 1986, 193). Critics argue that even where a causal connection was claimed by the researchers the approach was still flawed because it measured 'artificial responses to artificial stimuli in artificial situations' (Buckingham 1993a, 11). This focus on scientific 'proof' is a drawback, according to Hodge and Tripp (1986, 211-2), and is one of the significant inadequacies of the media effects paradigm. It is a bias:

> towards proof rather than insight … (and) it is not helpful to see any aspect of television content as an autonomous cause with consistent effects irrespective of the social conditions of the viewer. (1986, 211-2)

One of the key proponents of the dangerous impact of violence in television throughout the second half of the 20th century was George Gerbner. While acknowledging the difficulty of pinpointing direct effects of TV violence in causing crime and violence, he nonetheless extensively wrote about, and condemned, the 'saturation of modern cultures with mass-produced images of violence and terror' (Gerbner 1988, 21). His argument for the influence of such saturation was more sophisticated than the direct effects model. He developed the 'cultivation theory' which suggested, as Gauntlett (2005, 55) points out, 'the exposure to television programmes will, over time, have a cumulative influence on viewers' perceptions of the world and their place in it', an approach which shared the 'notion of television as a "cultural form" with pro-social effects research'. Gerbner's (1988) research, however, did not look at 'pro-social' effects. While suggesting that television attitudes and representations would influence heavy viewers over time, he focused almost entirely on the representations of violence. In some cases his language was as hyperbolic as the dramatic media coverage of violence itself: 'For most groups of viewers, television's mean and dangerous world tends to cultivate a relative sense of fear, of victimization, mistrust, insecurity, and dependence, and – despite its supposedly "entertaining" nature – of alienation and gloom' (1988, 26). Gerbner (1988, 27) argued that because television is ubiquitous, 'television violence is inescapable', and as a result it stimulates a general sense of fear and anxiety, particularly in 'heavy viewers'. But as Wober and Gunter (1982) argue in their critical appraisal of Gerbner's findings, there are other variables which could contribute to such anxiety. After examining and comparing other research across a number of variables, they found Gerbner's arguments could not be sustained and that:

the present results suggest that personality variables which characterize television viewers at deeper levels than measures of social perception may also need to be considered in explaining relationships superficially demonstrated between amounts of television viewing and allegedly paranoid conceptions of social reality'. (1982, 246)

Once again, these findings support an argument for looking at television in a broader social and cultural context.

Hodge and Tripp (1986, 202-3), as did Gauntlett (2005, 118), found Gerbner's overall framework interesting and suggested that it provided 'promising methods and models for the future'. But in Gerbner's analysis of the 'violent content' of television, they found his model did not take account effectively enough of audiences' perceptions of what is 'real' in television and what is 'fantasy'.

Gerbner and Gross's (1976, 184) measurements of 'violent' content on television certainly do appear to be both limited and limiting, particularly in relation to cartoons. In his content analysis, Gerbner uses the same definitions of violence for all types of television programs, whether fact or fiction, whether for adults or children. There is no distinction made between a real-life murder scene shown on the news, or a cartoon sequence of Tom flattening Jerry with a cast-iron pan. Violent content is in all categories of programs identified as 'the overt expression of physical force over the self or other, compelling action against one's will on pain of being hurt or killed, or actually hurting or killing' (Gerbner and Gross 1976, 184). Not surprisingly with these indicators, Gerbner (1988, 17) finds that 'Children's programmes on American television have always been saturated with violence. Children in 1984–1985 were entertained with 27 violent incidents per hour'. The American animated cartoon *Tom and Jerry*, in some episodes, would no doubt eclipse a number of action films in counts of violence per second of airtime with these measurements. The application of this type of content analysis to cartoons has always stirred up the moral panics around television that have generated calls for action, from banning the shows to cutting out the violence – which in the case of *Tom and Jerry* would leave little to watch. As Hodge and Tripp (1986, 102) note:

> As a result of these horrific figures, cartoon violence, in which characters like Tom and Jerry suffer violent death and deformity at an alarming rate per programme, has become a favourite target of lobbyists on children's television.

One of the underlying assumptions behind the notion that cartoon violence is harmful to children is the belief that they are too young and developmentally immature to tell the difference between fact and fiction. They will be frightened unduly as a result of watching such violence, they will 'learn' that this is the way the world works, and thus come to believe that this is the way they should act. Hodge and Tripp's (1986, 9) research with children, however, demonstrated that:

> far from the fantastic nature of cartoons causing confusion between fantasy and reality, the largeness of the gap is helpful to young children in building up precisely this capacity to discriminate.

They go on to argue that children actually need explicit fantasy programs – including cartoons – 'in order to develop a confident and discriminating modality system' (1986, 130). Buckingham's (1993a, 218) work with children supports these findings: 'the boundary between fantasy and reality is of central significance' for children and they explore this in their 'pretend play'. He argues that 'while "pretend play" may often permit children to try out forbidden roles and behaviours, children understand that it offers this licence precisely because it is not real' (1993a, 218).

As we have seen above, despite the failure to find the proof so persistently and anxiously sought that violent content in television causes children to behave violently, researchers in this tradition continue to characterise television as problematic because it is full of violence. Gauntlett (2005, 130-1) argues that:

> The academic and political discourses about television violence, as well as the more popular forms of moral panic, tend to present a picture of television as filled with a never-ending array of gratuitously violent programmes.

George Comstock and Erica Scharrer (2007, 98) continue in this tradition, writing in *Media and the American Child* that 'Children and teenagers are exposed to astonishing amounts of violence on television and in other media'. In the same section they focus on the 'violent' content of children's television and films as well as TV commercials and video games. The suggestion is always that this is a concern because of the potential that children will imitate the aggression and violence that they see on the screen: 'The use of physical or even verbal aggression to solve a problem … is not the life lesson that most adults want young people to learn' (Comstock and Scharrer 2007, 98). What this analysis of violent content fails to take into account is how the violence is incorporated in the story, whether it is part of the action, the humour, or the narrative, or whether in the end the violence is rewarded or punished. All of this makes a clear difference to the way the program – and the violence contained in the program – are understood by the viewer (Gauntlett 2005, 150). Despite their criticisms of the extensive violence in children's television, even Comstock and Scharrer (2007, 103) admit that, in connection with cartoons, the violence was 'combined with humour' and that while 'children's television contains a comparatively large amount of violence … that violence is frequently shown in a manner that detracts from its gravity and the harm it can cause'. As the critics of content analysis have pointed out, a simple analysis of the content cannot explain the diverse readings of particular audiences (Buckingham 1998a; Gauntlett 2005).

> Content analysis does not help us to respond to the individual programme, nor, more importantly, the viewing session; it does not help us with matters of interpretations nor with how we respond to the complex significance and subtleties of the television text. (Fiske and Hartley 2003, 21)

Gerbner's work is true to the effects tradition noted above in that it assumes that the negative influence of television affects 'other' people, and that the popular medium is implicitly assumed to be inferior to more sophisticated modes of communication. Gerbner's (1988, 26) work into cultivation effects identifies the 'other' as being most in danger of being engulfed in the gloom of the 'mean and dangerous world'. 'The information poor (children and less well-educated adults) are again the entertainment-rich held in thrall by the myths and legends of a new electronic priesthood' (Gerbner and Gross 1976, 176). It is not Gerbner and Gross themselves, but children and 'less well-educated' adults who will be negatively affected by television; they are obviously incapable of resisting the wizardry of this pernicious modern medium.

Couch Potatoes

Gerbner's viewers who are 'held in thrall' presumably also have little capacity to exercise choice. They are captured by the all-powerful screen. Comstock and Scharrer (2007, 46-8) elaborate on this idea of a largely passive audience, though from a slightly different angle. Rather than being in thrall, they suggest that viewers watch television largely with indifference and with low involvement, while still spending significant amounts of time in front of the screen. These viewers don't exercise choice by actively seeking out favourite programs at particular times of the day; they watch simply because it is there – and it is on.

Comstock and Scharrer (2007, 46) call this form of watching television 'ritualistic viewing' and they draw on data from a 12-nation UNESCO time-study to support their argument that audiences largely watch television simply because it is readily available; the UNESCO study showed that television sets across the countries were turned on 'for about the same number of minutes each day regardless of the programs'. This finding that audiences are 'indifferent' to content is supported, they argue, by scientific findings that pleasure derived from television is related to processing by the right-side of the brain – a part of the brain which is responsible for 'non-verbal, noncritical, and nonanalytic' processing (p. 47). These arguments emphasise the uncritical, potentially mindless aspect of viewers' engagement with television, thus privileging the negative over the positive, and the passive over the active. In fact, Comstock and Scharrer (2007, 45) do acknowledge that 'viewing by the young occasionally will represent the instrumental pursuit of pleasures of particular interest and attraction' but they are insistent that this plays a small part in children and young people's viewing habits in general. Their approach is clearly indicated in their introduction which argues that:

> There is ample evidence that either the amount of time spent with particular media or the content viewed, read, or heard can have adverse effects. A great deal of research has convincingly linked either amount of media exposure or exposure to particular types of content with a range of important outcomes, including but not limited to performing poorly in school; learning aggression; behaving antisocially ... and increasing the odds that a child will be overweight. (2007, 1-2)

Both Gerbner's enthralled audience and Comstock and Scharrer's indifferent one are largely passive. They sit in front of the television soaking up the (mostly violent) content indiscriminately. They are also a gormless and fickle bunch: 'The popularity of specific programs is typically transitory; fashion rules' (Comstock and Scharrer 2007, 51). And they are demonstrably weak-minded: 'the affectively and cognitively undemanding nature of television makes monitoring sufficient to the task (most of the time television doesn't require much effort to achieve comprehension)' (Comstock and Scharrer 2007, 50). The picture is obviously not of the researchers themselves but the 'other' – the passive viewer captivated by the 'idiot box'. Gauntlett (2005, 119-20) argues that:

> the 'heavy viewer' is roundly (if unintentionally) demonized in the cultivation literature, and the cumulative picture which the research reports themselves cultivate is one of people who watch larger amounts of television as edgy, zombified individuals who are in a category quite removed from the researchers themselves, and who watch television in an entirely unselective way.

From this perspective there is no consideration of the possibility that viewers might watch television because they seek it out and enjoy it.

The passivity of a child sitting in front of the screen appears in part to provoke the concern about the undemanding nature of the

CHAPTER 1

medium; the immobility of the child suggesting a slow-down in mental processes. Comstock and Scharrer (2007) certainly argue that this is the case when presenting their 'content indifferent' viewer. It is interesting to note that a child slumped comfortably in an armchair, reading a book, does not provoke the same worries of mindless inactivity even though to the objective observer the scene is remarkably similar. A child with their head in a book is seen in this case to be completely absorbed and therefore actively engaged and concentrating. Sue Howard (1998, 72) points out this paradox and suggests a different interpretation of the television viewer: 'It's more likely that the child viewer's "bug-eyed" look comes from serious concentration and an intense scrutiny of the televisual'.

This portrayal of a largely undifferentiated audience as passive, of the weak and vulnerable viewer soaking up the violence and gloom of the screen, has been steadily undermined by a newer research tradition. Barker and Petley (2001, 22) argue that this newer approach seeks to talk to audiences themselves and explore through qualitative research their varied responses to television:

> The great strength of the recent rise of qualitative media audience research has been in the impetus which it has given to replacing figures of 'the audience' with detailed pictures of different kinds of audiences.

One of the early advocates of developing alternative approaches to examining how audiences engage with television was Ien Ang (1991). She powerfully articulated the inadequacies of 'empirical studies … [that] ignore the socio-cultural and institutional contexts in which audiences are constituted' (1991, 11). She argued that the empirical effects tradition researchers:

> establish a kind of knowledge that sheds light on 'television audience' from an exterior, objectifying perspective ... Such a perspective can only slight the insiders' dimensions of television audiencehood, as it were: the complex and contradictory ways in which television becomes meaningful in people's everyday lives. (1991, 11-12)

The major focus on violence and the other 'negative' influences of television, that inform the large body of work presented by such researchers as Gerbner, Comstock and Scharrer, obviously contributes to Hartley's 'fear' camp. Even if some of the approaches, such as the cultivation theory, would seem to provide an interesting methodological direction, the findings in this tradition of the influence and 'effects' of television are largely negative. The problem, as Hartley (2003, 52) sees it, is that this tradition seeks to 'pathologise its supposed effects'. In this view, there is nothing 'normal' in desiring to watch television. Even though Comstock and Scharrer (2007) have rather reluctantly admitted to the occasional pleasure that television might offer its audience, their focus and direction is on proving the negative effects of television – and newer screen media – on children. This leaves little room to seriously explore the deeper dimensions of why and how children enjoy television and how this informs their lives. For such an approach it is necessary to go beyond seeing the audience as a largely passive and undifferentiated 'ritualistic viewer' (Comstock and Scharrer 2007, 43-4).

Hartley (2008) puts the case for taking a different direction in studying television, suggesting we should be looking to the consumer for expert knowledge – not seeing them simply as objects of study by the academic 'expert'. But, as he points out, this is not an approach that is favoured by the establishment; an establishment which depends upon seeing both television and its audience (the weak-minded and vulnerable children, and the poorly-educated) as inferior.

> The most respectable forms of expert knowledge about television tend to be the ones that evaluate it most negatively. Knowledge about television is at a low premium if it is gained via the experiential immersion of the domestic consumer, or even via research into that experience. (Hartley 2008, 3)

Here again, popular culture and television are placed at the bottom of the pole; in a position where neither the content of the programs nor the voice of their consumers are valued.

Hartley's (2008) 'domestic consumers' are far from passive and in fact their engagement in television is highly complex. Interestingly he identifies himself as one of these consumers, unlike Gerbner and Gross (1976), who do not identify themselves as members of the audience that they fear are being harmed by television. In fact, Hartley (2008, 6) appears to celebrate both his and others' enjoyment of television:

> We are not consuming a product but using the imaginative resources of story, song, sight, and sound – some of the most powerful tools known to humanity – to think about identity, relationship, and community, in real time and space.

With all of this to examine and discuss, Hartley (2008, 10) argues 'that television going forward needs to be understood via the creativity and imagination of its viewers as a complex adaptive system'.

Approaches that engage with different audiences and move away from direct effects research have been increasingly taken up by researchers in the fields of media, film and cultural studies over the past three decades: 'This research, utilising increasingly sophisticated methodology, works from how those audiences themselves talk about or in other ways express their feelings about, responses to and relationships with different media' (Barker and Petley 2001, 22). There is now a significant body of work that considers how diverse audiences interact with television and indeed with popular culture in general. From investigating the manner in which fans creatively engage with their favourite television programs (Barker and Brooks 1998; Jenkins 2013) to how children build their relationships with others and construct their own identities through both talk and through creative practices such as making videos (Buckingham 1993a; Gauntlett 2007), these researchers have been developing richly-textured pictures of the ways in which audiences, including children, engage with television in their daily lives.

Buckingham's (1996) research into children's emotional responses to television is a good example of this work. He sought to move away from the 'cognitive bias' of much audience research 'in which emotion is either defined in terms of generalised categories such as "fright" or "enjoyment", or simply neglected altogether' (1996, 312) and widen the debate. He found in his research with children that:

> In describing how they feel about television, and in passing judgment on what they watch, children (like adults) are also making claims about themselves, and thereby constructing relationships with others. (1996, 7)

Buckingham argues forcefully that researchers must seek to 'make sense of children's experience of the media in their own terms, rather than in adults' terms' (Buckingham 2000, 116) in order to get a real insight into children and television. Much of the negative public discourse that dominates the discussion of children and television fails to take account of children's views; rarely are their views presented by adults, let alone by the children themselves. Buckingham (2000, 116) argues that it is essential in this context that we understand children's views and counter those who 'do not even see it as necessary to find out what children have to say'.

Listening to children, and interpreting their engagement with television through other research methods, including analysing their own creative productions (drawings, writing and video), has resulted in research which offers a far richer picture of the diverse ways in which children are influenced by television (Buckingham 1993a, 1996; Buckingham and De Block 2007; Gauntlett 2007; Götz et al. 2005). This is particularly apparent in the investigation of children's imaginative and creative responses to television. But as I discuss in the next section, this aspect of children's television is also a hotly disputed field.

Creativity and Imagination: Reading versus Television

In the public discourse, children's 'passivity' in front of the 'idiot box' is often seen as an indication that watching television stifles imagination, creativity and capacity for thought. Though such criticism features less frequently and with less intensity than that around violence and television, it is nevertheless a regular refrain. Quoting an Australian Senate Committee report of 1978, Hodge and Tripp (1986, 100) observed that a recurrent concern of parents was that 'the escapist material mainly watched by children is stifling children's imaginations and the development of their creative instincts'. Today this concern continues to be echoed in the news media. In one example, Lindsay Johns (2012) wrote in the *Daily Mail Australia* that 'TV more often than not deadens our senses and stifles young peoples' capacity for imagination and thought'. Often when such sentiments are expressed, as is the case in this story, the opinion is presented as 'fact' – as a simple matter of common sense. It is a 'myth' that is so obvious, in the Barthesian sense, that it is automatically assumed to be true.

Researchers in the media effects tradition have also promoted the argument that television is lightweight and undemanding; and deadens the critical faculties. A comparison is often drawn between watching television and reading; books are believed to stimulate while television simply induces a mindless state of inactivity. Marie Winn, who has written the popular book about children and television, *The Plug-in Drug* (1985), is one of the proponents of this notion, arguing that 'Reading involves a complex form of mental activity, trains the mind in concentration skills, develops the powers of imagination and inner visualization' (p. 66) while television is simply a 'plug-in drug'. Winn (1985, 66) also argues, albeit with flawed logic, that 'reading is a two-way process: the reader can also write; television viewing is a one-way street: the viewer cannot create television images'. Gavriel Salomon (1984, 647) promotes a similar case and has argued that 'television is "easy" and print is "tough"', suggesting his adherence to the 'passivity hypothesis that processing television requires little mental effort' (Valkenburg and Calvert 2012, p. 162). Both Winn and Salomon argue that reading is an 'active' pursuit, where the child engages her mind and imagination. Watching television, on the other hand, is seen as a mindless and passive occupation, which doesn't engage the critical faculties. This has strong similarities to Comstock and Scharrer's (2007) 'indifferent viewer'.

Neil Postman (2006) was another advocate of the mindless nature of television. He did acknowledge its capacity to entertain, but in his view this characteristic was a negative one; and it was the only characteristic of television. His opinion of television viewers too was

CHAPTER 1

negative as is evident in the title of one of his most widely-read books, *Amusing Ourselves to Death* (2006). Postman (2006, 28) did concede that this provision of entertainment could have 'value as a source of comfort and pleasure to the elderly, [and] the infirm … [and had the] potential for creating a theater for the masses'. But as with Winn and Salomon, in comparing television to the 'printed word', Postman (2006, 29) finds television far inferior, arguing that print formed our 'modern ideas about the uses of the intellect … [and] about education, knowledge, truth and information'. Television on the other hand offers only the 'Age of Show Business' (2006, 63).While these views of television have changed, in particular over the past two decades, with critical attention focusing on the literary, aesthetic and production qualities of 'high-end' drama such as *The Sopranos*, *Breaking Bad* and more recently *The Handmaid's Tale*, widely popular reality TV shows such as *The Bachelor* and *Big Brother* are still largely regarded as 'rubbish' (McNamara 2015).

It is interesting to note that even though both media rely on the use of narratives in much of their fictional content, stories on television are not given the same weight as those in books. To those who view reading stories as superior to watching them on television, the undemanding flow of images is seen to turn children into passive sponges soaking up a stream of mindless content. Jack Zipes (2009, 2013) has written extensively and insightfully about the role of narratives in children's lives but yet he argues that stories relayed through the 'screen' have little value compared to reading: 'The slow, deliberate, and reflective process that complex reading entails is being replaced by the quick images, instant recognition, and non-reflective viewing of the screen, big and little' (2009, 25). In this view it isn't just television that compares unfavourably with books: pictures don't measure up to the written word. It seems that the visual image compares unfavourably with the printed word in our 'print-literate, science-based intellectual universe' (Hartley 2008, 7). For Zipes, today's consumer culture drives the design and influence of the visual image. He argues that today's television programs and other 'consumer' products for children are all designed with a view to getting them hooked on consumption; and the ubiquitous 'image' is at the heart of this pursuit of the child consumer.

In these critical comments, Zipes does not seem to allow that television could also provide 'pleasure during leisure time' (2009, 8). While there is no doubt that today's culture does focus on generating and maintaining consumers, and children are very much a part of the target market, Zipes appears to assume that children are powerless to resist the 'malign' visual onslaught. The implication is that they no longer engage critically with the texts because these are visual; but even more significantly it also denies their agency. There is no suggestion that children could read and decipher visual texts, just as they might written texts. Or indeed that they might as 'mindlessly' engage with written material as they do with visual material, in order to relax and enjoy their leisure time.

As Gauntlett (1996, 45) argues, this sort of argument implies that:

> children are inadequate viewers who do not watch television for any meanings or experiences which might exercise their minds, but simply because they cannot resist the attractive flow of its images.

He goes on to observe that:

> many psychologists, including Albert Bandura (1977), Jerome Singer (1980) and Harvey Lesser (1977), have propagated

the view that children's interest in television is not held by the meaningful content of programmes, such as the script and characters, but is captured by formal features such as visual complexity, movement, zooms, cuts and sound effects. (Gauntlett 1996, 45)

Arizpe and Styles note in their book *Children Reading Pictures* (2003, 23) that 'despite the expanding visual base of contemporary culture, low status is still accorded to image'. Such criticism is based on an implicit assumption that images don't have the same value in our culture as the written word. This perception of the lesser value of the image has in fact been challenged by a number of researchers (Arizpe and Styles 2003; Robinson 1997) who have explored the question by seeking to understand how viewers engage with images, and what they 'read' from pictures. They go beyond a simple content analysis of television and look at the complexity of the viewer's interpretations. This research has some interesting findings, including that reading of the visual can actually precede, and support, reading of the printed word. In her book *Children Reading Print and Television*, Muriel Robinson (1997, 17) analyses a tradition of research that finds that 'illustrations teach children complex messages about the multilayered possibilities of narrative long before they [can] cope with these messages in written form'. Interestingly Helen Bromley (2003, 157) found from her research that children even learnt how to 'read' pictures in books from their experience of watching television. She goes on to argue that pictures actually contribute to the development of a child's critical understanding: 'For all the children in the study the pictures provided a means by which they could move from using talk for appreciation, to using talk for critical understanding' (2003, 158).

Far from being a mindless, and mind-numbing, pastime, it appears from this research with children that television does engage their attention, teaches them about the world and develops their critical understanding. These findings have been borne out too by other researchers. Buckingham (1993a, 1996), Götz et al. (2005), Lemish (2007) and Gauntlett (1996) have amply demonstrated the complex and quite sophisticated ways that children engage in 'reading' television; particularly when the research involves seeking their opinions. This research would seem to refute the arguments put forward by Winn (1985) and Salomon (1984) that only books can engage children's critical faculties. Stephen Kline (1995, 162) has observed, based on his research into children's television, that:

> Any observer of contemporary children's television must realise that this medium has become the great storyteller of post-modern culture ... Yet for too long the issues surrounding children's television have been framed in terms of what harm television does to kids – its potential to elicit violence and perpetuate stereotyped attitudes in children, rather that its potential to contribute to their lives.

The widely circulated view that television is inferior to reading, and that even its ability to entertain is suspect, reflects a bias which denigrates both the popular medium and popular culture. It illustrates Hartley's (2008, 7) observation that in the polarisation of high and low culture, television, and its viewers, are at the wrong end of the pole. The criticisms voiced by Winn (1985), Salomon (1984) and Postman (2006) fail to recognise, let alone examine, the potential of television to contribute positively to children's lives – and certainly fail to recognise any positive similarities between reading and watching television. All three assume that television viewers are passive and that they simply absorb, uncritically, the lightweight entertainment fare offered up to them. They talk about this 'audience' – made up of children, the 'elderly' and the 'infirm' – as though they had no views and no agency; and they regard the popular medium as inferior in all respects to the more highly-valued print medium. Of course, these audiences do not include Winn, Salomon and Postman themselves but fall squarely into the category of 'others'. The views of these researchers, however, are hugely popular and have contributed significantly to continuing the growth and spread of the negative public discourse around television. Postman's *Amusing Ourselves to Death* has sold 200,000 copies and been translated into eight languages (McCain 2003). Winn's book *The Plug-in Drug* has been published in multiple editions culminating in the 25th anniversary edition in 2002.

The negative comparisons drawn between reading and television often focus on television's mind-numbing qualities, and its capacity to stifle imagination and creativity. Academic research in the media effects tradition has taken up this question and the findings are both extensive and contradictory. Valkenburg and Van der Voort (1994, 334) reviewed a significant range of this research and found that 'Although decisive evidence of a causal relationship is absent, the weight of evidence favors the view that TV viewing fosters daydreaming and hinders creative imagination'. Having asserted this finding they go on to qualify it with a significant comment:

> Although there is no evidence that TV stimulates creative imagination, *it cannot be ruled out that specific types of TV programs may foster creative imagination.* In a related domain of TV research, no evidence was found that TV stimulates fantasy play; nonetheless, *it was shown that fantasy play could be*

encouraged through programs that were specifically designed to foster fantasy play'. (1994, 336) (italics mine)

The limits of effects research are, I would like to argue, particularly apparent in these statements. The findings are inconclusive and in fact contradictory. I would argue that this approach does not allow for exploring the varied ways in which children engage creatively or imaginatively with television programs. It is the failure of this research to illuminate such engagement that is broadly criticised by researchers in the fields of communication, media and cultural studies, who suggest that the effects tradition is limited in its capacity to reveal the complex and contradictory ways that television plays a role in children's social and psychological worlds (Barker and Petley 2001; Buckingham 1996, 2000; Gauntlett 2005). Götz et al. (2005, 15) point out that:

> these findings still leave us in the dark in terms of understanding the crucial role of media in children's everyday fantasy lives … The question remains as to whether something as complex as fantasy can be understood adequately without letting children themselves articulate it and taking seriously the natural social context in which fantasy occurs in their everyday life.

Götz et al. (2005) have taken an innovative approach to looking at how children use the media in their creative lives and they directly challenge the notion that television 'kills' the child's imagination. From direct research with children in four different countries, they demonstrated:

> the value of research projects such as this one in unveiling the complicated ways in which media are woven into the fabric of children's everyday lives … [and] the creative and sophisticated uses they make of their contents. (2005, xi)

CHAPTER 1

In directly addressing the question of whether television kills the child's imagination, Götz et al. (2005, 202) stated:

> Our study would certainly not support such a populist argument. Our findings suggest that the media are another resource in children's environments that they use in creating worlds of fantasy.

Creating imaginative worlds, or indeed imaginatively creating a new identity through play using the characters and stories of television, are among the pleasures of the medium for children (Götz et al. 2005) and also for adults, as can be seen in academic studies of fandom (Barker and Brooks 1998; Jenkins 2013). But the complexity of this pleasurable involvement is only apparent in research which engages, at least in part, directly with particular audiences and seeks their opinions. Götz et al. (2005, 20) argue that their 'research design facilitated the children's expression of their fantasy worlds and enabled the researchers to "read" those worlds – in pictures and in written and spoken language'.

The empirical scientific analysis that informs the effects tradition does not explore this terrain; its approaches do not value, and its methods cannot easily accommodate, an analysis of the subjective comments of individuals. In an effort to expand our understanding of audience engagement with television, qualitative research has been taken up extensively in recent years by researchers using a variety of sociological and ethnographic methods, and a rich body of knowledge has been developed. But the long and dominant tradition of effects research has undoubtedly had an impact on the direction of research into children and television. As mentioned above, so much time and money have been focused in finding proof of the harmful effects of television, particularly the dangers of its portrayal of violence, that the pleasures of watching television have been under-researched – particularly the pleasures that children find in the medium. There have of course been exceptions such as Howard and Roberts's (2002) research with under-twos watching the British preschool television series *Teletubbies*. Children's humour too has received some attention from researchers although again this is not a widely studied dimension of children's televisual experience (Bazalgette and Buckingham 1995; Davies, Buckingham and Kelley 2000; Götz et al. 2006).

In seeking to investigate these fields further, I believe that researchers have to break away from the dominant tradition of negative effects research and follow the newer approaches to audience research discussed above. Not only does this involve challenging some of the findings and directions of the effects research but it also involves questioning perceptions of cultural value. Such research openly questions the long-established and closely-guarded cultural traditions that place serious-minded intellectual pursuits above the 'childish' enjoyment of the sort of 'mindless' and 'trivial' pleasure that popular culture – and television – provide. In researching the role of television in children's lives, we need to step outside the constraints of effects research, and, as Bazalgette and Buckingham (1995, 10) argue, acknowledge both children's hierarchies of value and the importance of 'fun': 'We have to accept the values that drive children's cultural preferences and, in doing so, acknowledge our own needs for triviality and fun'. This is a major challenge given our modern day construction of childhood in western culture. In the next chapter I explore in detail how our investment in the 'innocence' and vulnerability of childhood, and our drive to protect such innocence from corruption while educating the child's 'reason', has a powerful influence on what we do – and more importantly don't – allow children to enjoy.

Chapter 2

INNOCENCE OR IGNORANCE? HOW WE SAFEGUARD CHILDREN IN OUR OWN INTEREST

So just why is television's capacity to entertain and provide pleasure to audiences, particularly children, regarded with such suspicion? A look at the historical developments that created today's western concept of childhood illuminates these fears. Examining these developments, I believe, highlights how pleasure has come to be set up in opposition to education in western educational discourse; and how children in particular have suffered the consequences of this notional conflict.

In his seminal work published in the mid-20th century, the French historian and sociologist Philippe Ariès (1973) undertook to articulate a modern culture of childhood by charting its emergence and growth from the Middle Ages through to the 20th century. Ariès's observations offer a useful insight into how today's largely negative views on children and television (in particular the pleasure they get from the medium) have developed and why they are so entrenched. He traces both the introduction of education into children's lives and its institutional development, and he charts the emergence of the regulation of children's 'pleasures'. These two developments in the history of childhood are interwoven in interesting ways that anticipate the dichotomy between the two that exists in our culture today; they also, I will argue, inform our negative views of the place of television in children's lives.

In *Centuries of Childhood* (1973), Ariès draws on historical evidence to show that children in the Middle Ages were involved in all aspects of adult life, including the pleasure pursuits, games and festivals which were an integral and significant part of life in that period. Far from being excluded from the bawdy, drunken and riotous celebrations, children were often given a role themselves:

> Children … took part in [the great seasonal and traditional festivals] on an equal footing with all the other members of society, and more often than not played a part in them which was reserved for them by tradition. (Ariès 1973, 70)

But this wasn't to remain so; the child was soon to be singled out as a separate category, a category that included the 'innocent' child, one who was cherished and revered as 'pure'. This innocence was both precious and vulnerable and had to be carefully protected, in particular from the insidious and corrupting pleasures that were increasingly coming to be seen as the domain of adults only.

Ariès (1973, 79) suggests that even in the Middle Ages a 'powerful and educated minority of rigid moralists' had condemned the pleasures of games and festivals and 'roundly denounced them as immoral' for all ages. But it wasn't until the 17th and 18th centuries that this attitude came to dominate, though with a compromise. Adults were still allowed to indulge, even if this indulgence was condemned by the 'rigid moralists', but children were to be excluded from unregulated pleasures of all sorts. The new attitude to the child involved:

a desire to safeguard its morality and also to educate it, by forbidding it to play games henceforth classified as evil and by encouraging it to play games henceforth recognized as good. (Ariès 1973, 79)

So it seems that one of the first drives underpinning the emerging concept of the child was to control its pleasures, protecting it from their corrupting influence.

The need to curb pleasures was driven by the major feature of this new concept of childhood: innocence. This innocence was both valuable and vulnerable; it could be corrupted and was therefore in need of protection. The emergence of this notion was, Ariès (1973, pp. 107-8) argues:

> a great movement which manifested itself on all sides, not only in a rich moral and pedagogic literature but also in devotional practices and a new religious iconography. An essential concept had won acceptance: that of the innocence of childhood.

The pure and romantic nature of this innocence was nowhere more strikingly or lovingly illustrated than in Jean-Jacques Rousseau's *Émile* (1969). For Rousseau the child was born innocent; but from that moment the infant was threatened by the society of men. As he writes in his opening sentence: 'God makes all things good; man meddles with them and they become evil' (p. 5). Anne Higonnet (1998, 26-7) observes that:

> Like other Enlightenment philosophers sceptical of traditional religious teachings, Rousseau advocated raising children as 'naturally' as possible, by which he meant gently, with toys and play, in simple, light, loose clothing, outdoors whenever possible.

But while Rousseau's approach might have treated the child gently, his focus was always on guiding and nurturing this precious creature, and preventing his being led astray by 'passion' or corrupted by adult secrets and sexuality. Vulnerability and weakness were associated from the beginning with the innocent child and while this child needed protection it also needed education in order to grow strong, and this was also a major focus of *Émile*. As Ariès (1973, p. 116) observes:

> the idea of childish innocence resulted in two kinds of attitude and behaviour towards childhood: firstly, safeguarding it against pollution by life, and particularly by the sexuality tolerated if not approved of among adults; and secondly, strengthening it by developing character and reason.

Pollution appears to have been associated directly with pleasures and passions; a child was to be strictly monitored to make sure it didn't overindulge in laughter or tears, and it was not to be permitted enjoyment from touching or cuddling – especially with anyone of the opposite sex or the lower classes. It was in this century that children were separated from sleeping with multiple others – servants, siblings, parents – in the interests of modesty and of preserving the innocence of the child from exposure to the dissolute passions of 'adult' sexuality (Ariès 1973; Jenkins 1998a, see intro.).

The new ban on pleasures focused also on popular entertainments and I would like to suggest that this anticipated our attitudes to the suspect pleasures of popular television. Ariès (1973, 114) observed that in the 18th century, 'plays, balls, dances' and the 'more ordinary entertainments' provided by 'jugglers, mountebanks and tightrope walkers' were forbidden; 'only educational games, that is to say games which had been integrated into the educational system, were permitted; all other games were and remained suspect'. The desire of adults to protect the innocence of childhood was a main feature of these sanctions and this resonates within our culture today.

CHAPTER 2

While some of the proscribed activities have changed, the attitude of control, for the preservation of innocence and the appropriate strengthening of character, remains intact. Today, for example, plays are seen as beneficial to the child, as are television dramas based on the classics; these now fit into an 'educational' category of entertainment for children (Davies 2001, 50-1). But our own category of 'jugglers and mountebanks' would likely include reality shows on commercial television and programs with any hint of sex or violence.

In an interesting twist, Hartley (2008, 183) has compared the hugely popular television reality show *Big Brother* with Shakespeare's *Taming of the Shrew*; both in their own times fall into the category of popular culture; both include sex, fraught relationships and 'bawdy humour' guaranteed to please a 'popular audience of mixed class, age, and gender'. Ironically, today Shakespeare's work has moved into an 'elite' category of art and been substituted by the popular television programs of our era (Hawkes 1973, 231). And it is these popular programs, particularly those enjoyed by children, that are seen to have no 'educational' value and that are most condemned.

As education developed as an institution that would build character and reason in the child while protecting its innocence, pleasure was excluded. Thus from the very beginning fun and pleasure were set up in opposition to education; unregulated pleasure in particular was not to be allowed to contaminate the purity of the child or its education. The institutions of education developed as places where children were confined until such time as they could join the adult world:

> Henceforth it was recognized that the child was not ready for life, and that he had to be subjected to a special treatment, a sort of quarantine, before he was allowed to join the adults. (Ariès 1973, 396)

According to Ariès, worse was to come:

> the school shut up a childhood which had hitherto been free within an increasingly severe disciplinary system, which culminated in the eighteenth and nineteenth centuries in the total claustration of the boarding-school.[1]

In his book *Sentimental Education*, James Donald (1992, 12) takes a critical look at the 'techniques of public and mass schooling that emerged in the nineteenth and twentieth centuries', showing, as Ariès does, the connection with this history and our desire to maintain the innocence of the child and nurture its reason. He argues that these techniques:

> persistently attempted to shape children to their measure by means of disciplines that claim, ... not only to understand the nature of the child, but to be able to emancipate it ... suggesting that this will recover for civil society the virtues of its uncorrupted state. (1992, 12)

The moral control of children through education was an integral part of the institution from the 19th century; such control focused on the production of an adult that would be of value to society. This drive to mould the future citizen continues to inform government investment in children today. Alan Prout (2000, 305) observes that 'absolutely central' to the UK government's investment in eradicating child poverty is the importance it attaches 'to children as an investment in the future'. The central focus, Prout argues, is on the better adult lives that will emerge as a result of this investment: 'it is not on the better lives that children will lead as children' (p. 305).

---

[1] It is worth noting here that these sanctions only applied to the children of the aristocracy and emergent middle classes – working class children were still being put to work in terrible conditions even into the late 19th century.

CHAPTER 2

As the 19th century progressed, social reformers, educationalists and others came to focus more critically on the 'dangerous' side to the innocent child, the unruly aspect which needed to be mastered for the sake of humanity. Buried in the cherubic exterior of the Victorian child was a barely contained demon and this needed to be tamed through a rigorous education (Ariès 1973; Donald 1992; Jenkins 1998a).

In this era, as the industrial revolution changed the demographics of society, the lower classes, and their children, became a particular focus of the education reformers. As a large urbanised working class emerged, reformers feared the potential for 'moral and social corruption' of the masses (Donald 1992, 23). In order to control this undesirable prospect, ways had to be devised of 'improving their welfare and so civilizing their morals' and this was to be largely the role of the provision of state education (Donald 1992, 23-4). Such education would keep the masses, and in particular their children, in line and out of trouble: protecting them from their own unruly behaviour and barely-controlled urges, as well as from possible contamination from others. Interestingly it was particularly the working class and their children that were at risk: both were seen as the 'other' by the dominant culture of the middle and upper classes. These weaker members of society were more vulnerable to pernicious and corrupting influences and had to be 'educated' for the benefit of maintaining the existing order of society. As Donald (1992, 24) goes on to elaborate, the working-class family was seen, as was the child, as dangerous because they were themselves 'in danger':

> The family and the child are thus set in place as the object, mechanism and justification of state intervention. The supposed benefits of this mix of control and welfare provision were the substance of the case for involving the state in popular education.

Education and Work versus Pleasure

Ariès (1973, 70) suggests that during the Middle Ages, when the enjoyment of games, major festivals and celebrations 'formed one of the principal means employed by a society to draw its collective bonds closer', work did not have as 'much importance in the public mind [as] we have given it for something like a hundred years'. It wasn't until the 19th century and the massive changes to work practices driven by the Industrial Revolution that the focus on making productive citizens of our children in order to maintain and feed the new industrial complex became paramount. The education system, as it had emerged at the end of the Middle Ages, was ready to take on the task of feeding this new enterprise; time-wasting pleasures would be curtailed and education would focus on turning out productive citizens. In the late 19th century the:

> broader curriculum in the elementary schools ... would ... provide training for citizenship through systematic instruction in social duty or lessons in civics, physical exercise and military-style drill for boys, and instruction in the responsibilities and techniques of domesticity and motherhood for girls. (Donald 1992, 27)

There was no room here for the distraction of pleasure in the serious business of education and work. As Stephen Kline (1998, 100) observes, 'It was at school ... that children would derive their first sense of their position in the broader social matrix of jobs, civic duty, social responsibility and moral choices'. This drive to turn children into productive adults also influenced the regulation of their leisure activities. Children were not to be allowed a free rein to indulge in unregulated pleasures, and even play had to be harnessed; it came to be seen as 'the "work of childhood" – the moral equivalent of labour' (Kline 1998, 100).

CHAPTER 2

Organisations such as the Boy Scouts and Girl Scouts emerged at this time as society hoped to 'institutionalize ideas about what constituted children's appropriate use of leisure time' (Spigel 1998, 113). Hanging around in an idle fashion was definitely out; children had to be kept engaged in 'doing'. When television arrived, it was a technology that invited children to sit and watch: apparently indulging in idleness. To the adult observer this appeared to be a passive pastime and the television quickly came to be seen as an evil that would turn children into 'couch potatoes' and hence unproductive members of society. Inherent in this criticism is the assumption that passivity is bad. As Ellen Seiter (1998, 312) argues:

> the notion of children watching television offends the widely held belief in the importance of the child *actively* achieving developmental tasks … today passive is the worst thing children can be.

If television was to be tolerated it had to serve a useful purpose: 'Television should not be entertaining children: on the contrary it should be part of the "work" they are expected to be doing when they are not at school' (Buckingham 2002a, 48). The connection between pleasure and work was inescapable and 'the idea that fun should promote industrious behaviour rather than passive reflection was paramount in critical discussions' (Spigel 1998, 121). These attitudes have informed our view of children's television into the 21st century, and today Máire Messenger Davies (2001, 58) notes that a children's television program is 'expected to serve functions over and above aesthetic excellence, entertainment and narrative engagement for its audience; it has to help children in the task of growing up'. *Teletubbies* is not to be tolerated, but *Sesame Street* at least is 'educational'.

Nurturing children to become productive citizens was one aspect of the drive to make every hour of their lives productive. But there was also an element of keeping them safe from corruption. For both adults and children, work has long been seen as a path to salvation of the soul. The Protestant worldview that valued consistent application to work developed in the 16th century according to Alain de Botton (2009, 96) to allow the ordinary worker access to such salvation and to 'redeem the value of everyday tasks'.

> Salvation could be worked out at the level of ordinary existence, not only in the grand, sacramental moments which Catholicism had privileged. Sweeping the yard and arranging the laundry cupboard were intimately related to the most significant themes of existence. (De Botton 2009, 96)

In her book, *Work's Intimacy* (2011), Melissa Gregg argues that modern technology has today fuelled the pervasive spread of work into all areas of life. She suggests (2011, 7) that our culture fosters a 'deliberate confusion of friendship and business interests' which began early in the 20th century and was manifest is such self-help books as Dale Carnegie's *How to Win Friends and Influence People* (1937). Importantly, Gregg (2011, 4-5) observes that this 'collapse' of 'the boundaries between work and play' is supported by a culture where 'middle-class professionals [have] been encouraged to see work as the most significant demonstration of their success and identity'.

But it is not only that work is seen a route to success. In fact work is celebrated for the pleasure it provides; today's 'cultural context … celebrates the status and rewards of creative work' (Gregg 2011, 5). Gregg suggests 'that professional work generates forms of pleasure and accomplishment that rival the markers of identity favoured in previous historical formations' (p. 5).

CHAPTER 2

That work is a powerful attraction and fundamental to our sense of wellbeing has of course been noted by others including Alain de Botton (2009). Not least of work's appeal is its ability to keep death at bay:

> Death is hard to keep in mind when there is work to be done: it seems not so much taboo as unlikely. Work does not by its nature permit us to do anything other than take it too seriously. It must destroy our sense of perspective, and we should be grateful to it for precisely that reason, for allowing us to mingle ourselves promiscuously with events, for letting us wear thoughts of our own death and the destruction of our enterprises with beautiful lightness, as mere intellectual propositions, while we travel to Paris to sell engine oil. (De Botton 2009, 324)

De Botton's beautiful hyperbole illuminates the depth of work's influence in our lives and explains its attraction. But Gregg (2011, 6) suggests that 'work's enticing and seductive dimensions' also have a corrosive effect. These dimensions, assisted by the technologies that reach into every corner and moment of our daily routine, have enabled work to govern our most intimate lives. Gregg (2011, 6) argues that this blurring of boundaries between the professional and the personal has resulted in a culture that is dominated by work and where the intimate enjoyment of pleasure and relationships is 'most regularly exercised in the pursuit of competitive professional profit', leaving us 'unable to appreciate the benefits of intimacy for unprofitable purposes'. She contends that this is 'what is at stake in the move to work-centered identities and cultures' (p. 6).

The appreciation of our intimate enjoyment of the pleasures of popular culture certainly appears to be a casualty of a culture that places such value on the significance of income-generating work. It is not that this worldview stops us from enjoying popular culture but that it makes us feel guilty about doing so. In her extensive 1980s research with women readers of romance fiction, Janice Radway (1991) found that the women felt guilty about the pleasure such reading afforded them. She suggested that:

> this guilt is the understandable result of their socialization within a culture that continues to value work above leisure and play, both of which still seem to carry connotations of frivolousness. (1991, 105)

The cultural dominance of the importance and value of work, and its greater merit over 'unprofitable' pleasure, afflicts the television viewer with the same feelings of shame. In their research with television viewers in the 1990s, Gauntlett and Hill (1999, 111) found that many often felt guilty about watching TV and believed that they should be doing something more productive: 'The assumption here is that watching television is not productive'.

Gary Steiner (1963, 56), in his extensive interviews with nearly 2,500 television viewers, found too that even though people enjoyed watching television and the majority said it made them feel relaxed and happy, they still qualified the enjoyment, perceiving it as 'a perfect way to relax for lazy people who should be doing something else'. The work ethic prevailed, making them feel guilty about spending time in front of the set. Interestingly, Steiner (1963, 66) also noted that:

> uneasiness about viewing seems once more to grow with schooling; and it seems to come largely from the laziness and passivity associated with what the educated seem to consider 'contented vegetation' in front of the tube. They also admit to being relaxed and entertained, but they are less happy about it.

Steiner here has observed the way in which our culture's drive to educate and develop the 'productive' child manifests itself in relation to the enjoyment of television. Although children continue, as they grow, to enjoy television, they learn the language and values of the dominant culture, and become 'less happy' about admitting to such enjoyment.

As Hartley (1992b, 10) suggests, the pervasive nature of this dominant discourse spreads guilt inescapably through our societies:

> a fair amount of critical distaste has found its way via schools and periodicals into the common-sense wisdom of the very people for whom popular culture is popular, permeating popular culture with guilt about its own practices.

The Threat of Popular Culture – and Bad Taste

Just as the games and festivals of the 17th century were singled out as corrupting influences, in the 19th century, popular culture – and popular politics – were seen as a major threat to the established order. According to Donald (1992) this fear drove the education agenda in the beginning of the 19th century. Interestingly, Donald (1992, 78) charts the subtle changes to these perceived threats, noting that later in the century they were reformulated to focus on the dangers of illiteracy and debased taste. Education is set up here as the protection against popular culture and bad taste; both of which are undesirable elements.

Popular culture, and the debased taste that appears to enjoy its pleasures, threaten a world that reveres the child's innocence and worries over its vulnerability. Allowing indulgence in pleasure and 'bad taste' endangers efforts to mould and direct the child. As a result, children's bad taste, which is often associated with their obvious enjoyment of television programs that adults don't like, frequently comes in for criticism. Ridicule of 'tasteless' children's television programs appears regularly in the media, and adult columnists even devote space to the assessment of their own children's failings: 'Actually all of the shows he likes are terrible. Believe me, my son has many wonderful qualities, but his taste in television is awful' (Mentzer 2014). The Melbourne *Herald Sun* ran a story on 'The ten worst kids TV characters', opening with the comment:

> We've all been there as parents: the children absolutely love that television show with its adorable characters but all you want to do is reach through the screen and strangle them until they sing and dance no more. (Campbell 2013b)

In this article, the journalist goes on to list a number of the most popular children's television shows on air, dismissing, in his disparagement, the pleasures of the children who enjoy the programs. In the process of judging children's taste (or lack of it), adults assert their authority. As Davies, Buckingham and Kelley (2000, 9) observe, 'drawing on Pierre Bourdieu's notion that aesthetic judgments cannot be divorced from social relations: distinctions of taste are a means of displaying and sustaining distinctions of class and social power'. The adult voicing these criticisms of bad taste television knows best. In a similar way, adults judge adult television and its viewers: today one can claim to be a fan of critically-acclaimed programs such as HBO's *The Sopranos* or *Breaking Bad*, but it would indicate bad taste to be a fan of *Keeping Up With the Kardashians*, which as James McNamara suggests is seen as being 'rubbish' (2015).

Children's humour is often dismissed as puerile or infantile and by implication of no value. And the sort of 'tasteless' programs kids laugh at are therefore also considered worthless. The adult world has its own idea of what children should be watching:

> What gives children's television value is not the fun stuff (the cartoons and comedies) but the factual programmes, the

literary adaptations and the 'socially relevant' contemporary drama. (Davies, Buckingham and Kelley 2000, 14)

Some of the criticism of children's television reflects a rather benign disapproval of shows that happen to irritate parents. But there is another aspect informing adult anxiety about tasteless television. This sort of television is often feared for its potential to allow inappropriate material to creep into the child's world. Jokes and innuendo about 'forbidden' adult secrets are a threat to the innocent child at worst, and at best offer only a time-wasting indulgence. It takes an effort to control children who seem 'to like the very things that adults deemed inappropriate' (Spigel 1998, 122) but providing such control over the questionable taste of children in our western culture has been seen as an important task. According to a magazine proffering advice to parents published in 1954, *Parents Magazine*, if children could be taught good taste this would protect them from the inevitable 'exposure to unwholesome influences' of popular television (Spigel 1998, 122).

This perception of children's inability – or refusal – to recognise and choose programs in 'good taste' reinforces the push to control what they watch.

> It seems to be assumed that, left to their own devices, children will choose to watch material that is not only morally damaging but also inherently lacking in cultural value … Children's 'natural' taste, it is argued, is for vulgarity and sensationalism, rather than restraint and subtlety; for simplistic stereotypes rather than complex, rounded characters; and it is led by the baser physical instincts rather than the higher sensibilities of the intellect. Children and 'good taste' are, it would seem, fundamentally incompatible. (Davies, Buckingham and Kelley 2000, 5-6)

Education and Popular Culture

Donald's (1992) writing is particularly illuminating where he considers the juxtaposition of the institution of education with the 'apparatuses' and 'practices' of popular culture. He shows that in fact there is a close connection between the two – despite our apparent desire to keep them separate. He makes an interesting observation that two seminal 20th century strategies for education – the Leavisites 'as opposition to mass civilization and the Reithian vision of the mass media as a channel for education' – were driven by the desire to control and guide the development of children in order to mould both the child and the society:

> both were concerned to institute structures of cultural and symbolic authority as a means of 'policing' a democratic population, its knowledge, its moral welfare and its potentially subversive pleasures. This unanimity of purpose producing radically different social strategies again underlines how blurred and permeable is the boundary between education and entertainment. (Donald 1992, 76)

Interestingly, one strategy cut popular culture out of the picture altogether, while the other sought to use the mass media for the purposes of control. This last approach has a resonance today in efforts to compel children to watch 'educational' programs and to eschew those with no obvious didactic value: the ones that only provide pleasure.

Donald's point is that the presentation of mass media and education in opposition to each other is not a true representation of the way they function in our culture. The two are more closely linked; the boundary 'permeable'. For people like Reith, this offers an opportunity for control in order to produce the desired cultural result

(Donald 1992, 75-6). But to others the weak interface presents a threat. Popular culture has the potential to seep into the cultures that we want to keep pristine: in particular the innocence of childhood.

Given the critical view of children and television that is dominant in the media and public discourses, it is perhaps predictable that the popular culture of television is still largely excluded from schools. A number of researchers have pointed to this use of education to keep popular culture and its 'subversive pleasures' at bay; schools are places where children can be safe from television and its threats. Schools and teachers, Bragg (2006, 140) argues, 'are constructed as the last line of defence against the encroachments of [the] shallow consumerism and American cultural imperialism' that is manifest in popular culture. Hodge and Tripp (1986), and Seiter (1999a), have examined how television is frowned upon in an educational setting. Far from including the latest popular TV reality show for study in the classroom, even informal discussion of television shows is often discouraged at school. Hodge and Tripp (1986, 177) draw on French sociologist Pierre Bourdieu's theories to illuminate the reasons behind the resistance to this form of popular culture:

> Bourdieu (1980) has pointed to the close affinity that the purely academic culture has to the culture of the politically powerful, arguing that the role of the academic culture is both to select what is to be considered tasteful, interesting, consequential and valuable, and to teach it primarily through the school curriculum.

The control here again is around marking out what is tasteful and valuable for the education of our children. Popular culture is not 'interesting, consequential' or 'valuable' and the fact that children might enjoy the pleasures of popular culture confirm in this worldview the need to keep it from the classroom.

As I argued earlier, the media effects tradition has a long and entrenched grip on the public discourse and Seiter (1999b, 89) argues that this influences teachers' opinions, reinforcing notions that children's enthusiasm for popular culture is best left outside the classroom:

> Holding a lay theory of deleterious media effects … may be linked to the closeting of popular culture tastes, and to the suppression of talk about television.

Today, although media studies has gained acceptance in the field of education as part of the curriculum (Bragg, Buckingham and Turnbull 2006), talk of television, particularly of the television shows that children enjoy, is still something that is largely discouraged in educational institutions. When media studies is taught in the classroom, the focus is often on directing discussion to meet educational outcomes with a focus on critical understanding: an approach that is not always appreciated or enjoyed by the students (Lealand and Zanker 2008).

Buckingham (2002a, 48) has noted that today 'television … is largely defined as anti-educational'. At the heart of this complaint against television is its capacity to provide pleasure. If television is to be recognised as having any value it should provide educational programs: 'Children's [television] drama is explicitly … required to be didactic' (Davies 2002, 124). Once again pleasure is set up in opposition to education; there is value in education but little if any in pleasure. Television, therefore, which so apparently provides pleasure, can only be tolerated in so far as it 'teaches'. Just as the games of the 17th century were tempered to meet the character-building drive of the emerging educational agenda of the 17th century (Ariès 1973), so today modern culture demands television provide 'educational' programs for children. Programs such as cartoons and slapstick humour, which are seen simply to provide pleasure, are frowned upon (Buckingham 2002a; Davies 1997; Seiter 1999b).

This means of course that the shows that children love and laugh at are mostly not seen by adults as educational. There are some exceptions, however, such as the American children television series *Sesame Street*. This series is popular both with parents and educators (it teaches letters and numbers) and with children. *Teletubbies* on the other hand is not regarded as being educational, and this British preschool children's series stirred up heated controversy when it was first aired (Howard and Roberts 1999), no doubt in part because it was hugely enjoyed by its young audience. Many cartoons watched by children are considered either a waste of time or positively harmful (Gerbner 1988) and yet children love them. And it seems that the shows that are most popular with children often provoke the most heated reactions. Even the rather benign British cartoon *Peppa Pig*, which is widely and wildly popular with young children, is condemned with such media headlines as 'Is Peppa Pig making children naughty?' (Faulkner 2012). This headline from *Daily Mail Australia* plays directly on the fear, often generated in the media discourse, of the corrupting influence of television on the young. Media coverage of this cartoon has on other occasions focused on this issue of the moral threat of its content. An article in *The Daily Telegraph* states: 'Shows for children, particularly those that purport to be somewhat educational like *Peppa Pig*, have a moral responsibility to, well, act morally' (Campbell 2013a). Television, education and morality are all in one sentence here: three dominant triggers of anxious concern about children. This sentence suggests we must get a grip on the corrupting influence of children's television programs and not be taken in by their misrepresentations about their ability to 'educate'; it also suggests that the shows themselves have an active and malign agency and refuse to 'act morally'. The headline for this second story is '*Peppa Pig*: The wildly popular little brat leading our kids astray' (Campbell 2013a). The clear implication is that the pleasure offered by this captivating little pig and her family is going to lead our kids off the straight and narrow.

Jackie Marsh (2005), Leonie Arthur (2005), and Roberts and Howard (2005) in examining popular culture and early childhood have noted the significant engagement of preschool children with the narratives of popular culture, through the media and consumer culture (especially toys). Drawing on evidence from research with parents of 2- and 3-year-olds, Arthur (2005) suggests that this engagement is a critical element of their development of literacy. Despite the evidence of such research findings, Marsh (2005, 39) notes the continued resistance from educators to the discourses centred on popular culture and she goes on to argue that this resistance is detrimental to children: 'Banning … [popular discourses] only serves to ask children that they cast off aspects of their identities as they move from home to school'. She goes on to suggest that 'this resistance would weaken if educators were clearer about the important role such narratives play in children's identity construction' (2005, 39). The importance of narrative in children's lives was the focus of Muriel Robinson's (1997) research with children in the 1990s. But Robinson didn't focus solely on research into traditional written narratives; she included television, arguing that popular culture has a clear role in the 'literacy development of young children' (Robinson and Turnbull 2005, 52). Her work convincingly illustrated the importance of both television and print narratives in the lives of children, arguing that narrative 'is particularly powerful … in children's development' (Robinson 1997, 44).

It would seem that, in the classroom, teachers are playing their part to support and maintain the modern construct of the innocent child. Their role is to support the development of reason in the child, to protect its innocence both through instruction and through guarding the child against its own malevolent tendencies. Pleasure in this scenario does not have a place and this includes the pleasure to be enjoyed from popular culture. As we have seen above, pleasure and education have diverged over the past three centuries. Popular culture has ended up on the opposite end of the pole to education and continues to be regarded with suspicion. The innocent child can be kept pure by keeping pleasures at bay throughout the vulnerable years of childhood and by providing serious education that focuses on strengthening character and reason and helps the child to avoid the pitfalls of thoughtless delight. Laughing so hard that we all fall down has no place in education; the closing scene of *Peppa Pig* is far too trivial for the schoolroom. *Peppa Pig* and her family do not meet the qualifications set by the demands of this culture of childhood, and the thousands of children who enjoy the collapse of the family onto their backs amid giggles and snorts must leave their enjoyment of such 'trivia' at home when they head off to school. Popular culture simply does not have 'cultural capital' (Bourdieu, 1984) in educational settings and so is excluded. This is not only a concern for the message it gives to children about our policing of pleasure but it also positions 'many children as outsiders' (Arthur 2005, 175). The popular culture that engages their leisure hours is not given any recognition within the school environment.

This is the point that Hodge and Tripp (1986, 175) make; by looking askance at popular culture, the educational establishment leaves children out in the cold, especially the children who particularly enjoy television shows:

> Although it seems that there are few teachers who actively punish pupils for using their television experience in class, the overall effect is to delegitimate it in school, and thus put at a disadvantage the pupil whose chief environmental enrichment has been the television.

But it is not just that children are left out: the denigration of television results in sending a message to children that 'if what they enjoy doing is not worthwhile, they cannot be worthwhile people' (Hodge and Tripp 1986, 176). This is particularly insidious in its undermining of children's sense of self-worth.

The exclusion of pleasure and popular culture from the educational sphere has been the focus of a number of researchers in both the US and the UK in the past two decades who have recommended that its presence be not only acknowledged but integrated into education settings. Seiter (1999b, 260) argues that 'more integration of popular culture into the early childhood curriculum may be an important strategy to make school more inviting to all children'.

Buckingham (1993a, 297) too suggests that:

> we need to recover a notion of critical pedagogy which does not reject or underestimate children's affective and social investments in the media, or seek merely to replace these with rationalistic analysis.

Getting pleasure back into the picture is an important though quite a daunting task. Much is invested in the stance of the critical television viewer seeking to 'assert a powerful subject position'

(Buckingham 1993a, 293). This viewer avoids admitting to liking anything on television: 'with the exception of documentaries, perhaps, or high-status "adult" movies' (we could add today 'high-quality' TV dramas such as *Game of Thrones*, *The Sopranos* or *Mad Men*) because this 'would be to run the risk of aligning … with the mass audience' (Buckingham 1993a, 293). As Buckingham (1993a, 293) notes: 'To distance oneself from the pleasures of "other people" – or indeed from one's own pleasures – is implicitly to assert one's own superiority'.

Parents as Police and Adult Secrets

As indicated above, pleasure does not have the cultural capital of intellectual pursuits and in this context time spent watching television is time wasted – particularly for children (Buckingham 1993b, 44). Watching television does not involve 'work' and it is not considered educational (with the exception of specially nominated 'educational' programs) (Buckingham 1993a, 105). This raises a concern for parents whose role on the front line of defence, in preserving the innocence while strengthening the reason of the child, is paramount. Policing children's television viewing, and in fact their access to all content on the various screens available today, is a major focus of parental concern. In its research, the Australian Communications and Media Authority (2015b, 13) found that 94% of surveyed families had rules in place about watching television. These primarily included time and content restrictions. But all screens attract restrictions for children, with three in four parents having rules about television, internet, mobile phones, and gaming (Australian Communications and Media Authority 2007, 13).

Parental rules around children's viewing habits are not always strictly enforced (Buckingham 1993a, 105) but nonetheless the dominant discourse demands constant vigilance on the part of the parent.

> Most adults watch television and most parents let their children watch television, but many mothers feel compelled to apologize for it and see regulating children's consumption of television as part of their job. (Seiter 1998, 314)

The pressure on parents to see this as 'their job' is still strong today, with the Australian Communications and Media Authority (2011, 58-9) finding in its latest research that 89% of adults believed that 'parents were responsible for preventing children from seeing content with too much sex and violence' on the internet. This is also supported by the answers from the children in my survey where 80% indicated they were not allowed to watch television as much as they wanted.

The task of controlling children's media consumption is a challenging one and fear of losing control is an ever-present concern. Children's apparent facility with new technologies seems to feed this fear while parents struggle to keep up with the latest developments (Luke and Luke 2001; Marsh 2004). Seiter (1999b, 88) points out the irony of the argument that is often made 'that children should be kept away from television because they cannot understand it, in fact it is often the ease with which they become media experts that may frighten adults'. As Faulkner (2011, 137) observes, 'The pace of the media is too fast and it makes us feel passive. In this context, the next generation becomes one more element slipping from our grasp'.

Faulkner (2011) argues that the enormous investment our culture has in the innocence of the child drives this heavy policing. Possessing what we all want (that tantalizing innocence), children have to be carefully handled, and as a result they 'are feared,

CHAPTER 2

controlled and protected, [and] worried about' (Faulkner 2011, 68). Ariès (1973, 395) too contends that 'our world is obsessed by the physical, moral and sexual problems of childhood'.

While the institutions of education have been developed and designed since the 17th century to nurture and protect the child, so too has the family's role been shaped according to the needs of maintaining this child's innocence. Ariès (1973) suggests that the concept of the family that was born in the 16th century has been closely linked to the emerging concept of childhood. By the 18th century not only the child's future 'but his presence and his very existence are of concern: the child has taken a central place in the family' (1973, 130). The value attached to the child within the family developed, according to Aries (1973, 397), into an internally focused and obsessive love and this in turn 'raised the wall of private life between the family and society'.

At the heart of this love is a desire to protect the child, in particular from adult sexuality and violence (Faulkner 2011; Higonnet 1998). 'The family cordons off childhood from the rigors and abuses of public adult life. Mother and father act as guardians' (Higonnet 1998, 223). It is a heavy responsibility but there is a lot of advice available for the uncertain parent. Martha Wolfenstein (1998) tracks the wealth of literature written for parents on how to guard the innocence of their child, and strengthen their character through, in particular, policing their fun and pleasure. Lynn Spigel (1998, 114) notes that 'it was the adult's responsibility to generate moral values in the young by guarding the gates to knowledge'. But the stakes are high and a mistake 'could prove fatal – not only for the individual child, but for the moral character of the entire nation' (Spigel 1998, 114). This point is made forcefully by Faulkner (2011, 67) who observes that

'Children are the volatile substance of politics that must be controlled and carefully handled, lest humanity lose its way'. The responsibility is onerous for parents; if they don't or can't control their children's television viewing they are failures or, even worse, they become a cause of the problem (Buckingham 1996, 71-2).

This burden has created a story, according to Kincaid (1998), that has immobilised parents. They cannot afford to simply indulge in their own and their child's happiness. In fact, he suggests, 'we are obsessed with its denial, with the outrageous withholding of happiness' and 'with the best of intentions [we] bury [our children] within corpulent and suffocating narratives of danger' (Kincaid 1998, 282).

Television was particularly threatening when it first arrived because it brought pleasure, with its suggestion of the potential enjoyment of adult secrets, into the private heart of the family. Radio had of course already been invented, but television had the captivating images, giving it a far greater presence in the living room. These broadcast media brought the outside world into the living room and as such it was an invasion of the public into the private sphere of Ariès's 18th century family. Television was seen as a threat to parents' capacity to protect their children from the sort of knowledge that would endanger and corrupt their youthful innocence. 'Television's immediate availability in the home threatened to abolish childhood by giving children equal access to the ideas and values circulated in the adult culture' (Spigel 1998, 119).

Catharine Lumby (1999, 15) argues that the mass media has provided a window from the private into the public sphere and notes 'the ongoing penetration of the media into almost every aspect of life'. This has no doubt contributed to its position as a disputed and controversial medium. As Lumby (1999, 10) observes, the site of the

CHAPTER 2

mass media in today's culture is 'a profoundly political arena, a place where a dizzying array of ideologies and ideas collide and interact on a visceral level'. Certainly this aspect of television, as a purveyor of potentially dangerous notions and knowledge, appears to be at the heart of a number of the conflicts that the children in my research spoke about in the interviews (see Chapter 5). But what also appears to make the access to knowledge even more aggravating to adults is that it is reached through entertainment. Lumby (1999, 15) suggests there is:

> enormous concern about the blurring of the lines between information and entertainment in popular culture. We're constantly told that we live in an era of trash culture, a time when entertainment values have replaced serious analysis of politics and economics.

The suggestion that 'entertainment values' have corroded the serious business of life is a pervasive discourse, and I examine its influence on our culture's negative view of entertainment in the next chapter.

A compelling example of how the efforts to keep a lid on children's sexuality and protect them from forbidden knowledge plays out in the public discourse today is the debate sparked by *The New Yorker* magazine's use of two famous children's television characters. In July 2013 the magazine published a picture of the *Sesame Street* characters Bert and Ernie on its front cover. The two characters from the long-running and highly popular children's television program were sitting with their arms around one another, watching the United States Supreme Court make its decision on same-sex couples. The court had just released its finding that 'equal liberty' should be granted to same-sex couples under the US Constitution's Fifth Amendment. The title of the cover image was 'Moment of Joy'. This suggestion of joy, pleasure and sexuality, brought together in a powerful image that was implicitly related to children, unleashed a furious debate. A one-line headline story in the *National Review Online* tapped into the dominant cultural position perfectly: 'Innocence. Lost.' was the heading, placed directly above a picture of *The New Yorker*'s cover (Lopez 2013). The image on *The New Yorker*'s cover was interpreted as a direct attack on the cultural notion of 'childhood innocence': an intrusion of the nasty adult secrets of sex into the child's world. The producers of the program, Sesame Workshop, obviously understood the tricky nature of this debate for them. When they were approached for a response to the outcry against the cover, they steadfastly refused to buy into the debate over the image. Instead Sesame Workshop's previously stated comments, from an airing of this debate two years earlier, were widely quoted: '[Bert and Ernie] were created to teach preschoolers that people can be good friends with those who are very different from themselves'. The statement had said:

> Even though they are identified as male characters and possess many human traits and characteristics (as most *Sesame Street* Muppets do), they remain puppets, and do not have a sexual orientation. (Idato 2013)

The producers of *Sesame Street* were acutely aware of the dangers of allowing sex to be seen to be appearing in their television program for children. They have managed over the years to position *Sesame Street* to fit carefully within the cultural construct of childhood; the show educates children while it entertains. The entertainment is also carefully managed to keep any suggestion of 'adult' secrets from its core and the main 'work' of the program is to support the education of our young. *Sesame Street* has managed to avoid the criticism aimed

CHAPTER 2

at other children's television programs – most often at cartoons – that they are full of bad taste, gratuitous violence and depravity.

It is interesting to see how the producers of *Sesame Street* have managed the often conflicting demands of the dominant culture and those of their young audience, for the program is popular with children around the world, *and* it appeals to the parents, educators and the arbiters of taste who attempt to control what children should watch. This achievement in meeting the standards of the dominant culture and appealing to the audience is no doubt part of the reason behind its longstanding and widespread success.

Many popular children's television producers do not set out to produce educational programs but rather to entertain their viewers. But success in achieving this goal comes at a cost. The producer of *Teletubbies* was furiously criticised when it became apparent that her show was hugely popular with very young children: and that she had designed it for exactly that purpose. As Buckingham (2002a, 48) points out 'for some critics, the very existence of a programme aimed at such a young audience seems to represent an affront to their fundamental ideas or fantasies about childhood'. The producer of the program, Anne Woods, strongly defended herself and the show, saying that 'children have the right to fun and entertainment just as much as adult viewers' (Buckingham 2002a, 49): a brave statement given that it flies in the face of the dominant cultural concepts of childhood.

Interestingly it didn't take long for criticism of the program to spread to fears about its unsuitable sexual content. One of the four Teletubbies, a large goofy-looking purple character carrying a handbag, was accused of being the 'first gay icon for preschoolers'. This 'scandal' caused a furore in the media though not without provoking some ironic humour (see Crockett 2014; Oliver 1998; Rosin 1999) at the ridiculous nature of such an allegation. But while it is possible to laugh at such exaggerated reactions to a preschoolers' television show, these suggestions do reflect a serious and deep-seated fear. Although the children who watched the show were patently absorbed in the 'pleasure and excitement' of the show as delightfully described by Howard and Roberts (2002, 334), adults were worrying about the dangers of offering such pleasure to the very young and were also concerned at the slightest hint that it might provide a window onto adult secrets.

Powerful 'Myths' and the Sexualisation of the Child

While children do appear to evade and avoid parental restrictions of their viewing as I discuss in the next section, what is certain is that our culture circulates the myth, in Roland Barthes's (1973) sense of myth, of the necessity for such parental control. Barthes (1973) argues that key cultural concepts become adopted as 'common sense' over time and with use, and that they come to be seen as 'normal' values that are taken for granted. The reasons that originally informed such adopted concepts are no longer examined but accepted at face value: the concept becomes myth. As Barthes (1973, 156) argues:

> myth acts economically: it abolishes the complexity of human acts, it gives them the simplicity of essences, it does away with all dialectics, with any going back beyond what is immediately visible, it organizes a world which is without contradictions because it is without depth, a world wide open and wallowing in the evident, it establishes a blissful clarity: things appear to mean something by themselves.

Barthes (1973) suggests that this process has a depoliticising effect and the concept becomes 'exnominated': it no longer has a name

CHAPTER 2

because it has become the 'natural' state. I would argue that parental control of children's television viewing is seen as 'natural' in this sense; it has the status of 'myth' and is not a concept that is questioned or examined in our everyday lives. This myth feeds into the broader 'myth' that it is part of the role of the parent to protect the child from all threats to its innocence. Television is a major site for the exercise of this control, with parents urged to regulate and monitor access and to guide and educate the child through encouraging only worthy and 'wholesome' viewing. This regulation is particularly imperative in guarding against one of television's greatest perceived dangers: its potential to 'expose children to sexuality' (Faulkner 2011, 14).

Kincaid (1998) and Faulkner (2011) argue that these parental myths are insidious and damaging to the very ones they claim to protect: the children. They go on to suggest that the arguments about the need for parents to control and regulate their children's behaviour in all respects have over the past century become increasingly tied up with the sexualisation of the child. 'It is because children are idealised as innocent, unworldly creatures that they have become the forbidden, most prized, fruit of adult desire (commercial and sexual)' (Faulkner 2011, 42). Kincaid (1998, 68-9) argues that the perpetuation of the 'parental myth' allows us to 'load on the parents powers, responsibilities, and rights'. But it is what this myth hides that is of most concern: 'we don't acknowledge that these powers, responsibilities, and rights are sneakily sexualised' (p. 69).

> The naughty child allows us … to slip unconsciously into an imaginative sexuality that is almost obligatory in our culture: we make the bad kid into the Other (much as men do women) in order to idealize, beat, and generally mold as we like, all in the name of duty. (Kincaid 1998, 144)

Higonnet (1998) too has charted the emergence of the 'sexualised' child over the past 200 years, through the child's representation in images. She argues that the portrayal of the desirable innocence of the 18th century child has led inevitably to a vision today of the sexual child.

> More and more sexual meanings are now being ascribed to photographs of children both past and present, whether because of what is in the photograph or what is in the eye of the beholder. (Higonnet 1998, 10)

She argues that the cultural drives to protect childhood innocence have corrupted our view of the real nature of individual children and as a result we deny the child's whole, human potential. It is a system, she argues, that 'protects children against sexuality on the grounds that they are asexual, against violence because they are weak, against deceit because they are guileless, against knowledge because they are innocent' (1998, 223). If we are to take 'our children seriously' we must recognise:

> childhood as a great human subject. Like all great subjects, it is bound to have its dark and turbulent side. Why, then, should we be surprised that childhood has the power to threaten as well as to delight, to repel as well as to rivet? (Higonnet 1998, 225)

Faulkner (2011, 7) too has argued that 'it is critical that we begin to explore alternative avenues for understanding and experiencing children'. But in order to do this we must listen to children and young people, and hear what they say. We 'require an attention to the views of children that is not yet evident in our culture', Faulkner (2011, 126) argues. But this approach faces quite a hurdle as 'creating such an opening for discussion means relinquishing our investment in the idea of childhood innocence, understood in terms of ignorance and protection' (Faulkner 2011, 126).

Our culture's determination that children's viewing of television should be monitored and policed – in particular by parents – is based on the notion of childhood innocence. It is not based on an examination of the real ways in which both children and their parents watch and enjoy television. Here again is evidence of its status as myth; in the public and media discourse there is no questioning of the belief that children's viewing must be controlled and regulated; there is no apparent reason to look behind such an 'obvious' statement.

Beyond the Myths

There are, however, those who do question the widely accepted norm that parents should police their children's television lest they come to harm. In the academic field researchers such as Buckingham (2001a, 42) have cast doubt on the negative attitudes that inform the myths, pointing out their futility:

> The debate about parents' and children's relationships with television has been dominated for much too long by negative arguments. It often seems as though the most responsible thing one can do as a parent is simply to throw out the TV set.

Buckingham highlights both the impracticality and the exaggeration behind the prevailing negative discourse, suggesting that the implementation of the established myths would result ultimately in nonsensical actions. This is an insight that parents themselves appear to share. Hodge and Tripp have pointed out that even though parents do believe the content of television is often 'trivial or even harmful', and feel they are not exercising enough control over their children's viewing, they don't stop their children from watching television (Hodge and Tripp 1986, 1). Rather perceptively, Hodge and Tripp (1986, 1) suggest that this 'belief that television is a bad influence is … hard to sustain in the face of the apparently robust and healthy enjoyment of television by one's own children'. In other words, observing the ways in which children actually *enjoy* television is one of the most potent ways of unsettling the prevailing myths.

It does appear as though, despite the pervasiveness and power of the myth of parental control, parents and their children do manage to evade its strictures in interesting, if possibly unacknowledged, ways. Children pursue the pleasure they get from television in defiance of cultural (and parental) sanctions; parents observe their children's pleasure and delight and let the sanctions slip away (Buckingham 1998b; Hodge and Tripp 1986). Even more remarkably, in some cases the parents actually come over to the child's side: 'Parents may control their children's media use through a range of styles of regulation, but in turn children introduce and then encourage parents to trust new media spaces' (Lealand and Zanker 2008, 48). Lealand and Zanker (2008, 49), in some interesting research with children and parents in New Zealand, have identified ways in which children have influenced adults' view of television, referring to 'parents' descriptions of how they have been transformed into fans of erstwhile frowned-upon popular culture'. Beyond the influence of these behaviours on the immediate families, Lealand and Zanker (2008, 51) see a potential for such family dynamics to have an impact on 'the shifting construction of childhood'. Such an impact, which recognises the agency of the child, can perhaps contribute to breaking down the stranglehold of the innocence myth and allow breathing space for the child to be happy, as Kincaid (1998, 282) has suggested, outside the suffocating control of parental concern.

The fear of allowing children to overindulge in pleasure, as we have seen above, is one of the driving forces behind our culture's anxieties about children and television. The child, weak and innocent as it is, cannot be expected to control its own pleasure; the parent must step in to regulate and protect. As with much of Buckingham's (1993a, 1996) research, his approach to talking to children themselves produces revealing insights into the reality of children's lives behind these myths. He demonstrates convincingly that:

> children actively learn to regulate their own emotional responses to television. They develop very definite ideas about what they can and cannot 'handle', and hence what they will or will not choose to watch. (1996, 254)

Echoing what Lealand and Zanker (2008) have suggested, Buckingham (1996, 253) argues that parents could actually learn about this regulation from their children. While parents can 'play a very constructive role in mediating their children's viewing, and in teaching them about television', emotional self-regulation is something that children could teach their parents (Buckingham 1996, 253).

Lealand and Zanker's (2008, 51) suggestion that 'media consumption mediates parent–child relationships in a range of ways' echoes Donald's (1992, 3) ideas about the 'performative aspect … of popular culture'. Quoting the French scholar Michel de Certeau, Donald (1992, 3) writes that:

> the practices of everyday life … 'present themselves essentially as "arts of making" this or that, i.e., as combinatory or utilizing modes of consumption.' It is this performative

aspect that (de Certeau) sees as the most important, and often underestimated, characteristic of popular culture.

Given this significant characteristic of popular culture, 'and the fluidity of the movement in which authoritative norms are enacted and translated in their use', Donald (1992, 3) suggests we should not allow popular culture to remain in second place: in a marginal or subversive relationship to education. He argues that we should look for the unexpected perspectives:

> for example, not only the performative aspects of popular culture, but also the pedagogic functions of national broadcasting systems ... The point to stress is that 'popular culture' does not mean just one thing. It refers both to an apparatus that disseminates certain narratives and images, and also to the practices through which these are consumed or rearticulated. (Donald 1992, 3)

One of the performative aspects of popular culture as far as children are concerned can be seen through the pleasure they take in the television programs they enjoy. But in order to look more closely at this aspect of their engagement we need to get away from the negative cultural stereotypes of television being seen at best as a time-wasting occupation, and at worst as corrupting. One way of doing this is to listen carefully to children themselves, and, as many researchers have found, this attention is illuminating, often in unexpected ways (Buckingham 1993a, 1996; Davies, Buckingham and Kelley 2000; Roberts and Howard 2005). Talking to children, whose own views are considered marginal in our culture if not potentially subversive, is important if we are to get a fuller picture of their engagement with popular culture (Faulkner 2011; Higonnet 1998). Faulkner (2011, 117) warns of the dangers of leaving it to the 'concerned adults (to) advocate children's interests, not because children have no place in politics, but

CHAPTER 2

because by invoking the sanctity of childhood, children's opinions and agency are effectively excluded'.

Unfortunately, Prout (2000) believes that children are being increasingly excluded from debate in public life and this is certainly true in the media discourse on children and television where their opinions and voices are rarely heard. He argues (2000, 304) that 'despite the recognition of children as persons in their own rights, public policy and practice is marked by an intensification of control, regulation and surveillance around children' which does not involve an engagement with children's own views. Instead the private sphere of the family has become the place where they 'are more allowed to express choice, exercise autonomy and work at their individual self-realisation' (Prout 2000, 311) albeit under the 'control' of their parents. A growing separation of the public and private spheres, Prout argues, is leading effectively to an exclusion of children from the broader society and fosters disenchantment on their part with such major institutions as government and education. I would suggest that it also contributes to ensuring that children's views on areas deemed to be outside the culturally 'important' structures of governance and education, such as popular culture, remain largely unrepresented and undervalued in the public discourse.

Nonetheless television's pleasures inform the cultural and social lives of children in fascinating and complex ways. Listening to their voices on such pleasures reveals insights into the ways in which children engage with popular culture that could productively inform public policy in other areas of their lives. But while children's views are shared within families – and despite the pressures of the dominant culture to 'control' perfidious pleasures, parents do hear and respond to these views – they are not heard in public life (Prout 2000).

The task of achieving such participation of children cannot be underestimated. But listening to the voices of children, on a subject that is central to their lives while all but invisible in the public sphere, might possibly shake the pervasive 'myths' of the dominant culture that suggest pleasure is bad for children, education is good and innocence above all must be preserved.

Play – Is It Fun?

As can be seen from this review of the development of the modern-day culture of childhood, pleasure is a suspect indulgence for children. Fun itself might be considered less harmful but it is still potentially time-wasting. As a result, I suggest, there has been little examination in either the public discourse or in academic research of children's own pursuit of fun. One childhood activity, in the study of which one might expect to find an exploration of fun and enjoyment, is play. But even here, as a brief review of the literature demonstrates, fun is not central to the academic research into this field.

Play is an activity which obviously provides children with hours of fun and it has been researched and studied extensively. Its study has 'been extremely important in many theories of development, education, therapy, socialization, and cognition' (Burghardt 2005, 66). This has resulted in a large body of research though Gordon Burghardt (2005, 8) points out that, while play has been 'endlessly classified', there has not been 'any consensus on its nature or role'. Looking at just four of Burghardt's (2005, 7) list of 16 different views on play gives an indication of the diversity of the findings:

> Play is the process most conducive to improved motor skills, learning ability, imagination, and educational attainments in infancy and childhood.

> Play, like idleness, is not only wasted time, but is also a process leading to the neglect of study and work.
>
> Play is serious behaviour in which the arts of war are learned.
>
> Play must be organized and controlled by governments or other adult institutions to control young people and channel them into responsible adulthood.

These views are particularly revealing in what they leave out. There is no indication of any significant research into children playing *because* it is fun nor much exploration of what this might mean for them. This is not to say that fun is not included as an inherent feature of play but that the fun is often seen as a means to an end; for example, as a way of enhancing a child's education: 'as an essential pathway to learning for all ... children' (Isenberg and Quisenberry 2002, 33). In his study of play Brian Sutton-Smith (1997) categorised the various theories of play from a wide range of different academic disciplines into seven 'rhetorics', only two of which touched on emotional responses to play: the categories of 'self' and 'frivolity'. The study of play as 'fun', in particular for children, is not identified as central to any of these rhetorics.

The large body of work examining children's play in fact seems to have been influenced by the dominant cultural discourses that have developed over the past 100 years and that I have reviewed above. As Kline (1998, 100) points out, in the late 19th century play came to be seen as the 'work of childhood'. Directionless fun was not encouraged; instead, 'structured game play [was] ... highly recommended as [a way] of preparing children for a competitive society' (Kline 1998, 100). This approach to childhood strengthened in the 20th century where 'the child-saving movement set out to regulate children's play [and] helped institutionalize ideas about what constituted children's appropriate use of leisure time' (Spigel 1998, 113). This culture of play – where the desired end was to develop and nurture the child for the future benefit of society – certainly appears to have influenced the direction of academic research in the 20th century, which largely reflects the drive to understand how play develops the moral and critical faculties of the child. This was cemented with Piaget's notion of play as the 'work of childhood' (1964). As Burghardt (2005, 140) notes, 'mainline psychologists downplayed motivational and emotional aspects of play for much of the 20th century ... Modern research questions such dogma, but the effect it had still lingers'.

By trying to categorise play according to its outcomes, perhaps we are missing the essence of what it means to children themselves in much the same way as Miss Havisham does in Charles Dickens's novel *Great Expectations* (1981, 49) when she issues her instruction to the two children, Pip and Estella:

> 'I am tired,' said Miss Havisham. 'I want diversion, and I have done with men and women. Play.'

The cruel edge of Miss Havisham's narcissistic and obtuse command is that it denies the children's agency in their own play. This blackly comic aspect of her instruction highlights the fact that play is simply not possible without the agency of the child. When talking to children it is apparent that this agency informs their enjoyment not only of play but of other leisure pursuits such as watching television. There is agency in having fun too and this is a large part of its value to children. James, Jenks and Prout (1998, 87) articulated the importance of this agency in their exploration of children's culture where they suggest that 'something which could be called 'children's culture' exists only in the spaces and times over which children have some degree of power and control'. Allison James (1998, 404) goes even further in suggesting that children deliberately celebrate and value that which adults judge unworthy, in order to mark out their own agency:

> Children, by the very nature of their position as a group outside adult society, have sought out an alternative system of meanings through which they can establish their own integrity. Adult order is manipulated so that what adults esteem is made to appear ridiculous; what adults despise is invested with prestige.

This is supported by Davies, Buckingham and Kelley (2000) whose research with children found that they categorised television programs that parents watched as 'boring' while their own favourite programs were 'cool' and 'funny'.

More recent studies of children and play have taken a more holistic approach to play than the dominant fields of the 20th century. These include a strong recognition of both the agency and the voice of children. Marilyn Fleer (2014, 160) has argued for the importance of recognising that 'children do have agency and do shape their own play' and that this agency should be 'valued, made visible and sanctioned'. But her approach too is focused on pursuing an understanding of role-play in order to promote the use of play in development, though importantly it seeks to include the children's voices and values in the research directed to this end. Her ultimate aim is to further understand how 'the cultural nature of role-play … develops children and societies' (p. 160). The pursuit of understanding children's engagement in play is not focused on the valorisation of the play itself or on the fun to be had by the children engaged in it.

Glenn et al. (2013, 195) attribute this absence of research into the 'fun' of play to the scarcity of analysis that focuses on children's own views: 'as researchers have sought to define and understand play they have primarily considered the views of parents, practitioners, and theorists'. Seeking to address this gap, Glenn et al. (2013, 192) undertook to seek out children's own views and from this research they noted 'the critical role of fun in children's choice of [play] activities'. They also observed that 'children did not depict play fulfilling a particular purpose or outcome' (p. 190). In other words, to children play was fun for its own sake.

While their article addresses a significant gap in the research into play by seeking out the views of children themselves, Glenn et al. (2013) do make one rather spurious connection to children's views on television. They note that children do not classify watching television as 'play'. This would seem to be quite understandable simply given the word's everyday definition and use. An adult in today's society would not call watching television 'play' either.[2] But Glenn et al. seek to make more of the observation, arguing that children don't classify television as play *because* it is boring. They cite no substantial evidence to support this assertion, referring only to passing comments from the children such as 'we don't really do anything in her house, just watch TV' (2013, 190). Their interpretation could well be explained in the context of the dominant discourse which pits 'active' outdoors play against 'passive' indoors television viewing. As I examine in the following chapter, children themselves perceive and understand the prevailing negative discourses around television and, as might be expected, often adopt the same language in their responses to

---

[2] The *OED* 3rd edition 2006 defines play as: to exercise or occupy oneself, to be engaged with some activity.

adult interlocutors. In these particular interviews, seeking their views on play, the children might have expected the researchers to view television as the negatively 'passive' opposite to 'active' play and they have responded accordingly. Unfortunately Glenn et al. have not made reference to the research involving children that finds most children in fact regard television as fun (Davies 2001; Palmer 1986; Sheldon and Loncar 1996). It is an unfortunate example of how the negative dominant discourses on children and television, and the myths these have created, pervade not only the public sphere but also the academic field.

Another researcher who has sought in the past decade to focus on children's own views of play is Johan Meire (2007a, 2007b). He too has noted that 'remarkably little research focuses explicitly on what play actually means to children' (2007b, 47) and he argues that 'any concept of play should include something of the fun or attraction that is so central in the experience of play' (p. 44). Meire (2007b, 44) believes a focus is needed not only on the effects (positive or negative) and outcomes of play on children but also on their own agency: 'part of the fun in play comes from the feeling of control'.

Meire (2007a, 2) proposes a definition of the 'fun in play' that recognises the centrality of agency:

> I would argue that the fun in play comes from … the feeling of control or challenge, from sharing or (more generally) being part of the social, material and imaginary environment, and/or from bodily sensations.

This approach could perhaps also inform an exploration of the fun that children get from television. In the following chapters, I look at how children actively seek out their own favourite shows, taking pleasure in sharing their enjoyment of these programs with their families and friends, and delighting also in a physical pleasure in their engagement with these favourites.

The United Nations Committee on the Rights of the Child is a major advocate for the agency and voice of children and it has noted that the enjoyment of play, recreation and leisure is still denied to many children around the world (Committee on the Rights of the Child 2013). Despite the fact that the right to play, recreation and leisure is enshrined in Article 31 of the United Nations Convention on the Rights of the Child, the Committee noted in 2013 that there is still 'poor recognition of their significance in the lives of children' (p. 3). The Committee (2013, 11) notes the lack of value attached to play: 'In many parts of the world, play is perceived as "deficit" time spent in frivolous or unproductive activity of no intrinsic worth'. It argues against this perspective, stating that play, recreation and leisure 'are a form of participation in everyday life, and are of intrinsic value to the child, purely in terms of *the enjoyment and pleasure* they afford'. (2013, 4) (italics mine)

While it is heartening to see in such research and advocacy over the past 20 years a growing recognition of the value of play to children themselves and of the fun and pleasure it provides them, the same cannot be said about the appreciation of the fun of television in children's lives. Television is undeniably a major leisure activity for children and in interviews with children themselves it is obvious that television programs provide them with hours of fun and enjoyment. Yet even the UN Committee tasked with oversight of the implementation of children's rights has failed to acknowledge the central and valuable role played by television in children's lives (Committee on the Rights of the Child 2013). Despite strongly advocating that we listen to children themselves, the Committee has failed to hear the voices of children which clearly proclaim their enjoyment of television as a significant and valued leisure activity. The Committee (2013, 14-15) instead has fallen under the influence of the effects tradition and adopted the prevailing language of its largely negative discourse and its disputed causal effects:

> Television is also contributing to the loss of many childhood games, songs, rhymes traditionally transmitted from generation to generation on the street and in the playground … [and] is thought to be associated with reduced levels of physical activity among children, poor sleep patterns, growing levels of obesity and other related illnesses.

The same report (2013, 19) also refers to the pervasive myth about television programs promoting violent behaviour in children. There is no mention of the fun that children enjoy from watching television or the value it has for them as a significant leisure pursuit.

As can be seen from the literature, play has been extensively studied for more than 100 years, though largely in order to understand what it can 'do' for children rather than to promote any understanding of the intrinsic enjoyment it might provide them. Children's pursuit of fun itself has not attracted significant research or serious attention, although it has more recently been the subject of study into the value of play as understood by children themselves. It is significant that research conducted with children themselves, which seeks to elicit and understand children's own views both on play and television, has resulted in a recognition of the value and role of fun in such pursuits. Although this research is not extensive, its findings share a number of key points which have also been highlighted by leading researchers into the culture of childhood (James, Jenks and Prout 1998; Kincaid 1998): that fun has significant value to children; that agency is central to their enjoyment/happiness; that they seek to share this control with each other (Corsaro 2015, 152); and that there is a physical element to such joy (Meire 2007a, 2). This last element is illustrated in Kincaid's (1998,282) 'boisterously happy' child and in the 'delicious excitement' and 'barely controlled ecstasy' of the preschoolers watching *Teletubbies* in Howard and Roberts's (2002, 332) research. This physical enjoyment, however, doesn't necessarily have to be boisterous; it is apparent also in the sensation described by a 10-year-old boy in my research who lay back on his couch to watch television and to 'relax' as though he were 'on a vacation'.

After a lifetime career studying and writing about play, Sutton-Smith (2008) has reflected on the important differences between adult play centred on the 'creative' imagination of artists or scientists and children's imaginative play. He points out that the play of children is 'more heedless, more focussed on having fun' (2008, 99). This too appears to be true in the way in which children approach television; fun is a central element to them of its appeal and, left to their own choices, they will watch what they enjoy rather than what adults say is good for them.

But with this attitude, children come up against a powerful discourse. While play has been seen to be of use in children's development, and in their social and cultural learning, the element of pure fun in play has not been highly regarded. As James and James (2008, 99) note 'in the childhood context then, play appears to lose some of its associations with freedom and spontaneity and becomes a more obligatory activity for children'. Academic research into play has largely investigated what play can 'do' for children and this study has revealed many facets of play, not least of which is the notion that children can learn from such activity. This has given play a higher status than television viewing within the western culture of childhood; it has more obvious potential to produce upright and educated citizens. Television on the other hand is seen more often as a purveyor of 'cheap and nasty' popular culture, 'a kind of toxic virus responsible for killing off "childhood"' (Messenger Davies 2010, 142). Although the 'right' programs can offer some educational value, the fun of television does not appear to have any worth. As Davies, Buckingham and Kelley (2000, 14) perceptively note, very few 'contemporary critics of children's television … seem prepared to stand up for children's right to just "have a laugh"'. Children having fun watching TV simply does not have status on any level.

Drawing on the albeit scarce elements in the literature on play that focus on fun and in particular on the fun that children speak about themselves can perhaps give some valuable insights into how we might understand the value to children of the fun of television. Above all, it appears that to children, in their own cultural hierarchy, the 'fun' is the thing. They pursue this element consistently in relation to watching television as is apparent in research that includes children themselves (Davies 2001; Götz 2006, 2011; Messenger Davies 2010; Palmer 1986) including my own. Central to this element of fun is the child's own agency; fun is not fun without agency just as play under instruction from an adult, such as Miss Havisham, is not play. Choosing their own favourite programs, enjoying these on their own and sharing with both friends and family; these elements of television viewing are an integral part of the enjoyment. As suggested above by Meire (2007a, 2), bodily sensations are also an element of joy to children in their play and this is apparent too in their responses to television viewing.

But there is another element to the enjoyment that children get out of television which is perhaps less obvious and less tangible. It is hinted at in Sutton-Smith's (2008, 95) subtle insight into the power of the pleasure of play and its reach into our fuller existence:

> [the] positive pleasure [of play] typically transfers to our feelings about the rest of our everyday existence and makes it possible to live more fully in the world, no matter how boring or painful or even dangerous ordinary reality might seem.

Within my own research with children this element is poignantly captured by an 8-year-old girl who, in answer to the question 'Why do you watch television?', explained quite simply 'because it chse (cheers) you up when you are sad'.[3]

This insight into the way that pleasure and fun is central to our daily lives is, I believe, profoundly valuable in seeking to understand how children engage with television. But as I have already noted, academic research into such questions as thrown up by this insight is significantly limited. The value of fun in particular has scant appeal, it seems, in the field of academic research.

There is, however, an exception to this pattern of sidelining fun. Academic research into the field of entertainment provides some interesting observations of the essential role played in our lives by the joys of such leisure pastimes. It is to this field that I turn in the next chapter in order to draw out some insights that might further promote understanding of the ways in which children enjoy television, and of how this pleasure informs their lives. I explore some of the key literature on entertainment, acknowledging that this field too is

---

[3] I have kept the children's own spelling in the answers to the survey questions throughout the book. Where it might not be easily understood I include the correct spelling in parentheses.

CHAPTER 2

undermined by the dominant negative discourses that surround the pursuit of fun. I also consider from an analysis of my own research how children accommodate the negative public discourses on children and television while still expressing, confidently and clearly, their own pleasure in the medium.

Chapter 3

LET'S JUST HAVE FUN: ENTERTAINMENT AND WHY IT MATTERS

The valuing of 'high' culture over 'popular' culture, of 'serious' intellectual pursuits above pleasure, and of 'innocent' childhood as a pristine and uncorrupted state has informed the public discourse around children's television viewing in western culture for much of the second half of the 20th century. These cultural imperatives have also had an impact on the direction of academic research into the question of how children enjoy the pleasures of television. Buckingham (1993a, 13) points out that cognitive research has held the upper hand and has concentrated 'almost exclusively on the intellectual aspects of children's understanding of television'. He argues that this has had the unfortunate effect of driving a focus on '"meaning" … while neglecting the central question of "pleasure"'. But the influence of valuing cognitive understanding of television over pleasure goes further. It is ultimately promoted as a protection against pleasure: taking a rational approach to understanding television will protect from its pernicious influence; children won't be taken in by its insidious messages or corrupted by its unsuitable low-class morality. As Buckingham (1993a, 260) argues, 'In this formulation, pleasure becomes the soft underbelly which lies beneath the hard shell of cynicism: if we could only disavow or overcome pleasure, we would be wholly protected'. But a more fruitful approach to understanding children's engagement with television he suggests would be to look instead at the cultural preferences of children themselves and accept the values they place on affective responses to television (Bazalgette and Buckingham 1995, 10; Buckingham 1995). Certainly I would argue in support of this that such an approach could provide a richer picture of children's complex relationship to televisual programs.

In his book *Moving Images* (1996, 2), Buckingham writes about 'children's emotional responses to television – and more specifically, about what might be termed "negative" responses – what frightens them but also what they find moving and worrying'. While Buckingham (1996) focuses largely on what he terms 'negative' responses, these responses are closely tied to pleasure; as he points out, being 'scared' by a television program can provoke a visceral pleasure in the viewer. This is a central insight into children's engagement with the screen. I believe that the fun and pleasure of television is essential to children's own view of its cultural value, and I go beyond Buckingham's exploration of their 'negative' responses to explore the ways in which children *enjoy* programs. In this chapter, I will look at how they talk about their delight in television, but also at how they accommodate – and interpret – the pervasive adult criticisms of their engagement with the 'demon' screen.

Research with children, including Buckingham's, has revealed the pleasure and joy children experience in watching television (Davies 2001; Howard and Roberts 2002; Messenger Davies 2010; Palmer 1986). But while Buckingham has observed this pleasure (see, for example, Buckingham 1995), his work has not included an extensive examination of this aspect of children's television viewing.

CHAPTER 3

While he has significantly illuminated the debates around children and television, he has looked out from his research with children to the broader debates. This has driven his focus on countering the jeremiads against children watching television. Even in his book *Moving Images* (1996) he considers pleasure and children's affective relationship with television from the focus of 'negative responses', examining, for example, the value – and pleasure – that children get from watching horror. My focus instead is on an examination of the fun that children so demonstrably get out of television. The value children themselves placed on this response to their favourite television programs emerged throughout my research, in their conversations and in their written stories and drawings, and I look at these responses in this chapter.

But first, in order to illuminate the notion of fun and thus to better understand the pleasure and enjoyment that children get from television, I would like to explore how and where the subject of fun, and of fun in entertainment, is considered in academia. While this is not a comprehensive literature review of the field, I will draw on the work of some key theorists who I believe offer significant insights that shed light on my own research.

I will then go on to consider the evidence that children themselves place the fun of television high in their own hierarchy of values. This does not mean that they are not influenced by the negative public discourses. In fact it was apparent from my own research with children that they do not blithely, nor ignorantly, either accept or deny these negative discourses. Instead, in rather unexpected and curious ways, they incorporate such views into their own embrace of the medium. This hypothesis is supported by Rebekah Willett's (2015) analysis of research from an ethnographic study of children in London. Willett found that 'children were navigating complex discourses around childhood, masculinity, surveillance and media effects' during their engagement in 'media-referenced games' (p. 418). Certainly in my research I observed that children appear to rewrite the cultural landscape in ways that allow for their multifaceted engagement with the pleasures offered by their favourite television shows. Their delight in the fun of television, an examination of which is at the heart of my research, is what I will go on to explore in Chapters 4 and 5.

Where is Fun in the Picture?

Children's emotional reactions to television of course have been examined in depth across a number of disciplines but, as in the literature on play discussed in the last chapter, fun is rarely central to such study. It appears not to be taken seriously as an emotion of value. In her review of the literature in this field, Heike vom Orde (2008, 14) found that existing research 'not only covers a limited spectrum of questions, but also a limited number of emotions. The majority of international studies concentrate on so-called "negative" emotions'. I would argue that such a focus reflects the continued dominance within the study of children and television of the effects tradition, seeking as it does to discover how and why television is 'bad' for the viewer. Vom Orde (2008) did not uncover any research that focused on an exploration of children's enjoyment of the 'fun' of television.

This is not to say that researchers haven't recognised any positive emotional engagement of the audience with television. The uses and gratifications research tradition has a long history over 50 years of looking in particular at the ways in which television viewers use the medium to satisfy their own desires and psychological needs. In a recent article Anne Bartsch (2012, 267) continues in this tradition and considers 'the role of entertainment in psychosocial need satisfaction'. Her search is for a distinct purpose to explain why, for example, an individual might seek to watch a distressing or scary television program and how this might contribute to the viewer's 'eudaimonic wellbeing'. While this approach certainly focuses on the potential positive impact of television on the emotional life of the individual viewer, such research has significant limitations. These have been highlighted by academics such as Lewis (1991, chap. 1) and Buckingham. Buckingham (1993a, 16) argues that this approach:

> runs the risk of defining television viewing as a much more conscious, purposeful activity than it actually is ... uses and gratifications research largely fails to provide a fully social account of children's relationship with television.

He also points out that it fails to allow for the 'non-purposive' ways in which people interact with the medium. This casual approach to television was certainly evident in my research and is illustrated in the comment here from an 8-year-old girl:

> Yeah, it's not like – you don't really think about TV all the time. You mainly think about like what interests you. Sometimes when we watch singing films my mum and dad go to cook, my sister – my little sister – goes to read, my big sister does her homework and my brother does like his maths homework. I'm the only one actually watching the singing because I have like a thing for singing.

Here the 'non-purposive' nature of the television viewing within a family is delightfully captured by the young girl. There is no intense absorption in seeking out television to satisfy a desire or meet a psychological need and the child is not thinking 'about TV all the time'. The scene captures Hartley's (1987a, 256) notion of the way in which television offers a light 'brush' with the world, and shows how the young girl enjoys a 'solitary, private, comfortable' pleasure from within the safety and comfort of the family living room.

Barker and Brooks (1998, 91) argue that the uses and gratification approach does not allow for the viewer's simple enjoyment of the fun of television:

> There simply isn't space for understanding someone saying that they might like a programme or film or whatever because it is fun or funny. These are positive qualities, sought for their own sake, not because of a failing in a person's life.

In an interesting study of popular television, Frances Bonner (2003, 111) observes 'ordinary television's role of bringing pleasure [to] and being fun' for the viewer. The focus of her research is on 'light' television entertainment which she notes has not been taken seriously in academia. She argues that it is the

> lightweight, ephemeral character of the forms themselves that is the problem; examining them does nothing to counteract the impressions from the academy in general that television is too trivial to be worth studying. (2003, 2)

While her research deliberately excludes the category of children's television, it does highlight an interesting point: that television programs which might simply bring pleasure and fun to the viewer are not considered worth studying. These kinds of programs she argues are not valued in the wider culture; entertainment that simply provides 'fun and pleasure' is not worth more than a passing thought.

But if television entertainment might be seen at best as benignly lightweight when consumed by adults, it is regarded as a potentially pernicious influence on children. As Kirsten Drotner (2005, 44) observes:

CHAPTER 3

> Society is described as overflowing with all sorts of superficial entertainment that pervades children's lives and leaves little or no room for introspection and depth, properties that are perceived as being essential for healthy child development.

Drotner suggests that our fears for our children are powerfully tied into discourses of cultural hierarchies and national dichotomies. The global spread of 'trashy' US television is not only a threat to our children but also to the 'lofty values and cultural traditions underpinning old Europe' (Drotner 2005, 44). This discourse resonates in Australia too – the historical colonial outpost of old Europe – and is reflected in a comment from a 10-year-old girl in my interviews: 'my mum isn't big on me watching Disney Channel and Nickelodeon … she calls it American rubbish'. Drotner (2005, 44) notes also that at the core of this denigration of US television and Hollywood film is a cultural notion that values print above the visual (see discussion in Chapter 1) and which particularly disparages the 'strong emotional appeal in which Hollywood excels'. She goes on to suggest that these 'perceived threats to established values, print media and children concoct a powerful cocktail that it takes potent measures to countervene' (2005, 44). It is perhaps remarkable that children can and do persist in the face of these 'potent' oppositions to not only continue to have fun watching television but also to celebrate it.

Fun is treated as lightweight in academia too. McKee (2008) has noted the reluctance of scholars to engage with the concept of fun itself. In reviewing the study of fun in the field of cultural science, he notes that:

> Debates about fun are not about the value of fun for fun's sake. Rather, they are about the possible political outcomes of fun.

> Is fun a distraction from political action? Or is fun, in itself, a form of resistance to political domination? (2008, 6)

Quite radically McKee (2008, 6) suggests that such outcomes shouldn't matter:

> The fun itself is the important thing. It doesn't matter if, by having fun, you are resisting capitalism. Having fun is the valuable end in itself. Politics is important only to the extent to which it enables more people to have more fun, more often.

A sustained study of entertainment, McKee, Collis and Hamley (2012) suggest, might be expected to examine the aspect of fun at its heart. As they point out:

> For entertainment, fun is an intrinsic good. It need not have any other purpose – the very fact of enjoying oneself is an end in itself, and one that is highly valued. (2012, 17)

But it seems that the very fact that fun is at the heart of entertainment has in part contributed to the academic world's lack of interest in its study. As McKee, Collis and Hamley (2012, 17) argue, 'academic accounts of valuable culture have traditionally had little time for fun'. McKee et al. (2014, 8-9) have found that 'globally there has been only a little academic attention to "entertainment" as a cultural category', though they point to Richard Dyer as one 'humanities writer who has engaged with the category in a sustained way'.

Dyer (1992, 2) himself has commented on the lack of serious attention that has been paid to entertainment, suggesting that part of the problem is that entertainment 'is born of a society that both considers leisure and pleasure to be secondary and even inferior to the businesses of producing and reproducing'. The irony that Dyer (1992, 2) points out is that, despite society's disdain for entertainment, it still 'invests much energy, desire and money' in the industry. McKee et al. (2014, 2) have also commented on this aspect of entertainment today: '[it] is not a small and isolated cultural phenomenon … it is at the centre of many cultures' self-articulation and understanding, and many people's leisure time'. I would like to suggest that this is true about the place of television entertainment in children's lives, and this is particularly clear when examining what they themselves say about it as I do in the next two chapters.

Dyer (2002) has sought to investigate the ways in which entertainment is central to our lives and has examined how popular entertainment creates a product focused on giving pleasure. In his study of American musicals he offers a critical vision of what entertainment does:

> [It] offers the image of 'something better' to escape into, or something we want deeply that our day-to-day lives don't provide … [it] presents, head-on as it were, what utopia would feel like rather than how it would be organized. It thus works at the level of sensibility, by which I mean an affective code. (2002, 20)

Dyer echoes Buckingham's (1993a, 13) point noted above, that a central 'question' of entertainment lies in its appeal to our emotions. As a 9-year-old girl said in the survey that I conducted during my research, she watches television programs because 'they are funny and make you feel good'. Another 8-year-old in an interview said 'The best thing about television is that you can smile and it's funny'. And in a gesture toward utopia, a 10-year-old girl said the best thing about television was that 'It means I can have a little world of monsters or anything'. The attraction of glimpsing what utopia might 'feel like' was apparent in my own research with children.

While Dyer has examined the role of pleasure and fun in entertainment, his work is rare in an academic world that appears to harbour disdain for such enjoyment. So why has fun come to be seen as so lacking in value? In his book on cultural hierarchies in the United States, Lawrence Levine (1988) explores the disappearance of fun from the cultural value system over the past 200 years. According to Levine (1988, chap. 2), fun was a casualty of the 19th century's 'sacralization' of culture. He traces the growing chasm that developed between 'serious' and 'popular' culture during this time, arguing that theatre and opera were gradually elevated beyond the reach of the masses by the educated elite. Seeking to set themselves and their culture apart from the rabble, the middle and upper classes ensured that culture became 'a manifestly serious and intricate endeavour that few could hope to master' (Levine 1988, 211). Pursuits such as the theatre which during Shakespeare's time had provided much 'mirth and merriment' (Hartley 2008, 183) to all classes of society were no longer a simple source of fun or enjoyment. In establishing the new cultural hierarchy, the widely accessible aspect of fun was relegated to an inferior status. This has made it difficult today to talk about simply enjoying television for the 'fun of it' as Buckingham (2001b) found out in his research into Disney programs. The participants in his research, who were all adults, found it difficult to acknowledge their enjoyment of Disney programs in the face of the dominant culture:

> It was much more difficult to argue that Disney was just innocent fun or entertainment, much less that it was any good for you … To proclaim one's enjoyment of mindless pleasure, to profess an enthusiasm for all things American, or to celebrate one's infantile desires are simply untenable positions – at least if one wishes to avoid the ridicule or disdain of others. (2001b, 284)

CHAPTER 3

Even today, when television is no longer dismissed as entirely trashy, and, in being recognised by critics, has turned into 'a medium reviewed in highbrow literary journals' (McNamara 2015), the emphasis continues to be on the value of watching 'high-quality' programs. While this does include programs of widespread popularity, which are obviously entertaining, such as *Game of Thrones* and *Breaking Bad*, it doesn't include equally popular programs such as *The Bachelor, Big Brother* or *Keeping Up with the Kardashians*. The value of the program does not depend on its capacity to entertain, nor on the fun it provides its audience, but on a perception of its literary and artistic merit. In the same way that Shakespeare's ribald, violent and funny entertainment, which delighted the bear pit in its day, has been elevated to a 'high art' as opposed to popular mass entertainment, so too has some of today's television. Mass entertainment 'popular' culture which includes such programs as *The Bachelor* is still 'low' culture – Hartley's dichotomy still applies (see discussion in chapter 1). It is largely seen as rubbish and a time-waster and, despite its obvious ability to entertain, of little worth. To 'avoid the ridicule of others' one would not be likely to admit to watching such television.

For children, however, such classifications do not seem to apply – rather 'fun' is what matters. While adults might be reluctant to admit to watching TV programs simply for the fun of it, children – when given an opportunity not only to speak but to be heard – do assert, and share, their own view of the value of fun in watching television (Götz et al. 2006; Götz et al. 2005; Messenger Davies 2010; Palmer 1986). Such fun appears to be regarded highly within their own culture and children seek it out, through watching television and through play, in the 'spaces and times over which [they] have some degree of power and control' (James, Jenks and Prout 1998, 87).

They appear to grab these moments in the time left free by the working lives of their adult carers (Solberg 1990, 132) or between the increasingly scheduled activities that 'regulate children's activities under an adult gaze, challenging them into forms considered developmentally healthy and productive' (Prout 2005, 33). It is quite an achievement that, within an adult culture so driven to protect and perfect the child, that children themselves should accord status to fun – for its own sake. I would suggest that television's place in this achievement, through the entertainment it offers children in its varied and complex ways, is central to such success.

This is not to suggest that children simply escape from the regulation of the adult world through watching television or sneaking a bit of extra time in front of the set to have a laugh. I would argue that children's engagement with television is a social and creative act of the kind articulated by James, Jenks and Prout in their book *Theorizing Childhood* (1998). These researchers have proposed that the essence of the 'culture of childhood' is 'a form of social action contextualized by the many different ways in which children choose to engage with the social institutions and structures that shape the form and process of their everyday lives' . Television is undoubtedly a major social institution that is woven into the 'form and process' of children's lives. Children choose many ways to engage with television and the joy it brings to them remains a central value in their lives. As Seiter (1999b, 87) observes, 'television is cheap, easy, plentiful, and children love to watch it'.

Hartley has captured the essence of the centrality of television in modern lives – and its capacity to entertain – in *The Uses of Television* (1999). He persuasively argues that:

CHAPTER 3

> Its rather simple and therefore frequently overlooked 'power' to bring social, geographical, environmental and demographic variety into the home makes television the greatest 'variety show' in history.

The 'variety show' of television appears to provide a rich source of entertainment for both adults and children; and part of this appeal appears to come from the insights it provides into everyday life. In his provocative (given the 'sacralization' of Shakespeare in our culture) comparison between Shakespeare's *Taming of the Shrew* and Endemol's reality television program *Big Brother*, Hartley (2008, chap. 9) argues that the success of these two entertainments, and also of television itself, is linked to the fact that the audiences relate directly to the characters and the scenes. They enjoy the drama and theatricality of the performances but they also see through this 'to the conduct of human relationships within' (Hartley 2008, 183). Drotner (2005, 49) has noted that the sitcoms and soap operas that are 'hugely popular' among children and young people are 'readily incorporated into a known everyday world … and their conflicts are immediately recognizable'. Terence Hawkes (1973, 240) makes a similar point, though more broadly, when he argues that 'television serves, as all communal art does, to confront a society with itself'.

For the children in my research this kind of 'learning' about society and the world from television was something they both enjoyed and valued. A 10-year-old boy in my survey explained that 'i watch TV to discover things' while a 9-year-old girl said she watched 'because its fun and interesting'. One 10-year-old boy whose favourite shows included two Australian reality TV shows called *My Kitchen Rules* and *The Block*, and an American sitcom called *The Big Bang Theory*, said the reason he liked these shows was because 'they a funny and teach you things'.

This kind of learning, however, does not appear to fit into the notion of education that our culture expects for our children, as I discussed in the last chapter. There is no space within this cultural understanding for an acknowledgment that children might actually learn something of value from a soap opera. This is not to say that there is no appreciation of the ways in which children can learn from television but that the focus is on the learning being educational in the sense of supplementing the work of the modern school curriculum. *Sesame Street*, for example, is a children's television program that has long been regarded as educational because it 'teaches' children such obvious educational tools as the alphabet and numbers. 'Learning' about the 'immediately recognizable' conflicts of the 'everyday world' (Drotner 2005, 49) and of the 'conduct of human relationships' (Hartley 2008, 183) from reality TV does not count as learning in this schoolroom and has no value within such a tradition. Underlying this view is a suspicion of pleasure and fun and a belief that any form of entertainment with these attractions at their heart cannot be of any real value. Fun has no place apparently in the serious business of understanding life.

The effects tradition of research into television's influence on children has, I would argue, reinforced this perspective with its negative view of the influence of television on the child. The mindless pleasures of television are potentially damaging and the effects of watching violence are definitely harmful (Gerbner 1988). In this tradition, 'exposure' to 'educational' programs can be beneficial (Comstock and Scharrer 2007, 137-146) but such exposure must be to sound educational programs such as *Sesame Street, Mister Rogers'*

CHAPTER 3

Neighborhood and *Dora the Explorer* (Anderson et al. 2001; Center on Media for Child Health 2005) and not to 'aggressive cartoons such a *Batman* and *Superman*' (Comstock and Scharrer 2007, 143). The focus of this research tradition is informed by a culture that sees education in a carefully circumscribed field – one which includes such subjects as spelling, arithmetic, history and possibly a foreign language. This tradition doesn't ask children themselves what they learn from television but considers rather what adults believe television should teach in order that children might in a timely fashion take up their approved places in the adult world. It's an approach that is strongly underpinned by a suspicion of the entertainment value of television. As Davies (1997, 146) notes, 'Entertainment – the main reason given by most TV viewers for watching the medium – has rarely been seen as a legitimate educational goal'.

While a number of researchers have studied the ways in which television's pleasures are central to adults' engagement with the medium, particularly in the study of fandom (Barker and Brooks 1998; Bonner 2003; Gray 2008), there is no corresponding body of research into children's embrace of the fun of TV. In fact, children's apparent pleasure in television has been largely denigrated, not only in the public discourse, but also in many academic studies (Comstock and Scharrer 2007; Postman 2006; Rich 2014; Winn 1985). Hartley (1987a) suggests a possible reason for this attitude: that the pleasure to be had from television is seen as being slightly disreputable. Critiquing Todd Gitlin's (1983) book *Inside Prime Time*, which 'finds TV wanting' (Hartley 1987a, 251), Hartley argues that Gitlin 'fears that [television viewers'] solitary, private, comfortable pleasures are neither respectable nor productive' (1987a, 256). In suggesting that television is also used as a way to stay in touch 'as a nation', Hartley

(1987a, 256) points out that Gitlin disapproves of this too and sees it as 'little short of mass deviancy, producing not fine upstanding citizens, but, behind the suburban drapes, a nation of *frotteurs*'. In a mischievous twist, Hartley turns this disapproval on its head, arguing that the pleasure of a *frotteur* is something to be celebrated. He suggests that the pleasure of television 'is akin to frottage … a glimpse, a frisson of excitement provoked by taking private pleasure from public contact' (1992b, 166).

> The idea of television as frottage captures perfectly the slightly shameful practice of taking private pleasures in public places: One sense of the word refers to the desire for contact between the clothed bodies of oneself and another. (Hartley 1987a, 256)

Celebrating this aspect of television will perhaps do little to quell the cultural anxieties that inform our desire to keep our children innocent of adult secrets. But it is something that Hartley suggests we should embrace. In my research with children, this 'frisson of excitement' is certainly apparent in the way the children talk about their enjoyment of their favourite shows – and this is abundantly evident in the next two chapters.

Fandom and Its Pleasures

As I have suggested above, the disdain of pleasure in popular culture as a 'serious' interest has led to a dearth of academic research into its value and importance to both children and adults. Exceptions to this rule exist in the study of entertainment and this includes a body of literature on fandom. This particular area of research, which examines adults' participation in fandom, has explored the pleasures fans enjoy in their engagement with popular culture. It has been studied in some depth over the past two decades, in particular by Henry Jenkins

CHAPTER 3

(1992, 2013), and Martin Barker and Kate Brooks (1998). Although Jenkins (2013, 286) warns against drawing on research into fandom as a means of 'developing a new theory of media consumption' and notes the significant differences between fans and the average media consumer, nonetheless the extensive research into the pleasures of this form of media consumption offers some useful insights for my research with children.

After finding little available research on the 'differences in pleasures, let alone differences in their languages of expression', Barker and Brooks (1998, 133, 143) set out to map possible 'vocabularies of involvement and pleasure' that would illuminate the ways in which they might investigate the pleasures of the fans of the American science fiction action film *Judge Dredd*. In order to do this they came up with a number of suggestions about the 'ways in which pleasure might be talked about' (p. 143) that offer a way of looking at my own research into the pleasures children enjoy from television.

Barker and Brooks's (1998, 143-5) suggestions for thinking about 'the practices of pleasure' include: physical satisfaction, joining a crowd, being free of pressures and obligations, making imaginative worlds, game-playing and role-playing, taking risks, rule-breaking, being in company/sharing, and critical appreciation including setting out to learn. These categories, I believe, are useful not only to investigate the pleasures of fans in film, but also of children in television.

While fans and children might appear to have little in common, Barker and Brooks (1998, 12) have astutely observed that:

> children are not different in principle from other audiences, despite all the social fears that surround them; they are in fact often using the media as part of learning how to be members of their culture generally, and more particularly of their local groups.

This is not to deny the differences between fans and other television viewers. As Jenkins (2013, 286) warns, 'fan culture differs in a qualitative way from the cultural experiences of media consumption for the bulk of the population'. Barker and Brooks's (1998, 155-75) use of their 'practices of pleasure' to theorise a number of culturally-generated 'SPACES' in which their fans operate does take their research in a direction that diverges from mine. Their six SPACES identify different types of interest in, and engagement with, favourite movies and their characters which involve an intensity that is not shared by the average television viewer. Participating in fan culture involves a significantly greater commitment of time and energy on the part of the fans, who also often actively define themselves as part of a specific group. The children in my research were not engaged in television, or with a specific program or film, to the extent suggested here by Barker and Brooks. But they undeniably got pleasure out of watching their favourite shows: an element shared across the board with fans. Many of these pleasures are reflected in Barker and Brooks's (1998, 143-5) 'practices of pleasure' and I will examine this further when I analyse my own research with children in the next two chapters.

While acknowledging therefore that fandom may have its own culturally-specific characteristics, research into fandom can, I believe, illuminate the ways in which children *enjoy* television. Jenkins (2013, 287) observes that a study of fandom reveals the ways in which audiences have 'a more active relationship [with] textual materials [which] are appropriated and fit to personal experience'. Certainly this way of engaging with television, appropriating favourite television characters and stories, for example, to 'fit' with personal experience, was also apparent in my research with children, and again I will consider this more closely in the following chapters.

CHAPTER 3

'It's fun and interesting': Children Negotiating the Negative Public Discourses

Television's ability to entertain and provide a good laugh is what many children appear to love about it. The researchers who have conducted research with children directly, both listening to and observing what they do with, react to and say about television, have often commented on this aspect of children's engagement with the medium. In her extensive interviews with children in the early 1980s, Palmer (1986, 33) found that 'nearly every child who was interviewed watched TV programs because they were "funny"'. She found that 'children watched TV for fun and excitement and to learn about things not usually accessible to them'. Máire Messenger Davies (2004) observed too that children found their favourite shows funny but they also saw television as a window onto a larger world. She noted that children in her research thought the American animated sitcom *The Simpsons* was hilarious but that 'they also valued it because "it reflects some things from life"'. It was seen as socially useful' (2004, 429). From a group of children aged 6–7 and 10–11, Davies, Buckingham and Kelley (2000, 16) found: 'In response to our somewhat earnest questions about why a programme was chosen or preferred, the most common answer across both age groups was simply that it was 'funny". Götz et al. (2005, 202) found that media played a rich role in the make-believe worlds of children and that in these worlds there was a strong search for 'excitement and fun'.

Although this research into the fun and pleasure that children get out of television is limited, it does appear from its findings that fun is a central element of children's engagement with the medium, and that favourite programs are particularly important to children. But, as discussed in the earlier chapters, the negative public discourse is a powerful influence on the way we regard children and television; and it largely denies the value of the fun of such entertainment. Given the pervasiveness and power of this discourse, I thought it important to examine its influence on children themselves. In order to do this I have analysed in this section the responses of the children in my own research to a number of questions about television.[4]

The results from the survey that I conducted with 77 primary school children showed similar results to those found by the researchers mentioned above. In response to the question 'Why do you watch television?', a total of 51% said it was fun or entertaining with 8% stating explicitly that it was funny. Another 24% said that they watched television because it was interesting or educational: as one 10-year-old wrote, 'i watch TV to discover things'. A further 23% said they watched TV if they were 'bored' or had nothing else to do: a response which I consider in more detail in Chapter 5.

I would like to look more closely at the answers to this survey question, and to compare it with two other similar questions from the same survey. In doing this, I would like to suggest that children do indeed, as Buckingham (1995) has suggested, have their own hierarchy of values and cultural preferences, and that they do assert these in their own lives. It is also possible to see from their answers that they use entertainment to enjoy glimpses of the world: Hartley's 'frottage' (1987a, 256). But this engagement with television does not happen in a social or cultural vacuum, any more than it does for adults. As I will show from the children's responses, they are acutely aware of the dominant negative discourses around television; they

---

[4]   Details of the methods and extent of my research are included in the appendix.

CHAPTER 3

are after all on the receiving end of the sometimes panicked efforts to get control over the screens that allegedly threaten their health, intelligence and morals. Children do appear to understand that their hierarchy of values is not that which is promoted by the 'adult world'. What is interesting is how they negotiate, resist and accommodate these differences; and how in the process they still manage to enjoy and find pleasure in the much maligned 'idiot box'.

In talking about TV, I would suggest that children incorporate the negative public discourses with their own emotional responses to television programs, creating interpretations and meanings adapted to their own social and emotional context. In arguing this I am drawing on Buckingham's (1993a) well-established research and his observation that talk – including children's talk – about television is not simply an objective or factual account of what a person thinks or feels. What children say about TV is influenced by their social context and crucially by 'the way in which that context is perceived' by the children themselves (Buckingham 1993a, 291). This does not make their comments any less real or valuable in contributing to an understanding of children's engagement with the medium. In fact, Buckingham (1993a, 36) argues this talk is 'a central aspect of the process by which [television's] meanings are established and circulated'. With this in mind, I would like to compare and contrast the responses of the children in my survey to three questions and argue that the answers to these questions – and the ways in which these responses vary – have been influenced by the children's negotiations with the dominant negative discourses on television and by their drive to establish their own 'meanings' and cultural criteria for the popular medium that is such an integral part of their lives.

Both at home and at school, children learn the negative discourses concerning television early. Parental regulation of television viewing starts from a young age and is largely related to efforts to control access to content that might teach the child 'bad habits, language or ideas' and that could 'have a bad or negative effect on the child' (Cupitt 1996, 48). Parents also voice concerns that their children should allow time for other activities and in particular that they should do their homework first (Cupitt 1996, 35). In my survey, 80% of the children answered that they were not allowed to watch television as much as they wanted; close to 50% replied they could only watch 'after doing homework'. In its extensive and latest research with Australian children and families, the Australian Communications and Media Authority (ACMA) (2009, 13) found similar figures: 87% of parents said they regulated the hours their children could watch television. Parental regulation of viewing then, at least according to these accounts, is still in force in family life.

On the school front, too, television is carefully circumscribed. As I discussed in the last chapter, school is a place for education, for the improvement of the child, and not for popular culture. In educational settings, television's cheap popular entertainment is mostly ignored but sometimes denigrated (Hodge and Tripp 1986; Lealand and Zanker 2008; Seiter 1999a, 1999b). It is not something that is seen as being of much value. The fact that children understand and react to this discourse was illustrated by a rather wistful comment made during my interview with an 8-year-old boy: 'If I could create a TV I'd make a TV that was good for you and you could watch it whenever you wanted'. In the survey, a 7-year-old girl responded to the question about what is the best thing about television in the common language of the negative discourse: 'Some of it isn't bad

CHAPTER 3

for you or rubbish'. Directly addressing the negatives, this young girl redraws the boundaries and asserts a stand: the best thing about television is that it really is not all 'rubbish'.

While the children's answers to certain questions reflected the dominant discourses around the need to control the potentially damaging medium of television, they did also demonstrate a desire and a capacity to express their own views about television. I would like to argue that throughout the survey, children were negotiating their own meanings. These incorporated their understandings of the largely negative views circulated within the institutional school setting and implied in parental efforts to control how much and what they watched on television. But it was also driven by the children's strong sense of their own pleasures in the medium which they confidently promoted at various opportunities in both the survey and the interviews during my research.

A comparison between the answers to three of the survey questions listed below reveals the children's engagement with the dominant negative discourses. All three questions were seeking information from children about what they liked and enjoyed about television, but they were phrased and worded differently and, importantly, were preceded by different questions. The three questions were:

Question 7 Why do you watch television? (discussed above)

Question 12 Do you think television is good? Why?

Question 16 What do you like about these programs?

The first of these, Question 7, directly followed questions about age, year group, gender and family demographics: the type of questions that would have been familiar to these children. Children in western cultures are commonly categorised according to age and gender and from their first days at school they learn to respond frequently to such questions. By primary school, answering these questions is a routine and uncontroversial task. But the very process of answering them would have reminded the children of their context: they were undertaking a task set in school. As discussed earlier, school is an environment even today that is potentially hostile, or at the very least indifferent, to the popular culture of television and certainly to its pleasures. It was within this environment that the children answered Question 7, and I believe their answers reflect the influence within this space of negative attitudes to television.

When I introduced myself to the children before they started the survey, I explained to them that we were interested in their own views about television, not those of the adults around them. But I was still an adult, I was standing in their classroom and I was accompanied by a teacher. This all helped to reinforce the school context. It was perhaps surprising therefore that in answer to Question 7 just over half still said they watched television for 'fun', thus acknowledging the pleasure it gave them. One 8-year-old boy quite explicitly stated that he watched television 'just for fun'. One 9-year-old girl wasn't quite as brave, qualifying her response slightly: 'its fun and interesting'.

While television was fun for the majority, nearly a quarter of the children who responded to this question said they watched television because it was interesting or educational. One 10-year-old girl wrote, 'some tv helps u lern for school and they r intresting'. At the age of 10, this girl had already understood that television is more acceptable if it can offer a serious contribution to life, such as to a child's education. But despite having written that she watched television because it 'helps u lern', later in the survey she listed her favourite shows as *Friends*, *Bad Education* and *Adventure Time*. The first two of these are, respectively, American and British popular sitcoms, the third is an American animated cartoon that according to *The New Yorker* magazine is seriously wacky and can best be described 'as a cartoon about a hero who fights villains, with fun violence, the occasional fart joke, and a slight edge of Bushwick cool-kid hipness' (Nussbaum 2014). From none of these shows would you be likely to learn anything related to the school curriculum. The reason she gives for enjoying her favourites is because 'they r funny'. Despite the obvious pleasure this child gets from her favourite shows, she felt she had to take a stand as a critic of television: a position which was at odds with her own pleasure in the medium. This stance was further reflected in her answer to the question 'Do you think television is good?', where she wrote: 'not really because u do not need tv because some programs r not good for u because theyr inapropreat'. She was well-versed in the discourse which presents television as a corrupting influence that harbours 'inappropriate' adult secrets. In adopting the dominant discourse, this 10-year-old was putting into practice something that Valerie Walkerdine (1989) has astutely observed: television pleasures are something we must rationalise and intellectualise; to simply enjoy these pleasures is regarded as 'perverse'. Walkerdine (1989, 196) goes on to explain the basis of these fears that are apparent in the public discourse:

> There exist among the bourgeoisie a terror of the pleasures of the flesh, of the body, of the animal passions seen to be burning darkly in sexuality and also in violent uprisings. No surprise then that the regulation of children's consumption of the modern media focuses so obsessively on sex and violence.

Based on other researchers' work with children (Buckingham 1993a, 1996; Davies 2001; Seiter 1999b, chap. 4) and on my own observations during my research, I believe that the children's answers in this survey reflect the influence and constraints imposed by the common public discourses on children and television; and I would suggest that the children's answers in my survey reflect how they are influenced by such discourses. These children have picked up on the notion that television is only of value if it contributes in some way to their 'improvement' and 'education'; and that its pleasures are suspect and have to be explained away. In their responses to Question 7, coming as it did early in a survey that was conducted in the school setting, they did not feel they could admit to watching TV for something as trivial as having a good laugh. Only 8% at this point in the survey said they watched television because it was 'funny'. What is interesting is that these responses changed as the survey continued, as the children became more relaxed, and particularly when the opportunity arose to discuss their favourite programs. I will consider this below but first I would like to examine the answers to Question 12: 'Do you think television is good? Why?'

'Do you think television is good?'

This question came after three which were about controls around television viewing: 'How much, when, where, are you allowed to watch?' Such questions would have reminded the children about parental regulation: something which is tied closely to the negative discourse on television. As Buckingham (1996, 65) has noted, the way in which parents talk about their regulation of their children's television viewing positions them as 'good' or 'bad' parents. Leaving a child to its own unfettered enjoyment of the screen is seen in public debates as a mark of negligent and irresponsible parenting. From the responses of the children in my survey, it was clear a large majority

CHAPTER 3

of their parents were mindful of this debate. They were taking this responsibility seriously and in theory at least laying down the rules. Nearly 80% of the children said they were not allowed to watch television whenever they wanted. A total of 42% were allowed to watch only after doing homework, and 32% were only allowed to watch at the weekend. Just how far these regulations were actually enforced was not a question this survey sought to answer. But Buckingham (1993a) has noted that there is considerable negotiation and debate around such parental regulations. Television is a contested site within the family 'characterized by struggles for power and control' and not all the battles are won by the parents (Buckingham 1993a, 125). Curiously parents are occasionally drawn to share the fun of television with their own children, choosing to watch favourite shows together. This is an aspect of television that I consider in Chapter 5.

One of the underlying rationales for regulation of children's television viewing appears to be an attempt to control indulgence in the, at best time-wasting, at worst corrupting, temptations of pleasure. As Buckingham (1993a, 126) writes, 'If children cannot be weaned off television completely, they can perhaps be turned into self-regulating viewers, whose pleasures are subject to rational control'. Pleasure is something to be regulated, not enjoyed. As I discussed in the last chapter, childhood in our western culture is precious; its innocence demands our protection and careful nurturing. While this culture of childhood is one that has been developed and perpetuated in the adult world, its message is something that children have acutely perceived and understood.

Not surprisingly then, the children's answers to Question 12, 'Do you think television is good? Why?', focused largely on TV's 'educational' value. It was obvious from the children's answers that they had picked up on the dominant discourses. In answer to Question 12, one 7-year-old girl wrote that 'It is good for you because you learn things'. Another 10-year-old girl obviously understood the implication of 'good' in this light. Her response reflected her understanding of the need for television to be educational if it is to be good, though she did put up an argument first for her own preferences: 'I think television is good because it shows heaps of cool shows and some can be educational'. I am not suggesting that children don't find pleasure themselves in learning from television and that in these responses they were only parroting the dominant discourse. It is clear, not only in the findings in my research but also in that of others in this field (Buckingham 1993a; Davies 2001; Palmer 1986), that children do get pleasure from learning things from television. This learning, however, is not perhaps the same as that understood by those who promote 'serious' education as the antithesis to popular culture.

The highest percentage of responses given to Question 12 suggested that television was good because it was educational. More than 40% of the children gave this answer. This is a large increase on the 24% who gave a similar answer to Question 7. The presence of the word 'good' in the question would no doubt have had an impact on the children's responses. Rarely in the public discourse is television promoted as being 'good' for you; school is 'good' for you, exercise is 'good' for you, television is not. Only that which protects and nurtures childhood can be claimed as good. In the dominant discourse there is no talk of television being good for you because it is pleasurable or simply fun: it has to be educational.

This discourse does appear to have influenced the children's responses to the question. A total of 15% answered Question 12 by saying that television was *not* good for you. These children obviously felt they could not say that television was good for you at all, let alone give an explanation of why this might be so. One 7-year-old girl did try to accommodate both labels. Having obviously felt she had to qualify her initial positive response that it was good, she wrote:

> i think television is good because they have some good shows but i also think its bad if you watch TV for to long its bad for your brain and your eyes.

One of the most revealing statistics from the responses to Question 12 was that only 10% said it was good because it was funny. I would suggest that there is little room in the public discourse on television for the notion that 'funny' television could be 'good' for you: it certainly couldn't be considered educational and such pleasure is surely suspect. What is perhaps surprising is that even 10% of the children, under these circumstances, said this was the case and were prepared to assert such a position.

Favourites: 'What do you like about these programs?'

The third question in my comparison, Question 16, resulted in some markedly different responses to the first two. The question, 'What do you like about these programs?', followed immediately upon one which appeared to engage the children's attention and enthusiasm: 'What are the names of your favourite television programs?' While they were answering these two questions, I observed a number of children turning to a friend and discussing favourite shows, comparing and competing over which were the best, who knew the most, and how many they watched. Their conversations were in some cases quite animated. Not all of the children discussed this question, however; some were simply too absorbed in writing their answers.

Their concentration was a testament to their interest. Some children were so interested in getting the answers right that they even asked both the teacher and me for help with the correct spellings of the program names. By the time they got to the follow-up question, 'What do you like about these programs?', I believe that they had moved somewhat out of range of the negative discourses around television that had influenced their answers to the earlier questions. The school context too had receded as they were absorbed in remembering and recounting their television worlds. The emotions they felt when watching their favourite shows came to the fore and were reflected in their answers. The sheer ebullience of this joy in a favourite program is revealed in one 9-year-old's response to Question 16: 'They are all hilarious & Mum is scared of adventure time!!!!!' A 9-year-old girl had a more introspective comment: 'They are funny and make you feel good'.

A total of 62% of the children explicitly stated that they liked their favourite programs because they were funny. This is a clear contrast to the answers to the earlier questions where 8% said they watched television because it was funny (Question 7) and 10% said television was good because it was funny (Question 12). It also echoes the same findings as Palmer (1986) and Davies, Buckingham and Kelley (2000) in their research with children, where 'funny' was at the top of the list of the pleasures of television.

Given that the children were talking about their own favourites here, I would argue that their answers to this question reflect more closely what they themselves value in television – rather that what adults think is best for them. Humour is obviously a major element of the television programs that a significant majority of children choose to watch.

CHAPTER 3

Excitement and action were also high on the list of the pleasures children enjoyed in their favourite shows, with 21% referring to these elements. For one 10-year-old boy, the best part of his favourite programs was the action: 'thay fight thay die thay fight'. An 11-year-old girl wrote that what she enjoyed was that 'theres always something going on'.

Reflecting Davies's (2004) findings that children also valued television for its ability to take them into a wider world, 10% said they watched their favourites because they were interesting or educational. Just what this learning from television means to them, I explore in Chapter 5.

No-one watched these chosen shows just 'for something to do'. When engaged in thinking of their favourite programs, these children appeared to abandon themselves to the pleasures of remembering their favourite television programs with great joy. When asked what he liked most about them, one 9-year-old boy could only say 'evrey thing'.

An interesting outlier in the survey was 'scary', with three children out of the 73 mentioning this word. One child chose her favourite programs because they *weren't* scary. Although she was already 12, her favourite programs were on ABC Kids – a television channel which targets a younger age demographic and typically would not run programs that might be at all scary. An 8-year-old girl, on the other hand, liked Harry Potter because it *was* scary. And an 8-year-old boy listed a famous American slasher movie, *Scream*, as one of his favourites because it was scary. Although the survey did not provide data that could illuminate these choices, they could perhaps be understood in the light of Buckingham's (1996) research into children's affective responses to television. He found that children 'actively choose to watch or read things that they know will upset or frighten them; and the sadness or fear is often inseparable from the pleasure' (1996, 2-3). He went on to suggest that children might also watch such programs as a way of coping with 'real-life anxieties and concerns' (1996, 3).

Out of 73 responses to this question, only two said they didn't have any favourite shows and one boy said he didn't watch television. These three responses only serve to emphasise the central role of television in children's lives – 96% of children in the survey reported a strong interest in and enjoyment of favourite programs.

The favourite programs mentioned by the children in my research were largely described with a small range of adjectives. 'Fun', 'funny', 'exciting' and 'entertaining' appeared frequently and were apparently words that circulated widely within the children's own discourse on television. It wasn't that these attributes weren't contested in talk about specific programs (not all children liked the same programs) but it was clear that the qualities of 'fun' and 'funny' were highly valued by almost all. The following remarks are an example of the comments that the children made about their favourite shows in the surveys and interviews:

> There funny, exciting, good, fun (7-year-old girl)
>
> some of them are funny and good to watch and they are all entertaining (8-year-old girl)
>
> it is all ways funny (7-year-old boy)
>
> there funny and amusing (8-year-old boy)
>
> they have humour action (10-year-old boy)

While the children were acutely aware of the lack of cultural value placed by the adult world on both television and fun, it was clear from their accounts that their favourite television programs were a source of considerable enjoyment and that they were prepared not only to acknowledge but to celebrate this fact. The following comment from an 8-year-old girl during one of our interviews reflects this reality quite clearly. She is talking about why she likes to watch her favourite show:

> Well it's just something that can entertain you for a while which is kinda weird to say because I know there are lots of things in the world to do than just sit down on the couch and watch television but um … [pause] I think it's because it's funny.

Here she begins her response rather apologetically – in deference to the prevailing discourse – but she gathers strength as she pauses to consider why she does in fact watch this favourite and with a quiet confidence she explains her reason: 'it's because it's funny'. Although at first she appears to be bending to the negative discourse, the tone of her voice at the end is confident and assertive. And she went on to share her enthusiasm for the show effusively with both her friend and with me during our interview.

To paraphrase McKee et al. (2014, 2), I would suggest that television entertainment plays a significant role in children's understanding and articulation of their own culture and it makes a significant contribution to their enjoyment of their leisure time. And in this embrace of their own pleasure in television, 'fun' and 'funny' are at the top of their hierarchy of values.

Children's Views about Television Being Bad for You

The questions discussed above were positioned and phrased in a number of different ways to allow for the children to articulate their opinions about what was 'good' about television and why they enjoyed watching it. There was also one question in the survey that asked children directly whether they thought television could be bad for you. This question immediately followed 'Do you think television is good? Why?' Its position in the list of questions and its wording situated it clearly within the dominant discourses that circulate in our culture around good versus bad, education versus pleasure, high culture versus low culture. The children's answers show that they are aware of these discourses and have taken on board the dominant and largely negative themes that circulate around children and television. Eighty per cent of the children answered 'yes' to this question, agreeing that television 'can be bad for you'. Interestingly, though, 12% said it was not bad for you while 7% negotiated a place in the middle, saying it was only bad 'sometimes'.

The answers the children gave as to why television was bad were particularly revealing of the impact of the negative public discourse on their opinions. The biggest single reason given was that it was bad for your eyes (33% of respondents). A total of 19% said television was bad if you watched for too long and 7% said it was bad for your brain. Five per cent referred to 'trashy' or 'rude' content, which appeared to cover sexual material that was rated for over-15s. Surprisingly, only one of the 75 respondents to this question touched directly on the violence debate. This 8-old-girl answered: 'it can make you agressive and make you want to watch more'.

It is not possible from this small survey to draw any definitive conclusions about the impact on children of the pervasive negative discourse about violence on television. But what is interesting to note from these survey responses is that, despite the extensive media coverage of the damaging effects of TV violence on children and the

CHAPTER 3

substantial interest in this area within academia (Barker and Petley 2001; Gentile 2003; Gerbner 1988; Warburton and Braunstein 2012), for children themselves the dangers of television violence did not loom large. This appears to confirm what Buckingham and Bazalgette (1995, 7) astutely observed:

> Children have considerable power to determine their own readings and pleasures. They may well refuse to occupy, or even fail to perceive, the positions our adult analysis identifies as being marked out for them.

Curiously the children in my survey focused largely on television being bad for your eyes and your brain. One 8-year-old girl explained: 'It herts your brain ceals [cells]'. Interestingly, this fear was reflected in contemporary media coverage. Tohoku University in Sendai in Japan had released a study at the end of 2013, not long before I conducted my research with the children, which according to the *Daily Mail Australia* found that 'Children who watch too much TV may have "damaged brain structures"' (Yapp 2014). Interestingly, despite the frightening headline, the article itself acknowledges that the study's findings 'highlighted an association between TV viewing and changes in the brain *but do not prove* that TV definitely caused the changes' (italics mine). A Google search (June 2015) revealed this story was picked up by a number of online news sites and blogs around the world.

Potential damage to children's brains from television was also covered in *The Sydney Morning Herald* with the headline stating 'Screen violence changing young brains: researchers' (Browne 2013). As I discuss earlier in my book (see chap. 1) the actual effect on a viewer's brain and whether the brain is 'damaged' by screen time is still strongly disputed.

Nonetheless, the debates about television's potential to injure the brain have gained considerable traction in the media discourse in recent years. These arguments have been fuelled particularly by the outspoken pharmacologist Baroness Susan Greenfield. In sometimes apocalyptic language she warns of the dangers of the screens – television being just one – that are invading our homes and damaging children's brains: dramatic statements that frequently get media coverage. In 2012, in *The Australian*, Greenfield was quoted in a story headlined 'Digital age is dumbing down our children' (Donnelly 2012). A *BBC News* story declared 'Screen use is bad for brain development, scientist claims' (Kleinman 2013) and an *ABC* news headline stated 'Neuroscientist Susan Greenfield warns young brains being re-wired by digital technology' (Rivett 2014). But Greenfield's suggestions have come under considerable attack, including from colleagues at Oxford University. In fact in 2015 a group of Oxford academics went public to challenge Greenfield's claims that watching screens and using the internet damages children's minds. An article in *The Telegraph* reported that 'Professor Bishop, Dr Bell and Dr Przybylski say there is no evidence to back any of her claims'. They went on to 'accuse Baroness Susan Greenfield of misleading the public and confusing parents with her views' (Knapton 2015).

These articles criticising children's screen time use sit squarely in the effects tradition, all warning of direct damage to our most vulnerable citizens – our children – from the threats of the screen. Given the pervasiveness of such claims, it is not surprising that children should echo them in their own comments.

What is more interesting perhaps is how irrelevant these statements about television being bad for your brain appear when the children

CHAPTER 3

are revelling in the joys of their favourite programs. The way they express their delight in, and avid engagement with, their favourites appears to bear no relation to their comments about 'bad' effects on eyes or brain, or from watching for too long. There is nothing apparently damaged in their explicit and, in some cases, acutely observed comments about why they like television:

it laughs with you not at you (10-year-old girl)

it helps my mum and I bond (10-year-old girl)

I would argue that in their responses to why television can be bad for you, the children appear to be drawing largely on the dominant effects discourse that pervades the media but circulates also in schools and within the discourse of parental regulation. When the children are talking about their favourite programs, however, they appear to move away from this space and inhabit a world where they are absorbed in their own emotional responses to television. This emotional engagement appears to be central to the way in which they connect with their favourite shows, and yet it is something that is rarely discussed in the negative media discourse.

As Dyer (2002, 20) suggests, entertainment is about 'sensibility' and takes you into a world that connects with the emotions. The focus on physical damage to brain and eyes does not allow for recognition of, let alone an understanding of, the complex emotions that children experience when watching television. As Buckingham (1996, 93) argues, 'Children's accounts of their emotional responses can provide a rich and often surprising indication of the complex roles that television plays in their lives'. In her research Palmer (1986, 114) noted the importance that favourite shows played in children's own definitions of television: 'Although children watched a number of programs, it was those they chose to watch and named as favourites which defined for them the experiences of television viewing'. Throughout my research, children turned invariably to talk of their favourites when given an opportunity to speak of their own interests in television.

Nonetheless, children themselves do also adopt the language of the negative discourse, though this talk does appear to be significantly dependent on the context. This is apparent in their answers to Question 13 ('Do you think television can be bad for you?') which in its wording quite obviously alerted the children to the dominant discourse. As I have mentioned above, the largest category of respondents said it could be bad for your eyes. While there was no major media coverage of television being bad for your eyes in the local media in the months immediately preceding this survey, the topic is nonetheless regularly covered. 'More children need glasses from hours glued to TV', a Brisbane headline warned in March 2012 (Vonow 2012). Australia's ABC radio covered a Sydney University study in April 2011 with the reporter saying that 'Researchers at Sydney University have found that children who watch too much TV have retinal damage' (Hipsley 2011). While there is no evidence that the children doing the survey, or their parents, had read this coverage, these stories do indicate that such issues circulate in the public discourse and are no doubt taken up within families and schools. One 8-year-old girl repeated an injunction common to the parents of the baby boomer generation that was used to warn children off television: 'it can give you squere eyes'. You can hear the admonishing, perhaps exasperated, voice of the adult resonating in the word 'square'.

The problem of watching too much television also surfaced in the children's answers to Question 13. Nineteen per cent said that watching too much was bad for you. No doubt the parental regulations mentioned above influenced the children's perceptions of this issue but this discourse also appears frequently in the media; watching too much TV apparently causes a wide range of problems for children. 'Kids' TV time linked to school woes' (Gardner 2010), 'Children who watch too much TV may have "damaged brain structures"' (Yapp 2014) and 'Inactive children "become middle-aged couch potatoes"' (Burns 2015) are representative examples of the headlines for such stories.

Interestingly, watching too much television is often seen as a problem facing 'other' people. I discussed this displacement of the 'evils' of television onto the 'other' in Chapter 1. For adults, it is children who watch too much, for the 'educated' or 'ruling' classes it is the 'lower' or 'more degenerate' social classes that are glued to the set (Petley 2001). For children, it is younger children, particularly younger siblings, who are at risk (Buckingham 1996, 80). In my survey a 10-year-old boy picks up on this discourse with his answer to the question of whether television can be bad for you: 'yes but it won't hurt me because i don't watch to much'. Implicit in this statement is the assertion that television is bad for others who watch too much, but not for 'me', because 'I' can regulate myself and my television viewing. This stance not only distances oneself from the negative effects of television but accords a higher status to the speaker, and children understand this as clearly as adults. As Buckingham (1996, 92) observes, 'The discourse of media effects is often used to support children's attempts to lay claim to "adult" status, or otherwise to distance themselves from what are seen to be "childish" inadequacies'. He suggests that this discourse:

enables its users to distinguish themselves from 'others' who are seen to be less intellectually capable or emotionally stable – in effect, less 'mature' – than they are, and hence more vulnerable to influence. (1996, 87)

The picture drawn by the children in my survey shows clearly that they understand and are influenced by the negative public discourses surrounding their engagement with television. But what emerges clearly from the examination above of both my survey data and other research (Buckingham 1995, 1996; Davies 2001; Palmer 1986) is that children nonetheless maintain a strong sense of their own pleasure in television and this is often focused on their favourite shows. It is the 'fun' of these shows, in their own words, that has obvious value for them. But just how does this manifest itself in their lives, and what aspects can we tease out to understand the ways in which this fun has meaning to them? How does it provide such pleasure? In the next two chapters I analyse my own research further to draw out answers to these questions from my interviews with the children and also from their own drawings and stories about their favourite television shows.

I divide these two chapters into themes that reflect the findings that emerged most strongly from my research of the ways in which children enjoy television. This includes consideration of children's physical and imaginative engagement with their favourite shows, how they believe they 'learn' from television, how they enjoy its humour and how their favourite shows offer them glimpses of the worlds they might wish for. This is a not a comprehensive list of why children enjoy television nor even of all the reasons that the children in my research indicated, but these were the themes that emerged most prominently and systematically from the analysis of my data.

CHAPTER 3

In examining these themes, I have sought to explore the evidence that points to the pleasure children get from television. Davies (1997, 144) argues that 'if shows like … *Sesame Street*, or … *Blue Peter* or *Neighbours* charm their leisure hours, then the importance of the pleasure that children take in these stories must be recognized'. I would add to this that not only should this pleasure be recognised but also understood, researched and valued – not only by children but also by adults. Hopefully the insights of the next two chapters might in some small part contribute to this understanding.

Chapter 4

'THE FUNNEST THING IN THE WORLD'

When we listen to children themselves talking about television, it is apparent that they enjoy television and that they seek it out for leisure, recreation and entertainment. It is, according to one 8-year-old boy whom I interviewed, 'the funnest thing in the world'. And yet, we seem reluctant to accept what children say about television and its meaning in their lives as either true or important. As discussed earlier in this book, watching television is largely regarded in western culture today as detrimental to the protection and nurture of the 'unformed' and 'innocent' child. As a result, it seems that even if television has value in the child's world and is her own choice as a leisure activity, we are uncomfortable with this reality. James Kincaid has written about this damaging view of childhood. He writes that 'the most moving and enspiriting thing I know is a laughing child, the total absorption of the child in the full altogether of its pleasure' (1998, 281) and he argues that through our obsession with the dangers threatening this child, and her subsequent sexualisation in our eyes, we have been responsible for the 'outrageous withholding' of this happiness: 'We have been so busy reinventing the child as a being at risk sexually that we have allowed the happy child to wander out of our range' (Kincaid 1998, 281-2).

But the 'happy' child is there within range – and she, quite regularly, sits in front of the television. Here she can discover 'a little world of monsters or anything' (10-year-old girl) or she can smile because 'it's funny' (8-year-old girl). She can even share the pleasure of tuning in to 'adult secrets' with the blessing and active participation of a parent. These are some of the insights that emerged from my research with children and that I will explore in this chapter and the next.

Children embrace television – not just figuratively and emotionally – but physically too. And this physical engagement appears to be interwoven closely with their imaginative experience of their favourite shows. So in this chapter I consider kids' physical and imaginative connection with television; I explore how excitement, thrills and action are part of this experience; and I look at the ways in which 'joining a crowd' (see Barker and Brooks (1998, 144) around the television provides a certain physical experience and pleasure not unlike that provided by the live theatre – something which has been astutely pointed out by Terence Hawkes (1973, chap. 12).

The second theme that I consider in this chapter is centred on the varied ways in which children share the fun of television with their friends: talking about it with each other, playing games associated with TV programs, jostling against each other to assert their own views of television. There is an element here of their using television 'to establish and negotiate social relationships' (Buckingham 1993a, 40) but in the analysis of my research this does not seem to be the dominant drive for the children. Instead the pursuit of fun appears to be at the heart of their shared enthusiasm for their favourite shows and a delight in the way the stories and characters thread their way through daily life.

CHAPTER 4

Finally in this chapter, I look at the ways children have fun talking about television not only to each other but to adults. In listening to the children it becomes apparent that they enjoy talking about television simply for the fun of it but it also shows how they negotiate their way through the different aspects of their own and adult perspectives on television.

Fun with TV: A Physical and Imaginative Experience

Television is not just about its programs but of course has a physical presence too in the home. Its arrival at the heart of the domestic world was highly noticeable and even from the start it provoked ambivalent attitudes from both critics and supporters. No doubt such a dramatic entrance, bringing a screen that shared its images from the 'outside' world, was bound to provoke concern and for some it was seen as a serious threat: 'TV penetrates every home in the land', Gerbner and Gross (1976, 175) ominously warned. Postman (1985, 80) argued that 'television erodes the dividing line between childhood and adulthood' and has made it 'impossible to withhold secrets'. The twin spectres of 'adult secrets' and 'mass-produced entertainment' were thus powerfully evoked as threats with the supporting image of the physical invasion of the set into the sanctity of the private domestic space.

While those who complained about television's 'invasion' of the home spoke in physical metaphors, they were not really concerned with the physical presence of the object in people's lives. Postman (2006, 83) describes an acquaintance who displayed 'her entire collection of Dickens, Flaubert, and Turgenev on the top of a 21-inch Westinghouse [television set]'. But his aim here was not to examine what television might mean to viewers in a broader sense; he did not comment on how proudly this woman apparently displayed the set along with her prized books, nor examine how it took its place, and had its own value, in her physical and social world. Rather, he shared this description as a metaphor in order to 'ridicule the hope harboured by some that television can be used to support the literate tradition' (Postman 2006, 83).

The arguments of Postman (2006), and Gerbner and Gross (1976), do recognise that television through its physical presence and the content of its programs is woven into the fabric of our lives; but for these researchers such a presence was a significantly negative reality. For others this presence is far more benign, perhaps even something to be celebrated. Hawkes (1973, 232-3) argues that television 'forms part of "real" life, and merges with it in the way that drama most effectively does', providing a 'level of immediacy' in its access to what's happening in the world – and of course providing a source of entertainment.

The way television was 'built into the rhythms of everyday life' was noted also by Raymond Williams (1989, 4) but for Williams this was not an entirely harmless feature of the new technology. Williams (1989, 12) argued that while television appears in our homes and becomes an intimate part of our lives, it is far more than a simple physical object; it is a:

> room on the stage ... where important things happen and where quite another order of importance arrives as news from a shut-off outside world; this room is a convention, now a habit, of theatre; but it is also, subtly and persistently, a personage, an actor: a set that defines us and can trap us: the alienated object that now represents us in the world. ... But more important than this has been a dynamic process when the room is dissolved, for scene is no longer external and yet

is still active, and what we see is a projection of observed, remembered, and desired images.

Williams suggests that the changes television brought were far more transformative and perhaps more questionable in their influence and impact than those suggested by Hawkes (1973, 232-3) and that they threaten to 'trap us'. There is a sense of foreboding in his 'projection of observed, remembered, and desired images'; certainly these images aren't presented as something simply to be enjoyed.

From the analysis of my research with children I would like to suggest, however, that no sense emerged of their being 'trapped' by the set; on the contrary I would argue that the children revelled in the merging of television with real life and sought out the pleasures of the 'observed, remembered and desired' images that circulate through the screen.

The fear of television's harmful influence is a factor that Hartley (1992a, 98) attempts to address with a novel approach that involves considering directly its physical presence. He suggests that an alternative way 'of looking at television's social impact' is to consider television's 'tactile power':

> Instead of fretting fruitlessly about the effect of TV on people's behaviour, morals or politico-aesthetic sensibilities, it is possible (with a good deal more certainty) to study the effect of television sets on people's living rooms. (Hartley 1992a, 98)

Hartley (1992a, 108) describes the way television sets in the early days were the centre of attraction in the home, a place where people placed 'their ornaments, trophies' and 'wedding pictures or formal portraits'. It also became 'the physical place … where you put the baby, the bride, or the pet for an intimate portrait' (p. 109). He goes on to suggest that 'the set is still personalized, but not as a family icon; more a familiar resource … in bedrooms, kitchens and studies' (p. 113). His descriptions echo Williams's in their hints that TV is both an object and a familiar 'personalised' member of the household; but they are distinctly different in their tone: menace is entirely missing from Hartley's television world.

Hartley's more light-hearted approach to television's presence in the home, and to its 'tactile power', is reflected by the children's comments in my research. On multiple levels it is apparent that their engagement with television involves enjoyment that includes an element of physical pleasure; a pleasure that is often connected both with the physical space of the television itself and a physical response to its programs. I would suggest that looking at these physical aspects as a unified whole gives a rich picture of children's relationship with television; and it is one that neither shows television as a 'trap' nor as a penetrating threat.

In his research into how children incorporate television into their play, Chris Richards observed the ways in which the physical set was inseparable from the program content for the young viewers. Watching his own children dance in front of the television, enjoying the music and images it displays, he comments on how:

> televisions can double, even simultaneously, as transmitters of images and as surfaces on which the viewer can watch herself watching, or dance to the dancing image and watch her own dancing body superimposed on the TV dancer. (1995, 141)

Richards's description of the young dancer evocatively captures the ways in which television merges the physical with the social and imaginative space of the child, but it also clearly demonstrates the child's agency: she is the one in control in front of the set. This agency

CHAPTER 4

obviously produces a large part of the pleasure of the entertainment; it is both physical and imaginative and it keeps the child free I would argue from any sense of being trapped. She is also far from the stereotypical 'passive' viewer.

Palmer (1986, 139) saw the physical excitement that some children demonstrated in front of the set as clear evidence of their active engagement with TV shows: 'the pace and energy of their physical and verbal activity around the TV comes as a shock to those expecting a placid viewer'. Palmer's observations quite contradict the views of those like Marie Winn, whose best-selling book *The Plug-in Drug* deplores the way in which children slump in front of television in a state of 'enforced passivity' (1985, 102). This view of 'enforced passivity' is not one that is supported by children's own talk about television; even when they are not dancing in front of the set as Richards's children do, by their own account they are actively absorbed in the programs. In one of my interviews an 8-year-old girl talked about her physical and mental state when watching a favourite show:

Interviewer: How would you describe yourself when you're watching TV?

Girl: Sometimes I get really distracted and if my parents are talking to me I don't always like hear them. And ... ah ... [pause]

Interviewer: Why?

Girl: Cos I'm too busy watching the TV. And [pause] ... But I don't like just like lie down and watch it.

Interviewer: It sounds like you're really concentrating.

Girl: Yeah I don't – I really like to watch the shows, I don't just like to relax and watch them, I am like very interested in them.

The intensity of this child's attention has a strong physical element. All her faculties are trained on the set so that she doesn't hear her parents when they talk to her. And while she might be sitting in front of the television – a pose that could attract the 'passive' epithet from an observer such as Winn – she is quite insistent that her attitude is not by any means inert or unreceptive. She is keen to emphasise this aspect of her viewing, as though she understands that the popular negative discourse might judge her behaviour adversely. She searches for the description of how she watches television quite carefully and thoughtfully, pausing to find the words. First she indicates that she doesn't 'like just lie down and watch it'. But then, perhaps feeling that she needs to add more clarity and an element of persuasion to her explanation, she has another go at describing her involvement with her favourite shows. Intently and with determination she continues: 'I don't just like to relax and watch them, I am like very interested in them'. She is not simply lying down and watching television in some passively indifferent manner; she is transfixed and absorbed and above all intensely enjoying the experience. There is no question here of 'enforced passivity'. This child's agency in her actions and choices is clearly evident, as is the physical intensity of her experience.

Physical satisfaction generated by a favourite television program was observed also in the 'barely controlled ecstasy' of the preschoolers watching the animated British TV show *Teletubbies* in Howard and Roberts's research. The children's physical pleasure was palpable:

CHAPTER 4

> They squirmed with glee, they bounced up and down, they beat their hands on the floor, they stood closer to the set and jigged – all the while their gaze was firmly on the television image. (2002, 332)

These are truly physical pleasures produced by a total engagement with the television program. The children appear to be in a state that echoes the 'Action/Adventure Space' described by Barker and Brooks in their research of fandom. They observed that fans seek out a 'sensuous, bodily' engagement with a film that actually produces physical pleasure 'in the present tense' (1998, 155).

This sensuous engagement with the action and thrills of a favourite television program was apparent also in my research. Two 10-year-old boys in particular demonstrated a keen physical engagement with their favourite action shows. One of these boys was an avid fan of an American animated television series called *Star Wars: The Clone Wars*. After I'd collected him from his classroom and as we were walking together to the room where we engaged in the interviews, he proudly shared with me the fact that he had *all* the DVDs of the series and a collection of Star Wars Lego. He was a quietly spoken boy with a gentle manner but his face lit up with eager excitement when he was talking about the series and the excitement apparently related to both his memory of previously-seen programs and the anticipation of watching them again.

Interviewer: Why do you think you like watching it? Just imagine you're sitting there and you're watching – what is it that makes you like it so much do you think?

Boy: [replies immediately] Action!

Interviewer: Really?

Boy:	Yep.
Interviewer:	You just love the action?
Boy:	Yeah … Action is my *thing*.
Interviewer:	Is it?
Boy:	Yeah, I like it *sooo* much … yeah that's why I like it, cos of the great action.

There is no mistaking this boy's active engagement in his favourite TV series. I had barely finished my sentence in the opening question before he leapt in with the answer 'Action'. The intensity he expresses in his emphasis on the words 'thing' and 'so' was in such contrast to his usual quietly spoken manner that it appeared quite physical. As a 10-year-old he wasn't going to jig up and down like the toddlers in Howard and Roberts's research but his face and voice expressed the same intense excitement and joy.

The other 10-year-old boy also conveyed a sense of physical engagement in his expressions of delight in his favourite show. Here he describes rapidly, almost hungrily, his favourite program – an American animated television series about superheroes called *Young Justice*:

Boy:	Then all their sidekicks become – join into a team to become Young Justice. And it's really actionative. And some of them are 'M', and really *scary*. But it's a cartoon … so … And I *love* watching it. And I watched every single one in three days yesterday.
Interviewer:	Why do you like watching it?
Boy:	It's just so exotic and so stretched out over so many different things.
Interviewer:	Like what?

CHAPTER 4

Boy: Like fighting, action, love, death – lots of death, death, more death, fighting, love, violence, death, death, death, violence, love, death, violence, death, love, death, violence. That's all. And it's really exciting [laugh].

It is apparent from his descriptions that this boy's engagement with the program is intense with a 'sensuous, bodily' element. He is on the edge of his seat explaining how he loves watching it. With a visceral enjoyment he describes the shows as 'really *scary*'. He too understands the negative discourse directed against such programs with their overt violence and he hastily adds, after admitting some are rated 'M' (recommended for mature audiences only), that it is only 'a cartoon'. But he can't curtail his enthusiasm for the program and lists the action that engages him. In describing the content of the show, he rattles off words with an intensity that mirrors his enjoyment of the excitement provided by this program. And again, at the end, in a nod to the dominant discourse condemning such over-passionate engagement with unsuitably 'sexual' and 'violent' programs, he lets out a slightly embarrassed laugh – apologising for the fact that he is so excited about potentially questionable television shows. He is slightly uncertain about revealing his unrestrained enthusiasm for the cartoon, and is deferential towards the adult in the room who might implicitly represent a criticism, in the language of the dominant negative discourse, of so much violence, sex and death.

While his descriptions themselves hint at a physical satisfaction and pleasure in the program, the 10-year-old's engagement with his favourite shows does also have a visibly physical expression. In another interview, the boy described how, after watching these shows, he would go down to the park by himself and play games based on the stories he had just seen. This re-creation of his own stories from the ones he watched on TV continued in the second interview session. In the story he wrote during this time, he placed himself at the centre of the action: 'I fight with a dagger and bow I can shout [shoot] a blue light out o my hands so this is how my story gous [goes]'. As do Barker and Brooks's fans, he obviously feels a 'sensuous, bodily' connection with his favourite programs; he becomes the one who can shoot 'a blue light' out of his own hands. When playing in the park, this imaginative engagement has a manifestly physical aspect but physical action is also central to his written story.

The elements of the TV shows that capture his attention and interest – that he finds exciting and sometimes 'scary' – thread their way through both his imaginative and physical life. The physical world (television and park), the physical satisfaction and pleasure generated by the anticipation of and enjoyment of the shows, the imaginative and emotional engagement in the TV stories and their characters, all overlap; and what binds them together is the enjoyment of television entertainment. For this boy, the television is Hawkes's modern theatre; he responds avidly to the immediacy and relevance of its 'drama'. Hawkes (1973, 235) argues that the medium of television 'demands – as "real life" does – a non-singular, "multiconscious" response on different but unanalysed levels'. The boy's responses to television are certainly 'multiconscious' and perhaps this is a part of their appeal: they present the opportunity to engage on multiple levels. Certainly this seems to be the view of the boy himself and is reflected in his astute observation of why he

CHAPTER 4

likes his favourite show: 'It's just so exotic and so stretched out over so many different things'.

This view of television encompasses what it means in our physical as well as our imaginative and social lives. It does not confine the medium to a comparison with a 'typographic tradition' (Postman 2006, 91) which, following Postman's argument, seeks to deny any value to television through completely ignoring the profound differences in the two mediums. Comparing television-viewing to reading a book is in fact, as Hawkes argues, 'an unjustifiable attempt to impose the alien structures of one medium on another, and consequently to violate the essential nature of the new medium' (1973, 235).

There are interesting parallels here to the research of Götz et al. (2005) into how children engage in their make-believe worlds. Their findings revealed nine categories of fantasy worlds which included 'conflict and threat … [and] sensual pleasure' (p. 43). 'Conflict and threat' involved 'worlds where great challenges have to be overcome in hazardous situations' and sensual pleasure involved 'delights to the senses' (p. 44). Certainly both these categories were evident in the 10-year-old boy's love of his favourite TV shows described above and the ways in which they engaged his interest and imagination. In his own written narrative from our second interview, which is based on one of these favourite shows, he faces 'great challenges' with obvious delight in the thrill of it:

> I was in the under world wahting for my friend Nico son of hades when and army of hell hond/bad wolves hedid towords me … I drow my sword and shout moonlight at them but I couldn't hold them so I run out of the underworld to somwere safe. As I ran I relised I left my freind so I run back.

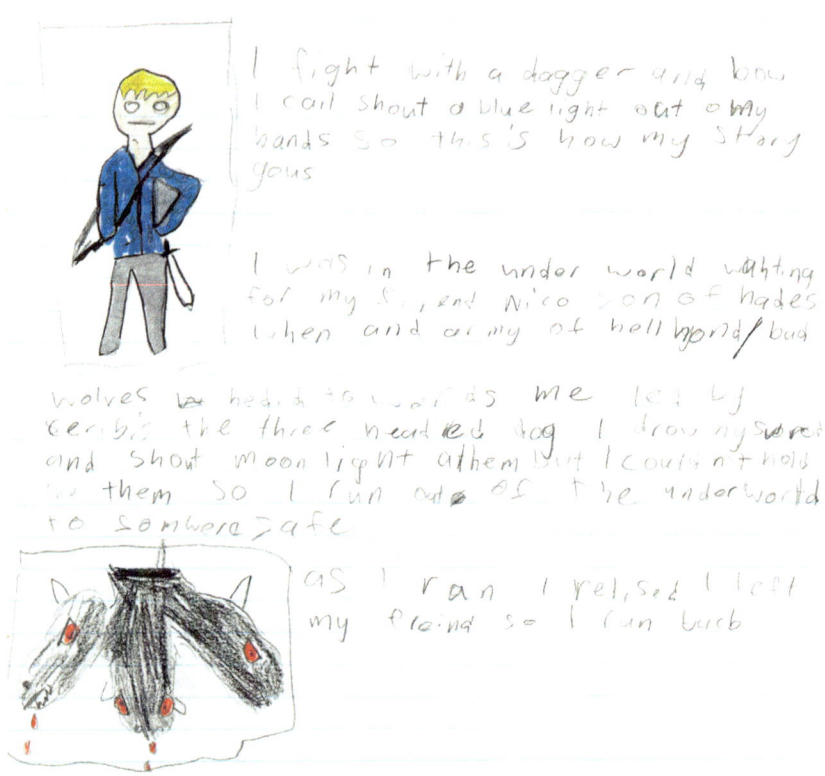

Story 1: 10-year-old boy's story of the underworld

CHAPTER 4

Götz et al. (2005, 67-8) observed how for children their imagined worlds provided a 'fantasy of thrill' and that this feeling 'is described by the children in very positive terms'. They also noted how their 'sense of fun is tied up with the thrill and the fear' (p. 68). While Götz et al. (2005, 81) were writing about the make-believe worlds created by children drawing on all available sources, they have noted that visual media, which includes television, does 'seem to have the most central role in children's stories'.

This certainly appeared to be true for the 10-year-old boy above whose intense enjoyment of his favourite shows, which included elements of thrill and fear, was evident throughout our interviews and particularly in his story. Here he is in the heart of the action shooting out 'moonlight', retreating to 'somewhere safe' and then having to head back into the thrill of the danger to rescue his 'freind'. This merging of his own imaginative world with a favourite television show is obviously an intensely positive, pleasurable and physical experience.

The anticipation of pleasure from the excitement and thrills of a favourite show is another element of fun that children revealed in my research and that appeared to have a physical element. Howard and Roberts (2002, 332) observed this anticipation of joy from a known favourite show: 'bodies, faces, voices all express intense excitement and a sense of "I know what's going to come and I can hardly wait"'. Götz et al. (2005, 67) too comment on the pleasure 'expressed in anticipation of the exciting and unknown'. A number of children reflected on this anticipation in my research when they spoke of their enjoyment of television serials that left off at an exciting moment and were 'to be continued' in the next episode. Here an 8-year-old girl somewhat breathlessly describes her delight in this aspect of a favourite show:

And it's one of those shows that has those signs that goes 'to be continued' so you all go 'Aww what happens next?', and you're like 'Oh I have to watch the show tomorrow' to see what's next and stuff.

For another 8-year-old, the convention of interrupting the story at a gripping moment, to be continued the following week, was a significant part of her pleasure in the program. She raised it herself as something she liked about the show, describing the details of how it worked in one particular episode.

> It's cool and … ah … it's … like and then they leave the episodes like at um a really exciting place like … and there is a demon trying to attack them. When they're about … on the last … second last episode they were about to say who um … the demon is and then they just stop it there. So you have to wait another week until you find out the next part.

The deferment of pleasure apparently generates its own excitement here; this young girl obviously enjoys the anticipation of having 'to wait another week until you find out the next part'.

Joining a Crowd, and Solitary Pleasures, around Television

Another pleasure that Barker and Brooks noted in their study of fans that has a physical aspect is the delight felt in 'joining a crowd' (1998, 144). In relation to television this manifests itself in the way audiences connect with each other while watching television in the home. Hawkes (1973, 233) observed that 'such an environment encourages audience participation, reinforced by the fact that the members of the audience usually constitute a group who know each other intimately'. Hawkes (1973, 219) has argued persuasively that

CHAPTER 4

this aspect of television viewing has turned the medium into the true theatre of today because:

> drama is a social, a communal medium. It depends on and results from interaction 'face to face' between people on the stage, people in the audience, and between stage and audience as well.

This 'face to face' interaction, the enjoyment of being in the crowd, was reflected in the ways children talk about watching television with their family and friends. One 10-year-old girl described watching TV in her family:

> Like sometimes I watch *My Kitchen Rules* with my nan in her bedroom, but most of the time I watch it in the living room either with my mum or by myself.

When asked who they watched television with, although 67% of the children in the survey said they watched it alone, around 50% said they watched also with family and friends. In my interviews one 10-year-old, rather thoughtfully, reflected on this aspect of television viewing:

> I like how it can just be like a bit of time for yourself [pause]. Yeah [pause]. But I also like how I can like talk to my family about how like it's really good or something.

This sharing, which is generated by the physical presence of the television within the family, and is an enjoyable element of being part of the 'crowd' in front of the set, occasionally goes beyond the actual moment of viewing. In a delightful description this 10-year-old girl tells of her enjoyment of a TV show that continued after the set had been switched off:

> when me and my Mum are going to bed we always like laugh about things cos we watch movies together and when we watch TV we always act out something.

As were the young dancers in Richards's (1995, 141) research mentioned earlier, mother and daughter here are engaged in a physical representation – that is also a conversation with each other – of the image and story of the television show.

In these accounts from the children in my research, the television and its programs are very much at the heart of family life. Despite the development of new screen technologies it appears that the television still has a central place, both physically and in the shared enjoyment of TV programs, within family life. The pleasure of this shared television space, which Stuart Hall (1986, 9) observed 30 years ago, is still evident today. He astutely noted that:

> we enjoy the way the televisual flow is incorporated into the 'flows' of everyday domestic life. ... Viewing can be used to provide the occasion for family interaction, or to 'create space', even when the living-room is crammed with other people. It can forge solidarities, establish alliances between family members or just provide a much-needed excuse for cuddling up. The medium thus has become integrated into the everyday processes and codes of family interaction.

As we saw above in the 8-year-old's description of being intently absorbed in a TV show, physical pleasure in television is not only produced by physical *activity*. Being slumped in front of television feeling 'free of pressures and obligations' (Barker and Brooks 1998, 144) is also potentially an enjoyable physical state and I would argue is not the passive condition either 'enforced' or 'indifferent' described by the critics of television (Comstock and Scharrer 2007, 46-8; Winn 1985, 102). Hartley (1987a, 256) writes about the 'solitary, private, comfortable pleasures' of the television viewer and in that comfort there is undoubtedly a pleasurable physical sensation. Viewers who are stretched out on a snug sofa watching a favourite program are not necessarily passive. Their engagement and enjoyment is simply not visible to the undiscerning, or the judgmental, eye.

Palmer noticed this still absorption in favourite programs among the children whom she observed in her extensive ethnographic study. She found that 'while some children will be most vocal and active during their best-loved programs, many choose these times to give their absorbed and intense concentration to the TV screen' (p. 139). They sit quietly in front of the television but, as Palmer (1986, 139) observes, 'their viewing is … being directed in a consistent and purposeful way'.

The children's descriptions of where they watched television particularly highlighted the multi-faceted ways in which they enjoy both a physical and emotional engagement with the medium and how it is woven into their 'everyday lives'. Here is a description from a 10-year-old boy:

> I watch it in like this room where there's a sofa. There's a room next to it which is the dining room. But I just sit on the couch and relax like it's a vacation. So then I just watch my favourite programs.

The physical space around the television is meticulously described by this boy who takes his place in the heart of it. From this concrete tangible space he is transported beyond the physical to an emotional place: which is 'like a vacation'. And that's where he enters the world of his 'favourite programs'. All the children I interviewed were quite specific about their physical relation to the television set and yet this position was not simply physical; the whole space overlapped with their dreams and fantasies and hinted at their wider emotional and social lives. Here is a description from another 10-year-old boy:

Boy:	Well, I just watch TV in the living room. Like – that's where my things are, toys and stuff, my old toys and stuff, and my little safe … and …
Interviewer:	What little safe?
Boy:	It holds my really special stuff.
Interviewer:	Cool. So, it's all there near the television, is it?
Boy:	Yeah, it's by a cupboard on the side. The television is nearby the door that we enter into the living room.
Interviewer:	And do you have a comfortable chair?
Boy:	Not a chair. I've got a couch.
Interviewer:	Ooo … That's really nice.
Boy:	Yeah, in the living room. And I get to eat dinner there sometimes, on the couch.

This 10-year-old boy was describing a world of his own which, as it were, grew out of the television viewing space. He was surrounded by his secret precious things, happily settled into the couch where in extra special moments he got 'to eat dinner … sometimes'. The space had been infused, not exactly by but because of the presence of the television, with a 'feel' of utopia (Dyer 2002, 20). The central place was his couch which, as he quickly pointed out to me, was not simply a chair. His special things were all carefully positioned in a cupboard by the side of the television. The television was an integral and enabling part of this world but it wasn't the whole picture. The child himself had a central role in creating this space for his own pleasure and enjoyment. Richards has noted this appropriation of the television space by children too: 'In some moments television is

CHAPTER 4

used to open up and reconstruct domestic space in the terms that children enjoy' (Richards 1995, 141).

It might seem an unlikely place to find solitude but children appear also to use television to 'reconstruct domestic space' around the set in such a manner as to create some room for themselves. This is apparent in the comments of the two 10-year-old boys above who described the nature of the physical space as they saw it around the set. It is also apparent in this 10-year-old boy's description in another interview:

> Well, my sister doesn't annoy me cos she's just sitting next to me watching it, so it gives me a chance of not being annoyed and just time to myself basically.

The 'family' is still part of the space, the boy's sister continues to sit next to him, but the television has enabled this boy to escape for the moment into his own world, a world he creates within the physical and imaginative spaces offered by the television.

The way in which television extends into both the physical and imaginative space, its quality of 'multi-consciousness' to borrow Hawkes's (1973, 235) term, was illuminated particularly in the drawing created by a 10-year-old girl during my research (see illustration on next page). She did not choose one particular TV show to write about, or to illustrate, in her own creation. Instead she drew a picture of a 'home'. In this drawing, a television set appears in a dominant place in the main room and its screen broadcasts 'News Breaking', a universally recognised television program. But there is also a cat pictured in the corner of the TV, which appears to be looking out of the set towards another cat, with silver hair and a pink dress walking through the front door.

SQUARE EYES

Drawing 1: 10-year-old girl's drawing of a room centred on the television

In this girl's picture the TV set is certainly in one physical place. But that is its only 'normal' aspect in this drawing. The television is drawn into a narrative created by the girl using aspects of her physical, social and imaginary life. Representations of physical reality are juxtaposed to imaginary characters in this picture; they overlap and merge in curious ways. The girl's family cat is *inside* the TV set while the fantasy cat character in the drawing is standing in the doorway. According to the young girl, the television itself is *talking* – she imitates its voice during our interview. And while the screen says 'News Breaking' the 'voice' of the television is talking about a popular American computer-animated children's movie called *Monsters Inc.*

> *Interviewer:* And what's this here. What's happening in this picture here? It looks like a television.
>
> *Girl:* Yeah … It is. And this cat is the, is *Monsters Inc* freaky zone
>
> *Interviewer:* Okay so the cat's come out of *Monsters Inc*?

CHAPTER 4

Girl: No. Well it's … the television is a [speaking in a different voice] 'What, *Monsters Inc* is on … Whaat?' It's like cuc-koo. She um is really weird cos she only watches TV when she hasn't got her shoes on.

For me as the interviewer, the flow of this conversation was hard to follow. I tried to impose some logic by asking if the cat in the set was part of *Monsters Inc*. The answer to this was quite emphatically 'no'. Elsewhere in the interview it becomes apparent that both cats in her drawing reflect the presence of her own family cat in her life; but its presence is not a simple depiction of reality; rather, it too is woven into the space around the television. In this interview segment, the girl steadfastly refuses to be interrupted by the demands of adult logic and continues with her own thoughts and her own involvement with this picture. She looks at the TV set and imitates what it is saying – which she does admit is slightly crazy (cuckoo). And then she jumps, with the disjointed effect of a stream of consciousness, to talk about the cat in the doorway who is 'really weird cos she only watches TV when she hasn't got her shoes on'. Here is another mention of the physical comforts associated with enjoying television, albeit attributed to an imaginary character.

In this girl's drawing, television characters people the room; real life characters (in this case the family cat) people the television set. And the imaginary characters are also curious mixtures; the cat in the doorway is part cat and part horse – one of the horses from a favourite television program, the Australian animated children's series *The Silver Brumby*. In the second interview the girl describes this character as one of the brown silver brumbies in the TV story:

> She's brown she's a brown cat … she's half cat and half horse … but she's wearing a dressing gown so you can't see [pause] but she can talk horse language and she can talk cat language.

A little later she continues the description of the same character as it develops in her imagination:

> Well it is really a silver brumby but she's got this stuff that keeps her warm and it's like protected fur in sheep's wool and she can keep warm.

When we talk about her picture again at a later interview this character has changed yet again and is now mostly a cat: 'it's sorta changed over time', she says in response to my comment that I thought it was a horse. The fluid interpretations of television characters and stories – what Hawkes (1973, 234-5) observes is 'an unwillingness to impose what obviously seems an arbitrary division between one programme and the 'next'' – is quite clearly visible in this girl's drawing. Programs merge on the television itself, but the stories and characters bleed across physical and imaginary boundaries, drawing in elements of real life along the way. This reflects what Jenkins (2013, 287) has observed about fans' relationship with favourite programs of 'a more active relationship in which textual materials are appropriated and fit to personal experience'.

The complex ways in which television, through both its physical presence and its content, weaves its way through children's lives was thus apparent in my research. In the moments when they did not feel constrained to respond within the framework of the dominant negative discourses, children revealed elements of what they enjoyed about television: time to themselves, a comfortable chair, a moment where 'like, it's a vacation', and a delight in the opportunities to dream that were offered by the porous physical and imaginative boundaries of the medium.

CHAPTER 4

The Fun of Sharing: TV in Children's Social and Cultural Lives

From the comments of the children that I interviewed and surveyed, it was clear that television had a central place in their social and cultural lives. Even with the proliferation of various portable electronic devices on which it is now possible to watch television programs, most of the children still said they watched television in a shared living space. In my survey 97% said they watched television 'in the living room'. This did not necessarily mean that they watched with other members of the family. Family life in some cases simply shared the same space, as in the scene so delightfully described by this 8-year-old girl who continued to watch the singing program on television as the others wandered away from the screen:

> Sometimes when we watch singing films my mum and dad go to cook, my sister – my little sister – goes to read, my big sister does her homework and my brother does like his maths homework. I'm the only one actually watching the singing because I have like a thing for singing.

The television here is part of the social life of the family and while some members have drifted away from the set, it still has a physical presence that weaves through daily life.

While the children often described the ways in which they were absorbed in the actual moment of watching their favourite shows, their engagement with the program also went beyond the instance of viewing and was woven into the social fabric of their lives in quite fascinating ways. Their accounts of this were often peppered with a sense of delight and enjoyment that could be shared also with friends, as can be seen in the following conversation with two 8-year-old girls in my research:

Girl 1:	Maybe my dad's pretty strong, except – and my mum's pretty strong as well. She's like – except every time, my brother is like 'Come on Dad, show your muscles,' at the dinner table [laugh]. And Dad's like, 'Nah.' Yeah. So he (Mr Incredible) is a bit like my dad because the dad doesn't want to show his muscles cos otherwise the kids would go like, 'Ohh, my dad's so strong,' and we like, they might know that he's Incredible. My dad's not that – my dad's not incredible [slight laugh].
Interviewer:	So you think of your dad as being Mr Incredible?
Girl 1:	Yes, sometimes, and my mum being Elastigirl – no, my sister being Elastigirl actually. I kind of want to be Dash cos I really like running.
Girl 2:	[unclear] I wanna …
Interviewer:	What did you want to be?
Girl 2:	I wanted to be Dash cos he can just run. He can actually run across the water cos he's going so fast.
Girl 1:	[eagerly] Yeah, yeah, he ran [unclear]. He's like whoosh …
Girl 2:	Because in the movie they were getting chased by these people and his eyes were closed and he just ran across the water. Then he looked down and he's like, 'Oh, I'm actually running on water.' [both girls laugh]

My conversation with these two 8-year-old girls had been quite free-ranging up to the start of this segment and included references to a number of favourite shows but also to observations of their families. The girls had mentioned some preferred programs and Girl 1 had already spoken about one of her particular favourites: an animated film of a family of superheroes called *The Incredibles*.

CHAPTER 4

In this film, Mr Incredible is the father of a family with supernatural abilities. He himself has wide-ranging powers and particularly large muscles. She had obviously identified quite closely with this family which lives a traditional suburban life, escaping every so often into adventures involving their superpowers. Talk of favourite shows had led to discussions of family life and relationships, which was a pattern that happened quite regularly with a number of the children in my research.

In this particular segment, the young girl transitions almost seamlessly from a discussion of the movie to sharing insights into her family life with her current audience. Although she doesn't mention the movie at the start of this segment, it appears that she is still remembering the fictional family when she rather suddenly starts talking about how strong her father is (adding quickly, so as not to offend, that her mother is strong too). This observation then reminds her of an exchange around the family dinner table. It's a rather typical scene; son both challenging and urging his father to 'show his muscles'; father resisting the appeal to him to show off his 'male' strength. The recollection of this scene reminds the 8-year-old of *The Incredibles* and in a rapid and fluid transition the girl is suddenly comparing her father to Mr Incredible, talking almost indistinguishably of one and then the other. The two families overlap in her conversation even within one sentence ('we like, they might') and have obviously been closely associated in her own mind. She has identified her dad with Mr Incredible. But as she is talking she suddenly realises how this might appear to her physically present audience – her friend and the interviewer (me). Recognising the boast inherent in the comparison, she rather deprecatingly adds, 'My dad's not incredible'. The girl has moved in and out of the movie, weaving the two families together and yet remaining squarely anchored in her social world. Her conversation is threaded with obvious delight – and a touch of wistfulness: 'I kinda wanna be Dash'. This child too is getting a glimpse of what 'utopia' might 'feel like' (Dyer 2002, 20) and it is a vision that is shared by her friend who would also like to be able to 'just run' like Dash.

The fun that these children enjoy from watching, talking about and dreaming of a favourite program suffuses the entire conversation. And this light-hearted mood carries them along to a delightfully funny exchange. Girl 2 recounts a comic moment in the movie where their favourite character Dash, who has been running wildly from some enemies with his eyes closed, looks down and suddenly realises that he's running on water. The joke is on him, because the audience has seen it coming, and the girls love it – erupting into laughter and enjoying the shared humour. In a way they are also laughing at their own fantasies of being like Dash, recognising the element of absurdity in such a dream.

Throughout this exchange, the children are revelling in their shared culture, and I've become a benign enough adult to be included as a listener. Part of their sense of enjoyment has been informed by and infused with their identification with Mr Incredible and his family and with their fantasies of having superpowers. It is a wonderful example of the way in which entertainment works, as Dyer (1992, 7) has so astutely observed:

> Entertainment … teaches us enjoyment – including the enjoyment of unruly delight. It works with the desires that circulate in a given society at a given time, neither wholly constructing those desires nor merely reflecting desires produced elsewhere; it plays a major role in the social construction of happiness. We have to understand it itself, neither take it as given nor assume that behind it lies something more important.

CHAPTER 4

It is interesting in this exchange between the 8-year-old girls to see how favourite programs are woven into the social and imaginary lives of children and the way they delight in moving in and out of the text – something that Buckingham (1993a, 240) has commented on:

> Much of the pleasure of fictional television may derive from this playful 'as if' relationship: viewers move into and out of the text, secure in the knowledge that it is not real, yet prepared, temporarily, to pretend that it is.

The way in which television reaches into diverse corners of children's social and emotional worlds is also illuminated by Hawkes's (1973, 233) keen observations about the nature of television viewing. He writes that:

> an 'evening' … spent watching television will have a quality of multifariousness within a much larger and more significant unity; that of the home, the known surroundings, the family or other 'setting' in which the response to television usually takes place … the screen itself sheds light on, and draws to itself a known and literally 'inhabited' environment.

For the young girl in the interview above, watching *The Incredibles* on television certainly has had a 'quality of multifariousness' that continues even beyond the moment of watching. Throughout the series of three interviews, the girl returns to features of this movie and its characters in her talk. For her the screening of this movie in her living room has shed light on the family and drawn it into its orbit. And her observation of this is something she is keen to share in our conversations. Family members have taken on the characteristics of their fictional counterparts albeit in imprecise and changeable ways; Elastigirl is first the mum and then the sister, the real life father doesn't quite have the muscles of the fictional dad.

She herself could be Dash; she does after all 'really like running'. The moment of viewing is woven into the social and imaginative life of the young viewer through her response to a favourite program – one which brings her much delight and enjoyment. The home and 'known surroundings' become a part of the narrative that emerges from but then envelopes the favourite program; this continues to extend into her conversation with her friend and with me during the interview. The physical, imaginative and social element of the child's engagement with the show is quite apparently a part of its attraction and of the ongoing pleasure she derives from watching it. It has become part of real life and has merged with it; which is a quality that Hawkes (1973, 231) suggests is part of television's 'universality'.

Sharing Talk with Friends: Competitive Critics or Partners in Pleasure?

Sharing the fun of a television show with friends appears to play a role in children's enjoyment of television. Talking about television, role-playing or game-playing based on favourite characters or shows offered a number of the children in my research significant pleasure and by their own account was 'fun'. This is something that was also observed by Palmer (1986, 92): 'Sharing talk about TV with friends or playing games based on TV programs was for some children an essential part of their viewing pleasure'. Buckingham (1993a) has researched the ways children talk about television extensively and he has observed from his interviews with groups of children that the sharing and 'retelling' of television stories 'provides an opportunity for re-living pleasurable moments' (p. 67).

During the course of my research, as the children became more confident that they could inhabit and enjoy their own pleasures

CHAPTER 4

in television, fun appeared to dominate; and they grabbed the opportunity to re-live these 'pleasurable moments' (Buckingham 1993a, 67). This pursuit of fun, and the priority given to it, emerged clearly from my research as can be seen in the following interviews. These are from the three interviews that I conducted with two girls, one 7-year-old (Girl 1) and one 8-year-old (Girl 2). Here the 7-year-old starts talking to her friend about her favourite show:

Girl 1: It actually is my favourite … my parents think it's horrible but …

Interviewer: Which one's that?

Girl 1: [slight pause] It's on ABC3 and [takes a deep breath] some of my friends say they don't like it, just to like, just to like make them, make them feel, make them like show off that they're, that they're big, that they're big enough to not to watch that but maybe like just most people just say they don't like it, they don't like it and one of the secrets is that they really like it.

The girl is tentative here in talking about her favourite program. Although this is our second interview, and she is with a friend, she hesitates at the start to even give the name of the TV show before first arguing the case for her choice. With a deep breath she launches into her defence with an explanation of why her peers condemn the show. It takes her some time to reach the crux of her argument as she builds up to her reason of why they don't like it: 'they like to show off … that they're big enough to not … watch'. Interestingly she explains their behaviour as a social act; she has understood what Buckingham (1993a, 182) observes, that talk about television is 'a means of asserting a 'subject position' and thereby of claiming social power'. In his research Buckingham (1993a, 235) found that children distanced themselves 'from programmes which were seen as "babyish" or "kids' stuff" ... thereby proclaiming their own maturity'.

Obviously this show does not meet the critical standards for an acceptable television program, either from the adults in her life or from her peers. She does not indicate why her parents don't like it; perhaps it is lacking in educational or cultural value, or is irritating to adult tastes. In any case the girl seems less concerned about her parents' opinion than her peers' as indicated by her comment 'my parents think it's horrible but ...'. She moves on quickly from announcing her parents' dislike of the show to tackling the criticisms of her peers.

Understanding that her friends' behaviour is driven by a need to assert their identities as mature 'critics' (Buckingham 1993a, 235), she confidently asserts her own interpretation of their negative reaction to the show: 'one of the secrets is that they really like it'. The show that the girl is referring to is a South Korean animated series called *YooHoo & Friends* and it is designed for preschool children; it would certainly lend itself to criticisms from primary school children of being 'babyish'. But it is also possible that older children find it boring, and that, as it turns out, is exactly what her friend (Girl 2) says in the next part of the same interview. A full two minutes after announcing 'it is actually my favourite', the 7-year-old finally reveals the name of the show:

Girl 1: My favourite show is like ... it's called ... it's called ... *Yoohoo & Friends*

Interviewer: *Yoohoo & Friends?*

Girl 2: Oh, I know that.

Interviewer: You know that, M____?

Girl 2: Yeah ... sometimes in the morning I watch it but I get really bored of it.

CHAPTER 4

In this exchange, the girl's friend does say she finds the show boring, but what is interesting is that the two girls go on to write their stories and create their drawings based on this particular program. The friend is apparently not trying to 'show off' her maturity and stake out her identity, so perhaps there is more room here to defer to her 7-year-old friend on this choice. It seems that Girl 2 does simply find the show dull. Her taste in television programs is in entertainment for older children including the American teenage fantasy sitcom *Wizards of Waverly Place*. Earlier in the interviews, she revealed that she is particularly enamoured of young female celebrity actors, especially Selena Gomez, who was a star of *Wizards of Waverly Place*. But even though her preferences for particular shows obviously differ significantly from her friend, she enjoys the sharing of laughs and insider knowledge of a television show that both of them know. *Yoohoo & Friends* is a favourite of only one of the two children, but both appear to equally enjoy the way it offers them an opportunity to have a laugh, to share their ideas of plot and to talk about their perceptions of various characters. The enjoyment of sharing talk and insights into a TV show has trumped any desire to stake out a superior critical stance and condemn 'babyish' programs. Although their favourite shows differed in both style and content, these two friends chose to sit at the same table and to write two 'episodes' based on the same TV program during our interview. While doing this, they talked almost continuously about the stories they were creating and the characters that they were drawing from the TV show. They were apparently quite immersed in the pleasure of moving in and out of the imaginative and social worlds that they created from their engagement with this cartoon.

Girl 2:   I think this one's cute. I like the tiny one … because the tiny one is a little bit nice … I think [rising inflection]

Girl 1:   He's the nicest.

Girl 2:   Yeah. But the, but the middle one, the large and medium are like mean.

Girl 1:   The biggest is the meanest, the middle one is the middle size meanest or something.

Girl 2:   Yeah, yeah [pause] and maybe the smallest is like nice to the thing

Girl 1:   Remember in *YooHoo & Friends* in one episode, the smallest, if you watched this one maybe you might recognise, the smallest, and the um, Chewoo, make friends cos they're the same size.

Girl 2:   Oh yeah, yeah.

Girl 1:   They make friends and they start going like, 'We're friends.' [imitating cartoon character's voice] This is what Chewoo said, 'We're friends, even though we're enemies.'

Interviewer: That's very funny.

[girls laugh together]

Girl 1:   And they're shaking each other's hands. That was funny cos they were actually like enemies except they were saying that they're friends.

Girl 2:   But they're enemies but they're nice to each other.

Girl 1:   [laughs at friend's comment then imitates cartoon character again] 'I can't believe we're friends even though we're enemies.' [laughter]

CHAPTER 4

At the start of this exchange Girl 2 defers to Girl 1 whose favourite show is the focus of their drawings. With a rising inflection at the end of her sentence, she tentatively puts forward an opinion of one of the animated characters from the TV program. She is obviously hoping that her friend will endorse her judgment of the character, of the 'tiny one' who 'is a little bit nice … I think'. The 7-year-old (Girl 1) rises to the occasion, happy to give her imprimatur to this assessment, and with a tone of authority asserts that 'He's the nicest'. This delights, and possibly relieves, her friend who responds instantly and with certainty now: 'Yeah'. But while one of the girls appears to have the authority in terms of being the 'expert' about the show within this relationship, it is obvious that both of them are having fun, and are enjoying sharing this sense of fun. Their talk is animated, they are absorbed in both their drawings and their conversation, and their exchanges are punctuated with laughter. They are talking about the TV show as they go along, sharing remembered scenes and working out the television characters' curious relationships.

Girl 1 recalls an episode where two 'enemies' find common ground when they realise they are both 'the same size'. This incongruity delights the two girls and sets off an entertaining discussion that reveals the joy in their exchanges about the cartoon. Girl 2 thoughtfully reflects on the two characters: 'they're enemies but they're nice to each other'. This fact is obviously interesting to her and highlights a value that she possibly shares. The cartoon characters' relationship is also funny in its unlikelihood, and this provokes a response from Girl 1 who, with a comic touch, imitates in a high-pitched voice what Chewoo might have said: 'I can't believe we're friends even though we're enemies'. At this point the two friends collapse with laughter. Their delight in sharing the fun in this entire exchange is clearly evident. And the shared knowledge of the television show and an appreciation of its stories and characters is an integral part of this enjoyment.

The two girls are drawing on the show in ways similar to those articulated by Götz et al. (2005, chap. 5) in their observations of children using media in creating their make-believe worlds. These researchers found that the children were 'selectively abstracting from [the media texts] various elements and features and integrating them together with ideas of their own to create new worlds of meaning' (2005, 99). Götz et al. also examined the content of these make-believe worlds and found that 'what dominated the content … were universal human themes of harmony, relationships, wish to overcome conflict, and search for excitement and fun' (p. 202). This is reflected in my research with these two girls. In this interview segment Girl 2 comments on the way the two 'enemies' overcome conflict by being 'nice to each other'. They have found common ground in their relationship 'cos they're the same size'. Of all the stories or anecdotes that these two girls could have discussed from the television show, this one obviously struck a chord. But they go on from these observations to find the fun at the heart of this remembered scene. They continue for the rest of the conversation to focus entirely on enjoying the elements of the scene that they find funny and creating their own humour out of it.

The whole conversation, both in tone and in content, is infused with a search for fun. The girls are so engrossed in what they are doing – talking, sharing stories, enjoying a laugh – that when I interject with a comment, they barely register my interruption. They don't respond but continue on with their discussion as though I hadn't intervened. Perhaps they have decided that I can't really participate

CHAPTER 4

in their conversation, not only because I am an adult but because I don't know the television program. They are happy for me to observe, I provide an interested audience and they seem to like this, but I am peripheral to their real enjoyment. Here they are not just 'talking' about what they like about a television program, or distancing themselves as critics: they are immersed in the fun of it.

Drawing 2: 7-year-old girl's front and back covers

In her research, Palmer (1986, 139) observed how 'children bring TV stories and events to life again in their talk, activity and games' and she commented on 'the sheer enjoyment and enthusiasm' they exhibited in their talk. In my final interview with these two girls, where they had an opportunity to talk about the drawings they had created in the previous interview, their enthusiasm and 'sheer enjoyment' is evident. And they have certainly brought the television stories to life in their own creations.

Drawing 3: 8-year-old girl's front and back covers

In this last interview with these two girls, the friends talked about how they had woven together characters from *YooHoo & Friends* and also used a part of the storyline from the American animated movie *Ice Age* to create their drawings. As can be seen in the illustrations above, they produced the front and back covers of two episodes of the same story. The 7-year-old's, episode 146, comes first. Her friend (Girl 2) has drawn the second part of the story and her cover indicates that it is episode 147. As they explained in the interview, they wanted their two stories to be connected.

Girl 1: We wanted ours to sort of be related together. We wanted it to sort of like be the same.

Interviewer: That's gorgeous.

Girl 1: So I'm going to make this have a bad ending so that she can continue with it and finish with a good ending so it's like one big story.

CHAPTER 4

Girl 2: [eagerly agreeing] Yep.

Interviewer: Ohh … Fantastic. So it's sort of like a serial, is it?

Girl 1: Yeah maybe at the end I'll make the Pookies win something because they're the bad guys and then they'll get it back in the second one maybe.

Interviewer: Okay so tell me a little bit about what's going on in your picture here.

Girl 1: Well they're trying to fix the hole, the crack in Mount Everest.

Interviewer: So this silver bit in the middle here that looks like a mountain is a crack, or is this the crack, the white and red?

Girl 2: That's the crack, that's the crack [eagerly]

Girl 1: Yeah that's the crack. It goes all the way up here.

Interviewer: I see. So the white and red is the crack all the way up through the silver mountain.

Girl 1: They're trying to stop the Ice Age from cracking. Then I think in the second one maybe they made it stick together a bit so the crack is littler maybe this time.

Interviewer: Okay, so in M_'s the crack has got a bit smaller.

Girl 2: Yeah.

Interviewer: So who are these characters here at the front?

Girl 1: That's YooHoo cos he's like sorta the boss.

Girl 2: Yeah.

Interviewer: Okay, the blue one.

Girl 1: And that's meant to be–

Girl 2: [interrupting] Chewoo.

Girl 1:	Chewoo, she's the funny one.
Girl 2:	And she's like hyper.
Girl 1:	And she's really weird cos she is just, she's just like the funny one and everyone and he's … I think he's my favourite character.
Interviewer:	The black and white one?
Girl 2:	Yeah.
Girl 1:	Because he's like really …
Girl 2:	Grumpy.
Girl 1:	He thinks, he thinks he's sensible but he's actually quite funny. He thinks he's sensible and he says everything is stupid and bad.
Interviewer:	So why do you like him?
Girl 1:	Cos he's like, I think he's like really funny. Then that guy that looks like a teddy bear [both girls laugh], this time he's playing with Pammee who hasn't been drawn yet and the butterfly is looking for Pammee. Then when I've drawn Pammee, Pammee is chasing the butterfly.
Interviewer:	How cute.
Girl 1:	And the butterfly isn't looking for him anymore. Then he's playing and he's meant to be – I forgot his name … [laughs]. He's meant to be um one that's really good at science and stuff and he's an inventor, and um … his name I just remembered his name is Roodee.
Girl 2:	yeah … It's like, Roodee is like has ruined some stuff. Like sometimes he says bad words like stupid and that's why um he's called Roodee cos …
Girl 1:	He can easily get into fights with Lemmee.

CHAPTER 4

As they talked, their excitement at being able to tell me about their drawings grew; it was an opportunity to enjoy once again being immersed in the stories and characters through explaining them to an interested listener. But as the conversation continued, it became apparent that their talk was not just a communication with me; they weren't simply answering my questions about their drawings. The two girls begin eagerly, almost impatiently, sharing descriptions of their favourite characters. At this point an element of competition appears. Girl 1 senses that Girl 2 might be challenging the superior knowledge of the show that she established at the start with the choice of the TV program and she quickly moves to take control of the conversation. Delighted that I have asked about her favourite character, Girl 2 has excitedly identified Chewoo. Her friend jumps in to show her own insight into this character, 'she's the funny one', but Girl 2 responds rapidly with 'she's the hyper one'. Girl 2's excitement about this character is audible in her voice.

Girl 1 at this stage makes a determined effort to re-assert her superior knowledge of the show. She changes the conversation, rather abruptly, to her own favourite character, continuing steadily through her friend's interjections to establish a full picture of this character who 'thinks he's sensible but actually he's quite funny'. But despite this competitive edge, the search for excitement and fun still gets the upper hand as is apparent in the laughter that punctuates the friends' talk. They are delighting in recreating the characters together and weaving them into their own stories, sharing these creations as they go. Each girl draws out the characteristics of their own favourites and, although their tastes differ, the building of the portraits together is a significant part of their enjoyment.

In this segment, the girls' talk becomes more animated as it appears to move out of the reach of the interviewer and her adult space. As they become immersed in their own world, my comments have less and less effect on the conversation. Girl 1 cursorily answers my question 'So why do you like him?' and my next comment 'how cute' appears to have barely registered and certainly isn't acknowledged. Meanwhile, their talk is infused with a heightened sense of excitement. Girl 1 describes a funny-looking character in her drawing, 'that looks like a teddy bear', and they both burst out laughing.

There is no doubt that there is an aspect of performance in this conversation, particularly as I have noted above in Girl 1's attempts to demonstrate her superior knowledge. Buckingham (1993a, 67) has observed this element in children's talk about television; it is a social event 'that takes the form of a demonstration for the benefit of others'. The 7-year-old (Girl 1) in particular has been eager to demonstrate to both her friend and me, the adult listener, her superior knowledge of the show. But what dominates the conversation is the girls' engagement with the world that they are creating from the television program and it is apparent that a large part of the fun is in sharing this in their talk and their drawings, and in creating their related stories.

In these interviews, the pleasure these children are enjoying in television reflects what Johan Meire (2007a) identified as central to the fun in play. As quoted earlier in this book such pleasure 'comes from the feeling of control or challenge, from sharing or (more generally) being part of the social, material and imaginary environment, and/or from bodily sensations' (Meire 2007a, 2).

That children's engagement in television is rich and varied is apparent throughout my research and is supported by others who have conducted research with children. Marsha Kinder (1995, 19) observes that the 12 contributors to her book *Kids' Media Culture* find that:

> children's reactions to media culture tend to be more active, variable, and negotiated than is usually realized; for such reception is often embedded in the context of play and other leisure activities, as well as in a complex network of social relations found at home within the family, at school among friends and teachers, and in the broader public sphere of the neighbourhood, region, and nation.

This is an apt description of the multi-faceted ways in which the two girls in my interview engaged with the television show *YooHoo & Friends*. But I would suggest also that a search for, and indulgence in, 'fun' was a dominant characteristic of their complex reactions to and engagement with television.

Television, Friends and Games

Of course the particular opportunity examined above, where the girls created their drawings of a favourite TV show together, was a situation generated by my research. The children did not sit down on their own and draw these pictures. But the research nonetheless presents an insight into the ways children engage with television, and such use of television shows in talk, games and activities has been observed by a number of other researchers (Buckingham 1993a; Götz et al. 2005; Palmer 1986).

In the course of my research, however, some of the children did explain the ways they drew on TV shows in their own games outside our shared interviews. One 10-year-old boy spoke about play-acting with his friends, based on a movie that he and his friends had watched on the TV screen. Here, too, the way in which fun is given top billing in this game is apparent in his comments.

Boy: When my friends come over, we always watch a movie and then go down to the park and play the movie that we just played – play the movie we just watched. And we're characters from the movie, everything. And it's *really*, really fun.

Interviewer: And do you make your own movies?

Boy: Well, once we went down to the park cos we all were wearing costumes and things. And my brother had a film camera. And we were doing a fighting scene. And then I accidentally kicked my friend in the part. And he started crying. So we had to go up. And so we just watched a movie. And then he started laughing so we went back down and we kept doing the scene. And it was really fun.

The boy's delight is in the fun here; he is pursuing the fun, it is at the centre of the way he tells the anecdote: 'it's *really*, really fun'. The characters of the movie have provided the jumping off point for the game in the park and the boys have focused on 'doing a fighting scene'. Fun for the boy appears to be closely related to excitement and action (his favourite TV program is an American animated television series about superheroes called *Young Justice*), and by doing a fighting scene the group of friends can focus on these elements. But accidents happen in games and when one boy is injured they all head back to the house. Here the friends automatically turn to the screen to bring the group together again. And the movie that they watch on the boy's television provides the fun which provokes the laughter that gets things back on track.

CHAPTER 4

With its humour, its action and its characters, this televisual experience weaves through the group's social engagement at many levels. The group uses the movie in their re-creation of games of make-believe, focusing in particular on the 'excitement and fun' identified by Götz et al. (2005, 202). But it is also interesting to observe in the context of this account by the 10-year-old boy how television 'has a quality of multifariousness' because it exists 'within a much larger and more significant unity; that of the home, the known surroundings, the family or other "setting" in which the response to television takes place' (Hawkes 1973, 233). Viewers step in and out of Hawkes's TV 'setting' in much the same way the boys do; they move from the playground, the games, to watching the television in the sitting room and through all of this they share the stories of the screen. Far from 'the stupefied viewer [being] hypnotized into silence by a malevolent magic box', Hawkes (1973, 230-1) argues that 'on the contrary, [television] does encourage a kind of group involvement and participation, vocal and positive which … reverses the popular image of itself'. Television and the entertainment it provides is at the heart of our lives; physically it often takes its place in the living room, in shared 'known surroundings', and, as Hawkes (1973, 233) notes, 'the members of the audience usually constitute a group who know each other intimately'. These boys are moving in and out of both the created worlds and the physical spaces surrounding the television, using its resources in their own social and imaginative lives. Nothing concrete comes necessarily from this use, it is ephemeral in its nature, but it is nonetheless contributing to their lives in a very real sense. In this boy's account, the shared television 'space' has played a central role in their social interactions and in their pleasure in such connections.

As can be seen in this research, sharing with friends, whether through talking or playing games, is a significant part of children's experience – and enjoyment – of television. It was remarkable in my research how eagerly children started talking about shows which they quickly understood that their 'pair' in the interviews would know as intimately as they did. Although tastes in TV shows sometimes differed within the interview pairs, none of the children were entirely unfamiliar with any of the programs that were mentioned in the discussions. When the pairs landed on a show that they both liked, it was not long before they started eagerly talking about comic twists in the plots or the quirks of the characters. They often had favourite characters who were obviously of interest to them because of their particular traits; these characteristics clearly related to their own sense of identity and to what they valued in their social worlds. This way of engaging with media texts has been noted by other researchers (see Götz et al. 2005 and Buckingham 1993a) including Willett (2015, 411) who found in her ethnographic research evidence 'that in the social context of playing with media texts, children participate in social processes of meaning-making and identification'.

In the interview segment above with the young girls, Girl 2's favourite character is Chewoo; she eagerly bursts in with her description of this favourite: 'she's like hyper'. While she was drawing Chewoo in an earlier interview she started singing along, saying 'Chewoo, me Chewoo', as the two girls chatted and drew together. And the reason she gave for liking the show itself was that 'I think it's funny because sometimes Chewoo always be silly a lot'. 'Funny' was also used by Girl 1 to describe her favourite character who is 'sensible but he's actually quite funny'. Interestingly her friend had a different view on this character, calling him the 'grumpy' one, but this was obviously not the significant characteristic for Girl 1. Her description is revealing of what appeals to her: 'He thinks he's sensible and he says everything is stupid and bad ... he's like really funny'. She apparently liked his more caustic wit. The two girls were obviously focusing on characters who spoke to them and to what they appreciated in personality traits, and perhaps reflected characteristics that they aspired to for themselves. What they drew out of the program were the bits that were relevant to them. This reflects what Hartley (2008, 5) has observed, that television is:

> for each viewer ... a 'history of me' ... everyone in modern society spends some of their time making themselves up as they go along, learning their own identity via stories, interactions, and relationships, often in those otherwise unproductive, ungoverned, and potentially risky moments when we're not doing much at all; just daydreaming on our own or getting up to mischief with peers.

This perfectly captures the two girls' enjoyment of *YooHoo & Friends*. As they draw, and talk about the television show, they are literally and figuratively, as Hartley suggests, 'making themselves up as they go along'. There is nothing difficult or serious about this: they are having fun as they do so, but part of the fun comes from the value and experience of being part of the culture of television with all that it offers them.

The children certainly appear to be engaged here in testing out and exploring their own identities. This is something that other researchers (Buckingham 1993a, chap. 8; Marsh 2005; Sefton-Green 1993) have examined in children's engagement with television. But the particular quality that dominates their talk, I would like to suggest, is that of pleasure and fun. The children are not engaging in the serious business of identity exploration in order to focus on developing the self; they are in no way trying to make television worthwhile in some fashion to appease the guardians of the western culture of childhood. In fact, they celebrate characteristics that might be condemned by more sober adults (the girl's parents think the show is 'horrible') who would not appreciate a character who was 'hyper' or one who 'says everything is stupid and bad'. For the children, it would seem, this element of exploring identity is simply part of the joy of television.

The analysis of my research here shows how these girls drift along, thinking and talking about the television show: sharing a laugh over a remembered story or pretending to be a favourite character. What is apparent from these conversations is that above all the girls are having fun; they are sharing their imaginative worlds, 'getting up to mischief with peers' (Hartley 2008, 5) and daydreaming, in this case, together. Looking at their engagement in this way presents quite a different view of children and television to the one characterised by researchers (Postman 1985, 2006; Winn 1985) who only see the corrupting and negative influence of the medium, and even to those researchers who endeavour to find something 'worthwhile' in television that might contribute to children's nurture and education (Anderson 1998; Kirkorian, Wartella and Anderson 2008). Once again it is apparent from this analysis that for the children in my research the central element of their engagement with television, and that to which they gave value, was 'fun' – as the 'valuable end in itself' (McKee 2008, 6). As I explore in the next section, it is this element too that informs their delight in talking about television, in this case to adults.

Talking about TV to Adults

In one of its ongoing reviews of the United Nations Convention on the Rights of the Child (CRC), the Committee on the Rights of the Child (2009, 29-30) noted that for the implementation of Article 12 to be 'effective and meaningful … the issues on which children have the right to express their views must be of real relevance to their lives'. As I have suggested earlier, television programs for children have 'real relevance', and in fact are central, to their social and cultural lives; we should therefore listen to what they themselves have to say about them. Yet the powerful concoction of fears that surround children and television (Drotner 2005, 44) has largely hindered us, I believe, from listening to children's own views on the medium. This appears to be particularly true in the public discourse where children's views are rarely heard (Gillard 2002, 76-77).

Given that mainstream academic research too has had little interest in the joys of television, this aspect of children's engagement with it has suffered from a lack of serious study. And yet, joy appears to pervade the multiple ways in which children engage with the medium, including in their talk about it. For many of the children that I interviewed in my research, talking about television – and having an adult listen attentively to them and without judgment – was both observably fun and fun according to their own accounts.

The pleasure of talking about television is delightfully captured in the exuberant responses of these two 10-year-old girls. They were speaking at the end of our final interview session.

> I've had lots of fun. It's really fun talking about what I love a lot. Because I love TV. Yeah.
>
> I like enjoyed like expressing about why I like to watch TV and stuff like that, sort of saying what I enjoy about it and stuff cos TV's getting more bigger.

The first girl's comment could not be more explicit. She just 'loves' TV and for her the logic is self-evident: of course it would be 'really fun talking about what I love a lot'. The second girl, who also enjoyed 'expressing' what she liked about television, went on to comment on the importance of talking about a medium that was only getting 'bigger' in our culture. She quite clearly recognises the centrality of television not only in her life but in others', and that its significance is likely to increase.

Over the period of nine months that I visited the school, it became apparent that the children who took part in my research enjoyed our interview sessions. One teacher commented to me that they had some difficulty in getting children to participate in research with visiting PhD students, but that for my research, into what they liked about television, the opposite was true. Many children were keen to participate. In fact, most of those I interviewed eagerly expressed their delight in leaving class to join me in talking about television. Occasionally, when I was passing through the playground, some of them would run over to ask excitedly when the next interview would be. While part of this enthusiasm reflected a desire to get out of class, it was apparent from their comments that most of them genuinely enjoyed the interview sessions. They liked being asked to talk about television in their own terms. This was something that rarely, if ever, happened either at school or at home. For most, television was mentioned only to be criticised. Lealand and Zanker (2008) found the same enthusiastic response from children to talking about television in their research in New Zealand. Often the children pleaded with the interviewer to stay longer: 'It appears that the open discussions led by student researchers tapped into the salience of popular culture for children' (Lealand and Zanker 2008, 46). In her interviews Palmer (1986, 17) found that 'most children were very interested, even enthusiastic during the interview. Basically, they loved to talk about their experience of watching television'.

CHAPTER 4

It is perhaps unsurprising that children should enjoy talking to adult researchers about television because in their everyday lives it seems television is rarely discussed in a positive manner. Suffering as it does from a perceived lack of worth, and even worse, as a potential harm in children's lives, television appears largely to attract only adverse comment in adults' conversations with children. When I asked children in my interviews if they ever talked about television with adults or whether they were asked their views on the medium, the recalled exchanges were frequently negative:

> The only person that asks me is my mum when she says you don't need to watch TV cos it doesn't do anything for your brain to help you with anything. And I'm always like I always say to her that some things, some programs are educational and you never watch 'em but I always watch them when I'm like – because they don't always have them at night time. (10-year-old girl)

This girl had spoken earlier about the great pleasure she enjoyed from television: 'When I watch *Seinfeld* I'll always be happy cos it's like one of the things I like enjoy doing the most'. Yet she seems to understand that promoting the pleasure it gives her will not win the argument with her mother. The only chance she has of persuading her mother to let her watch is to tout television's educational benefits. Interestingly she talks earlier in the interview with great affection of how she and her mother share jokes from the American adult sitcom *Seinfeld* as both of them love the show and they watch it together.

Nonetheless, her mother has voiced one of the common complaints about television: it offers nothing to 'stimulate' the brain – it isn't Shakespeare, or a good book, or any other form of high culture – 'it doesn't help you with anything'. It seems that the pervasive negative discourse surrounding television simply does not allow a 'good' parent to relax from her appointed role in protecting the child from the lures of television and from promoting the idea of educational alternatives. Perhaps this child's mother felt guilty herself about indulging in the time-wasting fun of television, and even worse about drawing her own child into this temptation, and thus felt the need to police it more effectively.

The relationship between this mother and daughter perhaps reflects the ways in which sociologist William Corsaro (2015, 26) has observed 'children are always participating in and are part of two cultures – children's and adults' – and these cultures are intricately interwoven'. I would suggest that television is a shared space of major significance in this cultural exchange. The girl here obviously enjoys the fun of television and in fact shares this fun with her mother. This aspect of television for children appears to be a central value within their own culture and they do share it across the generational divide as I discuss in the next chapter. But the girl here is also participating in adult culture both through her mother's shared insights into the adult humour of *Seinfeld* and also through her mother's anxious insistence on promoting the dominant negative discourses.

In her own talk, to her friend in the interview and to me, the young girl reworks the concern her mother has put forward, arguing that television can also be 'educational'. She recognises the cultural hierarchies in the adult world and has reached for one of its highest accolades in order to praise one of her own valued cultural products: 'some programs are educational,' she insists. In Corsaro's (2015, 18) terms, she is engaged in 'cultural reproduction' such as children do when they are 'creatively taking or appropriating information from the adult world to address their own peer concerns'. As Corsaro goes on to argue, 'the term *reproduction* captures the idea that children are not simply internalizing society and culture but are actively contributing to cultural production and change' (p. 18). In the next chapter I examine how children define the ways in which they 'learn' from television and the pleasure this brings them, another example of their influence on 'cultural reproduction'.

It was apparent in my research that the children were prepared to embrace the fun of television and this included the fun of talking about it. Many adults on the other hand fear the 'ridicule' of acknowledging the 'mindless pleasure' or even the 'innocent fun' of television (Buckingham 2001b, 284) let alone abandoning themselves to the joys of talking about it. The children in my research obviously enjoyed the chance to express their views on the medium even if they were surprised at being offered such an opportunity by an adult. Two 8-year-old girls were rather bemused about the process and both astonished and delighted that such an opportunity had presented itself.

Girl 2: Yeah, cos you usually get to talk about writing or something but you're actually talking about something that you like – like in real life.

Girl 1: Yeah. Sometimes you only get that opportunity at recess, but we get an extra opportunity.

Getting to talk to an adult about something that 'you like' in 'real life' – something that has value in their own cultural space – was a major anomaly to these girls. Usually they only get to talk about television in their 'real' lives – in the playground 'at recess', in the spaces left free from adult constraints – because in the adult world such topics are simply not discussed. Such topics are not serious enough to be worth the attention that is focused on 'writing or something'. These girls have clearly understood the cultural hierarchy of the adult world where print is at the top of the pole, television at the bottom.

Examining and understanding books, writing, 'or something like that', is valuable, but talking about television, thinking about what it means to them in their lives, is not given the same status. Only 'sometimes' you might get an 'opportunity' to talk about television 'at recess', certainly never in the classroom.

Interestingly the children saw the interviews in my research as not just offering them a chance to talk about their favourite programs, and to share stories with their friend and the interviewer. They also understood, and appreciated, the fact that they were being asked to think about what television meant to them. Here is another interview with two 8-year-old girls from another pair:

Girl 2:   Well I liked how you actually like made us talk about what we think about television.

Girl 1:   Rather than like–

Girl 2:   Just like saying what you know about television or stuff like that.

Girl 1:   Or like–

Girl 2:   It's kinda hard to explain.

Girl 1:   Like, like–

Girl 2:   Cos you wouldn't really know anything like if you asked, 'What do you know about television?', or if somebody asked me that question I'd think that they're asking like what kind of things, parts of a television, do you need to make one [laugh].

Interviewer: [laugh] To make it work?

Girl 2:   Yeah [laugh] and I'd just go – awww, I'm not quite sure [laugh].

Interviewer: I'm not an engineer [laugh].

CHAPTER 4

Girl 2: Yeah [laugh].

Girl 1: [laugh] Yeah, I don't know how to program these televisions [laugh], I'm only in school.

Girl 2: You've made this um [pause].

Girl 1: Fun.

Girl 2: Fun.

Girl 1: Interesting.

Girl 2: Interesting – and like you haven't made it like um really … boring.

In this exchange Girl 2 can't imagine that an adult would be asking them about something as trivial as the fun they get out of their favourite programs. A question about television would have to relate to something more concrete and more serious; perhaps the mechanical functions of the set itself. She goes on to attempt to articulate further what it is about the interview that she enjoyed and is helped out by her friend who quite simply says it was 'fun'. For my part, I was delighted to be awarded such high praise for my contribution to the discussion; I hadn't succumbed to that prevailing adult propensity of making things 'boring'.

It seems that part of what delighted the children in the conversations during my research was that they were able to share with an adult a glimpse of their own cultural spaces. Children do talk about television with their peers, in their own spaces such as the playground 'at recess', but they quite obviously enjoyed sharing, not only their views but the sense of enjoyment they get from television, with an adult. They appreciated also that an adult would appear to treat the topic as one that was worthy of both talking and thinking about.

For children, providing them with an opportunity to speak about television acknowledges their agency and affords them a chance to celebrate this agency themselves. 'They have a great deal they want to say; it can be fun' (Lansdown 2001, 8). On a number of occasions it was apparent that the children delighted in educating me and introducing me to their world through their talk of television. They described with obvious delight the funny incidents in a particular program or the peculiarities of an idiosyncratic favourite character; and part of the enjoyment was in entertaining, and perhaps provoking, the one adult listening. As Seiter (1998, 298) has noted, 'sometimes young children feel their knowledge and mastery of consumer culture to be a kind of power: something they know, but of which adults are ridiculously ignorant'. This was manifest in one of my interviews with the 7-year-old girl who loved *YooHoo & Friends*. I had just asked her if she had enjoyed taking part in my research.

Girl: Yeah I liked the way that we could just like do *YooHoo & Friends* and I liked the way that you like *learn* something, like by listening to it.

Interviewer: The way that I learnt something?

Girl: Yeah.

Interviewer: Yeah because I learnt about *YooHoo & Friends*.

Girl: And you wouldn't have learnt about *YooHoo & Friends* if we hadn't came and done this.

Interviewer: I wouldn't. You're absolutely right.

Girl: [pause] So, yes, I did like it.

This conversation had started with a question from me about whether the girls had enjoyed the interviews and the chance to talk

CHAPTER 4

about television. This girl's initial reply was 'It's really fun. I think it's really nice'. But given a bit of time and space to think about and articulate her feelings, she pursued two particular aspects of what she had enjoyed; she was particularly proud that she had been able to teach me something just because I was 'listening to' their talk, and she also appreciated the fact that I had created a space where she and her friend 'could just like do *YooHoo & Friends*', without criticism or judgment from the adult in the room. Her responses highlighted her own agency and that of her friend: it was clear they were the ones with the knowledge in this cultural sphere and they were proud to be able to share it with me. But her response also illuminates, I would suggest, the complex ways in which the discourses of television are negotiated between adults and children.

The analysis of my research here highlights the distinctly different if not entirely oppositional views of television held by adults and children. For children one of the highest values that can be attributed to television is that it is 'fun'; for adults, television is certainly not celebrated, if it is celebrated at all, for simply being fun. Children have a foot in both worlds of course and it is apparent that they comprehend the dominant negative discourses that circulate within the wider culture and that they mould these to their own understandings. They also create and share with each other a cultural space that values what is largely disparaged in the dominant public discourse. It is apparent from their talk that the entertainment value of television – the fun of it – is something that is worth pursuing even in the face of the challenges and restrictions they encounter from the adult world. These two worlds are of course theoretical concepts and, though useful in understanding the role of television in our lives, they can't capture the reality of the lived experiences of individual children and their families. It is in looking at these experiences that we can see how both children and adults negotiate the constraints of their own cultures, in the process both conforming to and challenging the dominant discourses. In these peripheral and negotiated spaces we can get a glimpse of the slightly furtive pleasures (Hartley 1992b, 166) which both adults and children enjoy around a medium that I would argue is a cultural institution that is central to our lives.

In the case of my research, it was the children whose shared accounts of television offered the glimpses of the ways in which television is enjoyed not only by themselves but by their parents; there is the mum who, from her daughter's description, just 'absolutely loves' the slapstick humour of *Horrible Histories*, the dad who conspires with his children to watch *Rocky*, the mother who shares *Seinfeld* jokes with her daughter. Children are, I would argue, acute observers of the ways in which adults enjoy TV; they are also happy to celebrate this fact, while adults largely are not. The enjoyment of sharing the joys of television across the two cultures emerged clearly from my research. Parents appear to be drawn into the world of popular culture (Lealand and Zanker 2008, 49) by children, and children delight in the knowledge shared, often by their parents, of 'forbidden' and deliciously enjoyable adult humour. This relationship is another one of the themes that I discuss in the next chapter. Despite the powerful cocktail of threats that Drotner (2005, 44) has observed surrounding entertainment, television and children and that curtail an open acknowledgment of the pleasures of television, I will argue that within families there is both the space and the inclination for a shared enjoyment of television.

CHAPTER 4

I also investigate in the next chapter the ways in which children 'learn' from television, approaching this through their own understanding of 'learning' from the medium. As I go on to argue, it is apparent from my research that for many children such learning is an integral part of the fun provided by their favourite shows. This leads finally into a consideration of the ways in which the fun of television provides the 'unruly delight' (Dyer 1992, 7) that is so precious to all of us, and that comes from the pleasure of enjoying entertainment.

Chapter 5

SHARING PLEASURE, HUMOUR AND THE 'FEEL' OF UTOPIA

As discussed earlier in this book, parents are often given the role in western culture today of enforcing the rules around their children's engagement with television. By and large they appear to accept this role but what is evident from the analysis of my own research and that of others is that the execution of the task is not always diligently undertaken. Often parents simply let the rules slip; but in other instances it appears that they join forces with their own children in subverting these cultural dictates – and that they enjoy doing so. The sharing of such pleasure in escaping the rules is I would suggest a rich source of enjoyment for both children and adults; children in particular appear to relish the chance to get a glimpse of forbidden territory through the complicity of their own parents. At the start of this chapter I look at how this evidence emerged from my research: how parents shared fun – and secrets – and how both parents and children delighted in this aspect of their television viewing. I look at the different ways in which the control of 'adult secrets' plays out in the lived lives of real families. This research shows how much more complex and rich – and how unexpected – are the relationships between parents and children around the TV screen.

In the second section I explore elements of what children find funny in television. During the analysis of my research it was apparent that many of their favourite programs appealed to the children's senses of humour. They abandoned themselves with glee to the sharing and recounting of, to them, hilariously funny scenes. I consider how the slapstick that children enjoy often provokes criticism and how the 'tastelessness' of their humour also seems to appal adults. To demonstrate, however, that television is not simply pursued for its ability to provide a good laugh, I consider, in juxtaposition to this analysis, the ways in which children also appreciate television's capacity to provide a way of passing time. This might be seen as a rather banal reason for watching television, but it is evidently something of value to children according to their own accounts.

The next theme that I investigate in this chapter was another that was flagged by the children themselves in my research. It became apparent in my analysis that a number of the children were drawn to their favourite shows because they felt they learnt something from them. I examine here what this means to them and how it apparently opens up for them insights into life that they appreciate and enjoy.

Learning about life from entertainment also offers us glimpses – as Dyer (2002) has so astutely observed – of how our lives might be better. So in the final section of this chapter I consider, through the analysis of my research with children, how entertainment offers the 'feel' of utopia (Dyer 2002, 20), and how it informs an understanding of happiness. This section highlights, I believe, the essential importance of television as a source of fun in children's lives.

CHAPTER 5

Parents and Children: Conspiring for Pleasure

What is perhaps more surprising than the discovery that children celebrate the fun of television is that parents and children appear to enjoy *sharing* this aspect of TV viewing. This is even more remarkable when we consider the dominance in our culture of the notion that parents should police and curtail children's pleasure in television, guarding closely the adult secrets that television brings into the home (see Chapter 2). As I examine in this section, parents never entirely escape the constraints of these cultural dictates, but they do nevertheless share moments of joy with their children in watching favourite, and possibly 'suspect', television shows. Such insights are more clearly visible through analysis of children's talk about television. The dominant negative discourses around television are too confronting, I would argue, for adults themselves to be able to express such joy. Admitting to – let alone celebrating – a mindless enjoyment of television appears beyond the reach of adults 'at least if one wishes to avoid the ridicule or disdain of others' (Buckingham 2001b, 284).

The negative effects of television on children are widely circulated in the dominant public discourse as I have examined in earlier chapters. Today's headlines, for example, largely warn parents of the dangers of television and the articles admonish them to maintain a close vigil on what and how often their children watch TV (Gardner 2010; News agencies 2014). There is no suggestion in this discourse that parents should sit down with their children and share a side-splitting laugh over a scene from some mindless or tasteless show. In fact adult commentators are often eager to point out the mind-numbing and tasteless fare that dominates our children's television screens and that beleaguered parents are keen to avoid (Mentzer 2014; Spohr 2015). In 'The 10 kids' TV shows more painful than childbirth', Kerry Parnell (2016) wonders 'if children's TV producers purposely make the most annoying programs they can just to torment parents'. The opposition between parents and children is firmly established in such media discourse. Interestingly this seems not always to have been the case. Spigel has noted that in mid-20th century America enthusiasm for television and its shared family pleasures was publicly celebrated. In her research Spigel (1998, 116) found that in 1949:

> *Parents Magazine* claimed, 'All the mothers I have talked to are enthusiastic about television for their children. Certainly it has brought back the family circle in the living room.'

She also refers to a 1950 study of families where 'one parent claimed that television "has given the children a happier home where they can laugh"'. The same pattern was observed in Australia where in the 1950s and 1960s: '"family" viewing was promoted as an incentive to purchase a TV set' (Gillard 2002, 64).

While this recognition of the shared joy of watching television within the family appears to be no longer celebrated in the media, a number of academic researchers in the past decade have observed its presence in children's own descriptions of their enjoyment of television and this is supported also by my own research. In his research with children, Buckingham (1993a, 110) found that 'Television was often described as part of a family ritual or outing: coming into your parents' bed on Sunday mornings to eat your breakfast cereal and watch *Dennis*, for example, or watching *Star Trek* with your mum while she does the ironing'. Lealand and Zanker (2008, 48) found there were 'many stories told by children

CHAPTER 5

about sharing popular consumer culture *with* their parents ... furthermore, children often shared pleasure in their parents' media pleasures'. But what was perhaps even more interesting was the influence that children had on their parents' enjoyment of popular television. Lealand and Zanker (2008, 49) found evidence of this influence in their research, noting 'parents' descriptions of how they have been transformed into fans of erstwhile frowned-upon popular culture ... watching the often-scatological local animation series *bro'Town* was a case in point'.

Richards (1995, 149-150) has also noted this 'reverse' influence, suggesting that, 'though parents do regulate the lives of their children, there is also a sense in which "parents" are remade by those they "bring up"' and he suggests that 'in looking more closely at what goes on around the TV, some hints of how this might be happening emerge and take a more definite form'.

While the research into this aspect of children's TV viewing is limited, Buckingham (1996) has conducted some research into the relations of children and parents around television. In his research he did find that parents were not always entirely constrained by the negative dominant discourse in their relations with their own children. He observed that parents in reality didn't simply try to apply basic rules but sought to intervene in their children's viewing 'not only in order to help them cope with upsetting experiences, but in an attempt to make it more pleasurable and more worthwhile' (1996, 299). This insight is reflected in the following comment from an 8-year-old girl in my research:

> Our parents don't want us just to not watch TV for a random reason just because like you're not allowed to or something. I think they're just trying to look after us.

Even Buckingham's research, however, did not seek to examine in any depth the ways in which parents and children enjoy television *together*. In the literature that I have reviewed I have found no detailed research into how parents might take pleasure in watching television with their children, though there is considerable advice for parents that they should watch with their children in order to protect, guide or encourage its educational possibilities (Anderson and Bryant 1983; Comstock and Scharrer 2007, chap. 4). This perhaps indicates how far outside the mainstream discourses is such a conception of an audience: the parent/child audience that has fun watching entertaining, and possibly 'mindless', programs *together*. While there is a genre of family movies, often shown on TV, that are specifically designed for adults and children to watch together, these did not feature strongly in my research. The shared tastes identified by the children were more surprising, and outside the boundaries designed for their protection. In fact, this seems in part to have fuelled their pleasure. The unexpected ways in which children and parents enjoy the same delight in television can be glimpsed in the following discussion by two 10-year-old girls in one of my interview pairs of a British sketch comedy series for children:

Girl 1: *Horrible Histories*, it's so funny, because there's this one where there's two guys–

Girl 2: [interrupting] Yeah! [laugh]

Girl 1: And they're trying to figure out how to stop all the poo from coming down onto everybody's heads and randomly there's like all this fake poop coming onto their fake wigs and they're just walking around. Then at the end of the discussion they hug, because it was such a good idea, and then this *huge* slob of poo and wee comes onto their face.

CHAPTER 5

Girl 2:　　　Was it real?

Girl 1:　　　No, it was fake poo; you could see that it was like chocolate fudge.

Interviewer: Do you think adults think that's funny?

Girl 1:　　　My mum she absolutely *loves* that show! [laugh]

Interviewer: Does she? [laugh]

Girl 1:　　　She thinks it's absolutely *hilarious* and she always wants to watch it whenever it's on … [slight pause] It's weird.

Girl 2:　　　Yeah, that's weird.

The two girls are thoroughly enjoying shared memories of the slapstick humour of this show and towards the end I interrupt with a question about whether adults would find this scene funny. Girl 1 bursts in on the end of my question with wild delight, eager to share the fact that her mother 'absolutely *loves*' the program. But what is interesting in this exchange is that it is clear this young girl understands the prevailing cultural discourses that denigrate the 'tasteless' humour of children's television shows and that set the adult world up in opposition to the popular TV that children enjoy. She pauses for a brief moment after describing her mother's enthusiasm for the program because she is suddenly struck by the incongruity of an adult finding such a show funny. 'It's weird,' she says, and is immediately supported in this assessment by her friend, who agrees emphatically, 'Yeah, that's weird'. I too was surprised by the response, having expected a quite contrary answer to my question. I felt that her parents might criticise such coarse slapstick – not indeed find it funny. Instead this mother, quite possibly introduced to the show by her daughter, has obviously given herself up to the sheer fun of its outrageous farce.

Drawing on their research with children, Davies, Buckingham and Kelley (2000, 13) have noted this complexity in how the 'opposition between parents and children' is expressed in the discourses around parental involvement in children's television. They found that:

> in some cases, the children made a clear distinction between 'parents' in the abstract and their *own* parent(s). While parents in general were seen to like 'boring stuff' such as *The News*, talk about their own family lives often involved anecdotes about their parents watching and enjoying the same kinds of programmes that they liked. (p. 13)

This unpredictable nature of possible reactions of television 'audiences' reflects what Ien Ang (1990, 1991) articulated in the early 1990s, radically exposing the flaws in the theoretical construction of the 'television audience'. She noted that:

> the social world of actual audiences consists of such a multifarious and intractable, ever expanding myriad of elements that their conversion into moments of a coherent discursive entity can never be complete. (1991, 14)

Her argument was largely directed against the television institutions' appropriation of the notion of television audience to their own, chiefly commercial, ends, but her arguments are a reminder that the discourses around television that circulate in society today also effectively categorise audiences in order to control. As Ang (1991, 14) argued, such categorisation fails to reveal the 'complexities of the social world of actual audiences'. Television audience research has expanded extensively since the 1990s into an investigation of such complexities through a range of methodologies including the ethnographic approach advocated by Ang. But I would argue that the restriction of audience categories continues to prevail in the public

CHAPTER 5

discourse, in particular in the construction of the child viewer, and that these discourses are driven by an attempt to control. What the analysis of my research reveals, I believe, is a glimpse of a world of 'actual audiences' and that this analysis indicates there is a space and time within families where the fun of television is shared and enjoyed – albeit somewhat surreptitiously and under the shadow of the dominant negative discourse.

My interview with the two girls talking about the British sketch comedy series *Horrible Histories* demonstrates that television entertainment can have a strong appeal both for children and their parents and, while we might not value such popular entertainment highly in our culture, it does appear to provoke the 'unruly delight' that Dyer (1992, 7) notes is central to our lives. This is an element of our lived daily lives that Dyer (1992, 13) argues we should recognise and in doing so understand its importance: 'the richness and variety of the actual forms of leisure suggest that leisure should also be seen as the creation of meaning in a world'. This is not to suggest that we should fall into the trap that Buckingham (1993a, 272) warns against of seeing 'the "pleasure" of audiences … as sacred and beyond criticism' but it is to acknowledge the value of seeking to further understand the ways entertainment and fun inform the social and cultural lives of children – and their parents – in complex and diverse ways.

That children valued the sharing of the fun of television with their parents was evident in the analysis of my research. Results from the survey indicated that 52% of these children watched television with their mother and 51% watched with their father so there are obviously opportunities within families for shared moments of enjoyment. Of course these survey statistics do not indicate whether the children are enjoying watching television with these parents. Certainly there might be times when a parent dominates the choice in a shared living room space and perhaps the children are simply watching the parent's preferred program rather than one they have chosen. But from the comments of the children throughout the interviews in my research, it was evident that there does exist between parents and children a rich shared pleasure in watching favourite programs together.

One 10-year-old girl, who said she watched television 'because it has great shows and mum and I watch a lot of TV shows together and it helps us bond', recounts sharing a laugh over a favourite show with her mother:

> One of the characters from *Tattoo Nightmares* does a tattoo for a guy and after the tattoo, he says 'I sat down for this, this is horrible, just joking!' And my mum and I were falling out of our seats!

The scene in the TV show that has provoked her laughter is obviously greatly funny to this girl; but what appears to add a whole new layer of pleasure and delight to this viewing moment is that her mother's intense enjoyment of the scene is equal to hers.

For the 10-year-old *Seinfeld* fan introduced in the last chapter, watching the show with her mother appeared to contribute significantly to her enjoyment of the program:

> sometimes there was something going on and my mum would make a joke and she'd be like do you know where that's from? And I'd always be like it's from *Seinfeld*... and when I watch [it] on TV *Seinfeld* has some jokes and like it's a bit like sometimes they're hard to get ... so my mum has to explain it and then a while after I'll learn cos they're really smart questions. They teach you things sometimes.

CHAPTER 5

Here the enjoyment of the TV show goes beyond the moment of watching for this young girl; she obviously loves the intimacy of sharing the humour afterwards with her mother. But the pleasure is not only in the shared laughter. She goes on to explain how her mother lets her in on the jokes by explaining those which she doesn't understand. Here's a moment where the parent is actually sharing those closely guarded adult secrets. The child delights in being allowed into the inner sanctum, as it were, but it is apparent from this interview that her enjoyment extends even beyond this satisfaction. She is happy too that she will 'learn' from this shared information 'cos they're really smart questions'. She thoughtfully concludes, in reference to television programs in general, though obviously with her own favourite in mind, that 'they teach you things sometimes'. Her account reveals multiple and varied levels of enjoyment: both those that are solitary and those shared with her mother. And it gives a glimpse of her mother's pleasure in the shared fun of this television show.

It was apparent in a number of my interviews that sharing television's 'adult secrets' with a parent was a particularly pleasurable experience for the children. This was evident in the interview above where the mother explains to her daughter the adult jokes in *Seinfeld*. The parent here is the co-conspirator and together they confound the proscriptions established by the dominant discourses around children's television viewing. Other researchers have noted the joy that children express in gaining access to adult secrets. In his study of children's enthusiasm for the British soap opera *EastEnders*, Buckingham (1987, 200) found that 'much of their fascination [with the series] arose from its inclusion of aspects of *adult* life from which they were normally "protected"'. But what is interesting in the relationship between the mother and daughter over *Seinfeld* in this interview is that the gatekeeper, the parent, is the one opening the door into these tightly-held secrets.

For another 10-year-old girl in my research, this entree into the adult world was given a delicious twist. The young girl was not simply given permission to watch such television by her mother but was actually introduced to it by the parent.

Girl: Um … there's this one comedian called Chris Lilley and he does a lot of really funny mockumentaries. And I have all the ones that he's done that have been released on DVD. I got them for Christmas from my mum last year. And um … the recent one was *Ja'mie: Private School Girl* which was rated MA, but I got my mum's permission because we watched it together.

Interviewer: Did you like it?

Girl: Yeah, it was really funny because it was actually how I got introduced to Chris Lilley, then Mum told me about heaps of other stuff. Then I got into Chris Lilley. And later this year, there's going to be a new Chris Lilley mockumentary which I'm looking forward to, which is um based on one of the characters from his biggest one, which was *Summer Heights High*, and um which is *Jonah*.

And like the ones that I have on DVD, two of them are M, which is *We Can Be Heroes*, which is the first one, *Summer Heights High*, the second one and the biggest one, they're both M. But the other two, which is *Ja'mie* and *Angry Boys*, they're both rated MA, but because my mum got them for me and she lets me watch them, it's like I've got permission from her to watch them, even though it's for like people older than 15 and I'm like 10,

CHAPTER 5

turning 11, at least I've got parental permission from my mum.

This avid fan of the Australian comedian and television producer, Chris Lilley, obviously thoroughly enjoys all of his edgy television comedies and she talks about how she loves the programs throughout the interviews. Here in this discussion a key element of her enjoyment rests in the relationship with her mother. She is delightfully proud of the fact that her mother introduced her to the shows. She recognises that this is a matter for comment because it challenges the established order: 'it was really funny because it was actually how I got introduced to Chris Lilley'. She relishes the fact that she and her mother are in this together, and that despite the adult M and MA classification ratings she can watch the shows 'because my mum got them for me and she lets me watch them'. She is aware that it is the adult in her life who has helped her to circumvent the adult rules that regulate children's television viewing. And perhaps most significantly of all, she has understood that her mother has introduced her to these 'adult' programs because her mother thought she would enjoy them.

Of course, this is not to suggest that children's choices of television programs are always – or even often – supported by parents. Nor is it to suggest that children's television viewing doesn't cause conflict within the family. In much of the research that has been conducted with either parents or children or both, tensions around choice of programs and disagreements about the 'ideal' amount of viewing time are almost always evident (Australian Communications and Media Authority 2011; Buckingham 1993a, 1996; Cupitt 1996). Children's television viewing, surrounded as it is by strong negative public discourses, is still apparently a flashpoint for family conflict. The conflict generated by the television, however, is not simply around arguments about the choice of a particular show or even about the amount of time spent in front of the screen – though these issues are most often quoted as the causes of concern by adults and particularly parents (Buckingham 1993a; Cupitt 1996). The tension that circulates around the television screen reflects broader and deeper cultural and social issues. It is about power and control. As Buckingham (1993a, 126) argues, the debates are 'not just about behaviour, but about knowledge. Ultimately, then, the relationship between children, parents and television is inherently political'.

The complexity of these family relationships is all part of the shared experience of television. But while there is no doubt plenty of room for conflict, there are more unexpectedly opportunities for shared pleasure across the generations. The ever-shifting and complex nature of these relationships around the television is endless but nonetheless some of its variety can be glimpsed in the analysis of my research with children.

In what is perhaps a testament to the powerful attraction of television entertainment, it appears that parents and children do manage to create their own spaces rich with social and cultural significance in spite of, or perhaps outside of, the powerful negative discourses. It is here that they can share such moments of humour as are enjoyed by the mothers and daughters watching *Tattoo Nightmares*, *Seinfeld* and Chris Lilley's comedies together. Television entertainment in these families has drawn the child and the parent into a shared world where they can both laugh at the program's humour and delight in the warmth of sharing 'adult' knowledge across the generations.

But even where a parent does not share the child's enthusiasm for a particular show – and bends under the hand of the dominant

CHAPTER 5

discourse – it seems that this discourse has a looser grip than might be expected. This reality is apparent in the following exchange between two 8-year-old girls in one of my interviews:

Girl 2: When we watch – well there's this show called *World's Craziest Fools* and it's really funny. But my mum doesn't like it because it's always like they're getting hurt. Because they're like falling off the back of motorbikes and stuff…

Girl 1: [interrupting the other girl with enthusiasm] Yeah! My mum doesn't like violent films either.

Girl 2: [continuing from where she left off before the interruption] She doesn't like that. Each week she says you shouldn't be watching TV, but then she goes and does her work on the computer.

Interviewer: And leaves you to watch it?

Girl 2: Yeah [laughs].

Interviewer: That is pretty funny.

Girl 1: Yeah, it's really funny cos my mum is basically like that. She's like every time … say *Rocky* … It's like this guy who's a boxer, but it's also quite sweet because like he has a girlfriend and a little dog, and the girlfriend has a pet shop and stuff. Yeah. Except my mum doesn't – as I say, she's like – and my dad said – last night we watched another *Rocky*, cos it's like *Rocky 6* – and then it was like we're not showing *Rocky*. And my mum's like 'I don't like this sort of stuff'. And then my dad has to kind of agree with my mum, so I have to go on the stairs when the boxing scenes come. Except my brother doesn't, and neither does my sister. Except my sister just covers her eyes.

The negative discourses surrounding television and children weave fascinating threads through this discussion with the effects discourse emerging early on. The mother of Girl 2 is apparently worried that *World's Craziest Fools* might set a bad example for her child. The people on the show are caught on camera doing foolish things and are often 'getting hurt': perhaps her concern is that her child might copy the behaviour. She expresses her anxiety, attempts to enforce some control over and protection from the offending television program and then, consciously or not, allows the rules to slip, possibly feeling guilty about heading off to her own screen but ultimately sensing that the danger or threat is not one that requires total policing. It's a dynamic altogether understood by the daughter who goes along with the routine knowing that in the end she will get to watch the program.

The topic of parental regulation was often a popular one in my interviews and here Girl 1 is eager to get in early on the conversation. Barely has Girl 2 mentioned *Worlds Craziest Fools* than she leaps into the discussion introducing another dominant effects discourse. Girl 1 tells us that her mother 'doesn't like violent films either'. The negative effect of screen violence on children, as discussed in Chapter 1, has been one of the longest running and most researched themes in the field and, not surprisingly given its extensive coverage also in the public discourse, appears promptly in this conversation about parental concerns about television.

Interestingly in this discussion, it is the hapless accidents in *World's Craziest Fools* that prompt Girl 1 to mention violence. Perhaps the common thread here is related to parental concerns that these physical representations on television might negatively influence the *behaviour* of their child. This is one of the arguments that is at the

CHAPTER 5

heart of the moral panics around television that pervade the public sphere. Such arguments are based on the effects discourse that attributes to television the power to cause the viewer to act in a way that is detrimental to their own or others' interests. As a number of researchers (Barker 2001; Barker and Brooks 1998, chap. 13; Buckingham 1996) have noted, this common sense 'myth' has taken on the status of a truth in the public discourse around television and not surprisingly parents too are influenced by it.

In this interview segment, both of the girls were keen to share their stories of how television was regulated in their families; curiously they seemed to be enjoying this discussion and having fun sharing their own parents' particular obsessions and – to them – not entirely rational responses to controlling television. For the girls it was part of the whole colourful 'inhabited' (Hawkes 1973, 233) world of television and they were eager to talk about it. Perhaps part of their enjoyment of the discussion came from their awareness that their parents' attempts to police the television had largely failed: both of the children apparently knew the offending shows in intimate detail. It seems also that these discussions are woven into the ways in which television is present in their lives and the conflicts themselves pervade the ways in which children, and their families, actually enjoy the medium. The rules are part of this shared space where children have fun with television; contributing in some cases to a gleeful sense of having escaped the parental decrees, as happened to Girl 2, and in others to a sense of frustration, as in the case of Girl 1, who much to her chagrin is forced to 'sit on the stairs when the boxing scenes come'.

The girls appeared to enjoy elements of these negotiations with their parents, particularly when they gained the upper hand.

The game that surrounds the politics of power and control itself apparently provides a certain degree of enjoyment. Girl 2 laughs conspiratorially when she acknowledges that she can watch the forbidden program because her mother withdraws to her computer. She is quite possibly aware of the irony of her mother disappearing to sit in front of her own preferred screen. But the negotiations between parents and children over television are often more complex and reach also into contested cultural and social spaces. Perhaps most importantly they include fights over knowledge and this is closely related to positions of power and status within the family as Buckingham (1993a, chap. 5) has noted. These struggles are evident in Girl 1's account of watching the Sylvester Stallone boxing film *Rocky*. This account is quite revealing of the family dynamics, the fluid nature of alliances and power sharing and how knowledge is at the heart of the struggle for power – and also the source of pleasure.

The young girl's mother obviously commands considerable influence within the family. She doesn't like violence on television and although she appears not to have watched *Rocky* in its entirety, if at all, she does know it contains 'violence' which includes boxing scenes. But the film and its sequels are apparently favourites with the rest of the family, including the father, and this greatly complicates the family dynamic and undermines her control. The father is complicit with the children in choosing *Rocky 6*. As the daughter notes, this allows the family to evade the mother's proscriptions; they are after all not *technically* watching the one she says she doesn't like – the original *Rocky*. But the father moves across to join forces with the mother when she asserts her authority in the face of this subversion, 'I don't like this sort of stuff', and as a result the youngest child in

CHAPTER 5

the family, Girl 2, is shunted off to the stairs when the boxing scenes appear. The girl's banishment is made even more galling by the fact that her brother and her sister escape this exile.

Perhaps one of the most illuminating segments of the young girl's account comes in the last section of this quoted passage. She picks up on a thought shared earlier in the conversation suggesting that her mother always criticises television: she 'is basically like that'. Her mother apparently believes the daughter watches too much television and should do something more 'productive' with her leisure time, such as reading a book. This reflects a common theme in the public discourse: television is lightweight, it is 'only' entertainment, and therefore a waste of time. Reading has higher status in our culture and is regarded as potentially educational (see discussion in Chapter 1). Entertainment, as Jonathan Gray (2008, 6) notes, is placed in 'clear opposition to information and education'. The girl's mother quite understandably is concerned that her child might waste her precious childhood watching worthless or, even worse, violent, television.

While the daughter doesn't criticise her mother's views openly, she nonetheless sharply observes their limitations. In this segment she begins to say that her mother hasn't watched the program she is currently condemning (*Rocky*) and that she doesn't like television generally: 'except my mum doesn't – as I say she's like –'. But her comments are cryptically elided. It's as though she doesn't want to overtly challenge her mother – either to herself or in front of her listeners. Nonetheless she knows her mother hasn't watched the movie and therefore can't judge it. In an effort possibly to marshal arguments against her mother's objections, if not to convert her to the movie then at least to neuter her criticism, the young girl starts talking about the story and the characters. But what begins as an attempt to persuade, by describing the 'real' story that her mother has missed, becomes a delightful description of what obviously captivates the young girl herself about the movie:

> It's like this guy who's a boxer, but it's also quite sweet because like he has a girlfriend and a little dog, and the girlfriend has a pet shop and stuff. Yeah.

It isn't the boxing or the violence that she sees; it is the 'sweet' story at the heart of it, the romance of the girlfriend, the charm of the 'little dog' and the utopian attraction of the 'pet shop' with its promise of adorable young animals. Here is entertainment's idea 'of what happiness might be' (Dyer 2002, 3). The movie obviously speaks to this young girl through these fragments, reflecting back to her elements of real life but infused with a 'feel' of utopia (Dyer 2002, 20). And her mother misses out on all of this. The unspoken, and perhaps unrealistic, hope is that if her mother watched it she too might enjoy, with the family, the entertaining appeal of the movie.

The 'pathologization' (Hartley 1999) of television thus apparently reaches deep into family dynamics and feeds the pressure on parents to both circumscribe viewing hours and curtail the watching of 'unsuitable' programs. My analysis reveals the indisputable joy that children and their families get from television but this pleasure only sneaks to the surface occasionally and almost inevitably encounters obstructions. This is perhaps because as Hartley (1999, 104) has suggested:

> there is no easily available or widely distributed discourse or framework of positive explanation for watching TV among the very people – i.e. the majority of the population – for whom it is still, after all these years, the top leisure pastime.

CHAPTER 5

We apparently cannot simply talk about the 'fun' of it. This limits our ability not only to talk about but also to examine such pleasure, as Hartley (1999, 104) goes on to argue:

> in such a climate, an attempt to understand what the social impact of TV might actually be, both historically and at the present time, is hard to contemplate beyond the terms of the bad reputation enjoyed by TV among its many critics.

This 'bad reputation' combined with the evident pleasure that children take from television apparently drives parents to attempt to control its influence. As Gray (2008, 6) observes, 'television entertainment has become a prime topic of suspicion … a cause of guilt or shame' and such a dominant cultural discourse is hard for a parent to withstand. It is perhaps not surprising then that efforts by parents to enforce control over their children's viewing habits aren't always as benign as the scenes described above. One 10-year-old boy in my interviews spoke about the regulations in his family:

> It's really annoying cos you only get like one hour a day of electronics, no matter what it is. And so once you've had like five minutes more than one hour your dad comes into the room, starts yelling at you and saying, no more TV for a week, or something.

As this young boy observes, the regulation is complicated by the power relationships within the family:

> The only good time is when my mum's not there, my dad just ignores me and just lets me watch it cos my dad's only listening to mum's ideas, not to his own opinion cos Dad can't come up to us and tell us when Mum's gone because he'll – he'll – be on it the whole time when Mum's gone.

It appears that in this family the fear of television's corrupting influence has created pressure on both parents to attempt to enforce regulation. But the father appears not to really believe in such rules and 'ignores' his son's viewing when the key family enforcer, in this case the mother, is away from home. He too retires to his own screen – 'he'll be on it the whole time' – possibly with a sense of 'guilt or shame' (Gray 2008, 6).

As the young boy indicates, his parents are not simply concerned about time regulations, they are also worried about unsuitable material. In the interview segment below, he has been talking about his favourite show, a cartoon series called *Young Justice* which is quite stereotypically full of violence and sex in the classic superhero mould:

Interviewer: What do your parents think of those sorts of television shows?

Boy: They don't know.

Interviewer: Do you think they'd like them?

Boy: No.

Interviewer: Why not?

Boy: Well, I think they'd like *SheZow* but I don't think they'd like *Young Justice*. *Young Justice* is just too violent, too deadly, too kiss-ie, too everything like that.

This 10-year-old boy understands quite plainly that the knowledge of 'adult secrets' divulged by *Young Justice* would simply be out of bounds; the show's content is 'just too violent' and 'too kiss-ie' for his parents to approve of it. So while his parents are laying down strict time regulations he believes they would also object to the content of the show he watches – if they knew about it. Unfortunately for

CHAPTER 5

this 10-year-old his favourite program contravenes the dominant discourses on two levels – it offers him both pleasure *and* prohibited knowledge. And in this family, it seems the parents have not watched the boy's favourite program – so there is no chance of them liking it. Their default position therefore is one of enforcer of the regulations. This example just serves to highlight the diversity of responses to television shows that exists within families; these parents' reactions are quite different to those demonstrated by the mother who introduces the Chris Lilley comedies to her daughter and also to the mothers who themselves love *Horrible Histories* and *Seinfeld*.

While it is not possible to generalise from the presentation here of the different responses to television and its adult secrets across a handful of families, what the analysis of my research does reveal is the deep and complex ways that television shows inform the leisure and pleasure lives of families. The positions and attitudes of both the children and their parents are steeped in the dominant negative discourses, but the complex ways in which they live with these prevailing cultural dictates are fascinating; and perhaps most remarkable of all are the ways that children and their parents conspire together to enjoy the fun and pleasure of television in the face of such prevailing forces.

Looking at the humour children enjoy in television continues to reveal this complexity in the ways in which children and adults negotiate the contested television space. In some cases it seems that parents are prepared to ignore the negative discourses when they themselves enjoy the show and in particular its humour (e.g. the mother who watches *Horrible Histories*). But, as I have mentioned earlier, some children's television humour is apparently aggravating to adults; fear of such humour revealing adult secrets is one aspect that informs this reaction but it also appears that often adults don't like children's television simply because the humour is not to their particular taste. In the next section of this chapter I consider the findings of my own research into what the children themselves indicated that they find 'funny'.

Humour

In response to my survey question about why they liked their favourite programs, 62% of the children stated that it was because they were 'funny': 'The best thing about television is that you can smile and it's funny and stuff like that' (8-year-old girl). Such comments are mirrored in the responses of the children in Davies, Buckingham and Kelley's (2000) research where they indicated that the children's most common reason for liking television was that it was 'funny'. The children's sheer delight in this aspect of television was manifest in a number of my interviews and in this section I look particularly at what they find funny. As a contrast, which serves not only to highlight their enthusiasm for humorous television but also to indicate the diversity of ways in which they engage with favourite shows, I look also at how children use television as a means of filling in time. This too is apparently something that they value.

The 'funny' scenes of television came up fairly regularly during the interview sessions with the children in my research. Often one child of the pair would start recounting a humorous anecdote from a favourite show, only to be enthusiastically joined in the conversation by the other child. Here two 8-year-old girls talk about a character from the British animated children's television series *The Octonauts*:

CHAPTER 5

Girl 1: And … I … think that um … it's my favourite show because also there's this little snot monster, [slightly embarrassed laugh] it's …

Interviewer: A snot monster?

Girl 1: Yeah and it trails snot.

Interviewer: Oooo …

Girl 1: … when it falls out of its tub it's like going along trailing the snot and then the cat runs after it and it slips [laughs] on the snot [laughs].

Interviewer: [laughs] What do you think about the snot monster?

Girl 2: It's okay, he's really funny because he's always like leaving snot wherever he goes. Like if he was playing hide and seek it would be easy to know where he was.

Interviewer: If he was playing hide and seek, what?

Girl 2: If he was playing hide and seek everyone would know where he went because he leaves a trail of snot.

Girl 1: Yeah he got caught by the snot.

Girl 2: So there's good things about it and bad things about it.

Though slightly hesitant at the start to share one of her favourite *Octonauts* stories with an adult, the girl who introduced the snot monster was encouraged by the support from the other child who not only immediately recalled the character but joined in with her own quirky observation of how it was both useful and a handicap in life to trail snot. She wryly pointed out that while it did deter the cat, it also meant the snot monster didn't do well at hide-and-seek. Like many children, these girls are thoroughly enjoying the humour and are delighted that 'it refuses the orderly discourse of good taste', as Bragg (2006, 140) so aptly describes it. Their gleeful exchange also highlights 'the complex and playful nature of children's judgments of taste' and even more significantly 'their understanding of taste as "cultural capital"' (Buckingham 2008, 232).

The young girl's hesitant embarrassment at sharing such a 'silly' scene with an adult indicates clearly that she is aware of the negative public discourses that surround television, particularly the judgments of the 'puerile' and 'infantile' nature of some children's television (Buckingham 2008, 232). Immediately after admitting to liking the 'little snot monster' she gives an embarrassed, almost an apologetic, laugh. This discussion came at the very start of our interviews; we had only just had time for introductions and the children were not sure what to expect from the as yet unknown visitor. So although I had explained we were going to talk about what they liked about television, the strength of the negative discourse was not to be overcome by some glib reassurance on my part that I *really* wanted to know what the children *really* liked. Admitting to having fun watching television, and to enjoying something as silly as a snot monster, which might also be considered tasteless, was a risky undertaking. Yet both of these children understood the cultural capital here; they together were 'in the know' and thus had an advantage over me, and their confidence in their position grew as they deliciously shared the humour of a favourite TV show.

In his book *Children Talking Television* (1993a, 182) Buckingham explores the nature and purpose of children talking about television and he argues persuasively that 'retelling is a social, discursive activity rather than a matter of individual cognitive processing'.

CHAPTER 5

The point he is making is that we should not judge children's 'competence' and understanding of television according to their capacity to retell the story according to an adult's 'reading of the author's intention'. Their own retelling is far richer and is 'primarily about re-living and sharing pleasure, in order to affect others and to define oneself' (Buckingham 1993a, 182). Buckingham (1993a) does, however, focus in particular on the uses of this talk for children; in forming identity and positioning themselves in a social hierarchy. But I would suggest that what we should be exploring further is the aspect of their television viewing that Buckingham mentions only in passing; that talking about television is 'primarily about re-living and sharing pleasure'. In the interview segment above, this is a dominant feature of the girls' talk. The sheer joy expressed by these girls while sharing their memories of the snot monster is one of the most striking features of the conversation.

One aspect of children's humour crops up regularly in the, albeit fairly limited, research into what children find funny about television. A number of scholars have noted the particular delight children take in the scatological (Davies, Buckingham and Kelley 2000; Lealand and Zanker 2008; Sheldon and Loncar 1996). According to a Sydney children's television producer, 'For kids, if there's a bum or poo joke in it, it can't fail, especially if it may annoy parents' (Sheldon and Loncar 1996, 29). This producer has identified two aspects of television that obviously appeal to children. The scatological humour is one but perhaps equally importantly is how this humour, which is looked down upon by 'adults', allows children their own space, free from adults. This control and agency over their own 'cultural spaces' is important to them as is the chance to share this control with each other (Corsaro 2009, 302).

SQUARE EYES

The following example from my interview with two 10-year-old girls illustrates the ways in which children share and enjoy such humour. Here is a longer version of the segment quoted earlier:

Girl 2: There's a show and everything called *Horrible Histories* and it's really good, but I really like watching it, cos it's really, really, funny.

Girl 1: Yeah-ah-ah! [laughs loudly].

Girl 2: [laughs loudly too].

Interviewer: There you are, you could learn history from television, M____?

Girl 1: *Horrible Histories* it's so funny, because there's this one where there's two guys–

Girl 2: [interrupting] Yeah! [laugh]

Girl 1: And they're trying to figure out how to stop all the poo from coming down onto everybody's heads and randomly there's like all this fake poop coming onto their fake wigs and they're just walking around. Then at the end of the discussion they hug, because it was such a good idea, and then this *huge* slob of poo and wee comes onto their face.

Girl 2: Was it real?

Girl 1: No, it was fake poo; you could see that it was like chocolate fudge.

There is no mistaking the girls' delight in and fascination with this scene. They are both barely suppressing their laughter throughout the exchange and the second girl is bursting to know if the 'poo' is 'real'. The scene that Girl 1 is recounting is apparently funny to the girls because it's 'gross'. This was an aspect of children's enjoyment of television that Sheldon and Loncar (1996, 87) identified in their research with Australian children: 'In general the attitude, "it's funny because it's disgusting" was prevalent'. The first girl is relishing being able to recount in all its glorious detail 'the huge slob of poo and wee' running down the adults' faces. It is clear that not only did she enjoy watching the scene herself but that now she is revelling in sharing this pleasure with her friend. It is the 'grossness' that they are enjoying, and the narrative is not even mentioned. In fact it is not possible to understand from her account how this scene fits into a story.

Horrible Histories is a show that appears to be seriously entertaining to children, as can be seen in its widespread popularity and ratings success (Hickman 2011). The producers of the show apparently recognised children's enjoyment of the scatological from the outset of the development of the program. According to the creator of the original books, Terry Deary: 'The feedback from the BBC was unambiguous: "We really like it, but we feel the poo quotient needs to be higher"' (Hickman 2011). Children's television producer Jesse Armstrong certainly believes this factor is a large part of the show's appeal: 'The key for me, though, is that the [show's production] team has been given leeway to do the subjects that really interest kids – death, shit, blood and piss' (Hickman 2011).

The sheer exuberance of the girls' exchange highlights the pleasure they get from watching such television: there is no mistaking the fun of it. But this interview also reveals the complexity of children's humour in relation to adults and the central importance to children of their own agency. A number of researchers have touched on the ways in which relations between children and adults play out in our culture today around television viewing (Buckingham 1995, 2000; Seiter 1998). Adults' efforts to control how much but also what children watch is the most overt manifestation of this relationship but there is also a 'deep concern on the part of adult groups to monitor their entertainment and survey their pleasure' (Spigel 1998, 114). Children resist this control in many and subtle ways; from claiming 'to prefer programs their parents found unwholesome' (Spigel 1998, 123) to finding pleasure in a television program 'precisely [because] … adults are excluded' and which they can enjoy 'without the slightest possibility of adult interest or interference' (Buckingham 1995, 58).

In the interview above, I had just been asking the children if they learnt anything from television, and this question appears to have prompted the reference to *Horrible Histories*, a program that has attracted support from adults because of its 'educational' historical content. I continued with this line of questioning in my response to the young girl's introduction of the show, suggesting 'you could learn history from television'. The girls completely ignored my comment; it had no relevance to what they were sharing at this moment. They were swept up in the fact that the remembered scene from *Horrible Histories* was riotously funny and they were sharing the 'gross' humour with delicious pleasure. They were determined not to allow an intrusion into this space from the adult in the room, with her perceived focus on the dominant 'adult' discourse. It was not that they didn't hear, or were not aware of the implications of my question; they were confidently asserting their own agency in this space and were determined to share a good laugh. This show might be promoted by adults for its potential educational value but for these two girls it was simply funny. Their exchange demonstrates what much 'scholarship on children's culture' has acknowledged and that is: 'the ways children resist, transform or redefine adult prerogatives, making their own uses of cultural materials' that are available to them (Jenkins 1998a, 27).

CHAPTER 5

Some of the aspects of the humour in this interview appear connected to the fact that the gross things are happening to adults; adults who are already foolishly decked out 'in fake wigs'. This aspect of children's enjoyment of television programs has been noted by other researchers including Davies, Buckingham and Kelley (2000, 17) who found that children 'focused particularly on the subversive or "carnivalesque" element of adults behaving like children and making fools of themselves'. John Fiske (1989, 242) has observed that 'cartoons and comedies frequently invert "normal" relationships and show the adult as incompetent, unable to understand, and the children as superior in insight and ability'. He goes on to point out the pleasure this provides: 'it is the pleasure of the subordinate escaping from the rules and conventions that are the agents of social control'. Disrupting the power hierarchy is no doubt satisfying in itself, and irritating parents by laughing at such humour appears to be part of the enjoyment of it all, but the subversive element is not the whole picture. Davies, Buckingham and Kelley (2000, 23) astutely observe that there is also an inherent acknowledgment by children of their own lowly position in the social order:

> When children laugh at the incompetent child-like adult in *Mr Bean* or the spectacle of adults humiliating themselves in *You've Been Framed*, it is partly because these programmes speak to their sense of their own powerlessness.

It seems that when children laugh at ridiculous adults they are staking out their own space in opposition to adult superiority and control, and, at least through their laughter, however briefly, they are disrupting the social order.

Seiter (1998) expands on the notion that children are resisting adult control and power in their choice of kitschy and commercial popular culture over more refined aesthetically-pleasing or educational materials. She suggests that children enjoy television programs that 'enact a rebellion against adult restriction' and that 'children's mass culture rejects the instrumental uses of toys and television for teaching and self-improvement preferred by parents' (Seiter 1998, 300-1). But pushing back against adult efforts to make their television viewing worthwhile is perhaps only part of the story. Buckingham has cautioned against overstating this 'rebellion' lest we miss recognising that 'children actually seem to like this mindless nonsense' (Buckingham 2000, 161). They choose to watch it largely because they enjoy it.

It is just this light-hearted but delicious sense of fun that comes through in the following interview with the 8-year-old girl who loves the slapstick humour of people (i.e. largely adults) accidentally hurting themselves:

Girl: Now there's *World's Craziest Fools*, which is really funny. You joke about that all the time.

Interviewer: Do you?

Girl: Yeah. Because there's like people blindfolded and they're driving their car but they crash into a wall and – yeah.

The conversation is not serious or pointed here – there is no sense of 'enacting a rebellion' – the girl is quite simply recounting her pleasure in having a good laugh at the slapstick.

One of the criticisms directed at shows that many children appear to enjoy is that they are tasteless. It does appear that parents are annoyed at a number of the programs that children enjoy and find funny, as is apparent in this news story's headline: '19 incredibly annoying characters on kids' TV shows' (Spohr 2015). But what is also clear

CHAPTER 5

is that adults are asserting their own superior taste by denigrating their children's. Here a columnist does just that: 'Actually all of the shows he likes are terrible. Believe me, my son has many wonderful qualities, but his taste in television is awful' (Mentzer 2014). But this is not a one-way street. Children too judge their parents' choices, belittling the 'boring' shows that adults watch.

In their research, Davies, Buckingham and Kelley (2000) found that children use the word 'boring' to express disapproval of a program and also to judge others' choices, particularly those of adults. They found that for the children 'boring [was] ... a cardinal signifier of a lack of cultural value' (p. 19). But when children used this description, Davies, Buckingham and Kelley found that they were doing more than just criticising their parent's preferences for programs such as the news. Rather, in this process of valorisation, 'the cultural hierarchy that elevates seriousness and civic responsibility is effectively inverted' by the children (Davies, Buckingham and Kelley 2000, 19). It would appear that 'funny' favourites win; 'boring' adult television loses.

In my research, the word 'funny' was used by the children to cover a range of attributes displayed by favourite television shows. It was commonly used in talking about characters that were not only funny but were particularly loved and obviously spoke to the children, as seen in the interviews with the 7- and 8-year-old girls in the last chapter who were talking about the cartoon characters in *YooHoo & Friends*. In the following interview, two 8-year-old girls, from a different interview pair, are talking about quite a different program: *Life with Boys* is a Canadian teenage sitcom, where one of the main characters is a teenage girl called Tess. At the beginning of the segment, the two girls are speaking about Tess's three brothers but they soon turn to their particular favourites.

Girl 2:	Yeah, like one of them's really dumb but he's the oldest.
Girl 1:	Yeah he's really like – he has 'babe' modes.
Girl 2:	Yeah, yeah, yeah, yeah [both girls laugh].
Girl 1:	And … um … ah … I think my favourite show out of *Life with Boys* would probably be the main character Tess or her best friend Allie.
Girl 2:	Yeah [thoughtfully].
Girl 1:	And they're both really silly.
Girl 2:	Yep [immediately agreeing] [both laugh].
Girl 1:	Like they're smart but silly, yeah they like to joke around and stuff.

Obviously these two girls find this show funny. It is a comedy and of course is designed to be humorous. But it is interesting that they turn fairly quickly in the conversation to selecting their favourite characters: both of whom are female. What appeals to the girls about these characters is the fact that they're 'both really silly': always no doubt providing a good laugh. But it is not that they are simple buffoons; these two girls in the TV show are also 'smart'. They demonstrate agency and are the ones who 'create' the humour: 'they like to joke around and stuff'. These characteristics quite clearly touch a chord with the two 8-year-old girls. They are completely absorbed in talking, thoughtfully in some moments, excitedly in others, about the characters. These are not arbitrarily humorous characters from a show the girls just happened to see; this teenage sitcom is a chosen favourite that apparently relates to their own lives and aspirations.

Far from being passive viewers who are largely indifferent to the content of what they watch (Comstock and Scharrer 2007,

CHAPTER 5

46-8), these children have actively chosen a show that connects to their interests and, significantly, provides them with moments of sheer joy. This aspect of children's engagement with television is something that Palmer (1986, 128) has also observed: 'Children hope for a great deal in their television shows. They want to be entertained, and they want to learn about the world and about relationships'. In the segment above there are glimpses of this; at the start of the discussion the girls are fascinated by the boys' behaviour in the television show. Girl 2 is talking about Gabe, the oldest brother of Tess who is the female star of the show. They are laughing at the way Gabe flirts with his girlfriends, adopting his 'babe' modes to impress the girls with his charm and smooth-talking, but they are even more interested in the smart, funny girl who often runs rings around her brothers. Both of the 8-year-old girls have brothers and possibly this adds to their enjoyment of a show where the sister in the family is the obvious winner – smarter than the boys *and* funny. It could be real but it is also a fantasy; possibly it suggests a wishful glimpse of a family life that is not really their own; and that no doubt is part of its attraction. It offers what Dyer (2002, 20) has observed:

> the image of 'something better' to escape into, or something we want deeply that our day-to-day lives don't provide … the sense that things could be better, that something other than what is can be imagined and maybe realized.

But in order to do this the television show has to relate in some way to the girls' own lives. This is something that these 8-year-old girls themselves articulated in another part of the interview. Thoughtfully, Girl 1 is trying to explain what it is she likes about her favourite programs:

Girl 1:	It's entertaining ... rather than watching the news which I do like sometimes ... it's like, sometimes you just feel in the mood for like humour and cartoons and things ... like cos they make like shows that are for you kinda, so they understand what you like and it's um ... it's nice.
...	
Girl 2:	I just think that I really wish I was a character and doing all that cool stuff.
Girl 1:	Some shows are easier like to imagine yourself in.
Girl 2:	Yeah.
Girl 1:	Than other shows.
Interviewer:	What sort of shows are they, A___?
Girl 1:	Um, kinda like maybe *Sam & Cat*, there's like–
Girl 2:	Yeah.
Girl 1:	Yeah you can imagine yourself.
Interviewer:	Because you can relate to some of the characters a bit more, is that why?
[both girls start eagerly talking at once]	
Girl 2:	Cos some of the characters are inside my parents.
Girl 1:	Yeah cos like in *The Amazing World of Gumball* you can't really relate cos they're like animated, they're cartoons, they're made up stories.
Interviewer:	Right.
Girl 2:	Yeah [pause]. Well so is any other TV show.
Girl 1:	Well, yeah but like–

CHAPTER 5

Interviewer: But some of them are a bit more related to what you are like?

Girl 1: Some of them are real … a bit more like reality kind of …

Once again one of the television programs that comes up in these girls' discussions is a teenage sitcom. *Sam & Cat* is an American show with two teenage girls (Sam and Cat) appearing as the main characters. Despite the fact that these characters are living together in a flat and have set up their own babysitting business, Girl 1 likes it because it is one of the shows that is 'easier like to imagine yourself in'. She is only eight, and is living at home with her family, but she obviously relates to the two girls who star in the show, fascinated by their teenage world. She suggests that the show is easier to imagine yourself in because it is 'real … a bit more like reality kind of'. While the humour and entertainment provided by the show draw her to it, as she says earlier in the interview, there is more to it than this. To paraphrase Hartley (2008, 182), she sees 'the "pleasing stuff"' but also sees 'through it to the conduct of human relationships within'. For Girl 1 the show possibly speaks to her through the friendships of Sam and Cat, and perhaps their relationship with the grandmother. For Girl 2, on the other hand, it is the wacky adventures and fun that she dreams of: 'I just think that I really wish I was a character and doing all that cool stuff'. She too, however, sees reflections of real life in the show and, as can be seen in the eagerness with which she makes the following comparison, she enjoys the potential humour of such similarities: 'cos some of the characters are inside my parents'.

The entertainment value of the show for the two girls is reflected in their eagerness to both examine and share what they like about the program. Their relationship with the show is rich and complex, and has a distinctly social element. Barker and Brooks (1998, 11) have remarked on the centrality of this element of audience engagement in television, arguing in fact that:

> audiences are always social: that is to say, there are no audiences who do not respond to the meanings produced as part of living their lives in and through social conditions, social groups and social possibilities.

They go on to suggest that:

> children are not different in principle from other audiences, despite all the social fears that surround them; they are in fact often using the media as part of learning how to be members of their culture generally, and more particularly of their local groups. (p. 12)

In her research with children, Davies found this also to be true. One of her groups of 12- to 13-year-olds loved *The Simpsons* because, they said, 'it's funny … it's hilarious', but 'they also valued it because "it reflects some things from life". It was seen as socially useful' (Davies 2004, 429).

I would suggest that children draw on the 'socially useful' aspects of television shows, not only through watching, but through talking about favourite programs with each other and with their families, enjoying themselves as they do so. In this way, the stories and characters of television are woven into their everyday lives. The very nature of television as the modern source of truly accessible entertainment and drama, 'a communal art' (Hawkes 1973, 231), provides this possibility and encourages as Hawkes (1973, 230) argues 'a kind of group involvement and participation, vocal and positive'.

CHAPTER 5

This picture is far from that drawn by Robert Putnam in his hugely popular and best-selling *Bowling Alone* (2001). Putnam regards television viewing as a passive and isolating leisure pursuit and he argues that such viewing reduces 'social capital' by taking away from social interaction. Real life relationships he argues are substituted with a 'pseudopersonal connection' (p. 242) to television celebrities and characters. But this is to miss the way audiences engage with entertainment, enjoying it as they go, as so perceptively observed by Hawkes (1973), Hartley (2008) and Dyer (2002). Certainly in my research, the children's involvement with each other and with their families and friends around television was clearly visible and their accounts demonstrated that, not least of all, this engagement with favourite programs in particular provides a rich source of humour and joy. There was little evidence of it being predominantly, as Putnam (2001, 241) has argued, 'a surprisingly unsatisfying experience … about as enjoyable as housework and cooking, ranking well below all other leisure activities'.

Passing the Time with Television

Perhaps Putnam is thinking about the ways in which both adults and children use television to pass the time, and believes, along with many others, that reading a book would be a far more worthwhile way of achieving this objective. But I would suggest that this is to miss the value of 'passing time' in front of television.

As we have seen above, children do actively enjoy the fun and humour of their favourite programs. But television is not always sought out for its ability to provide edge-of-the-seat excitement; it apparently provides another function in children's lives. It offers, from their own accounts, a relaxing way of filling in the idle moments of daily life. In response to the question in my survey, 'Why do you watch television?', a total of 22% of the children said they watched television sometimes because 'it passes time', or when they were 'bored'. One 9-year-old boy in my survey said he watched television 'because I sometimes feel bored in the weekends and got nothing entertaining to do and I just want to do something relaxing'.

This is echoed in others' research with children who have found they watch 'to pass time and relax' (Sheldon 1998, 79) and sometimes 'for something to do' (Palmer 1986, 45). Such viewing might seem to provide a fairly benign way to fill in the spare moments in a child's schedule but the easy availability is in fact judged harshly by some in the effects research tradition. The ubiquity of television is seen as a threat: 'It comes into the home ... [and provides] virtually unlimited access from cradle to grave' (Gerbner and Gross 1976, 176). Gerbner and Gross go on to argue that television is dangerous for the hypnotic effect it has on the passive viewer who is 'held in thrall'; these viewers, who include children and old people, are by implication weak-minded and feeble and are particularly at risk from the easy temptations of television: 'television is there to keep the elderly company when all else fails' (p. 176). There is no suggestion here that choosing to watch television when you have nothing else to do is an active, let alone a valuable, choice: that in fact the 'elderly' might welcome its 'company'.

Research with children, however, presents a rather different picture to Gerbner and Gross's malign hypnotist. In my survey a number of children commented on the *value* that television provided in passing time:

> Television is a good thing to do in your spare time. I usually use television to get ideas for stories and sometimes just watch television when i am bored (10-year-old girl)

CHAPTER 5

> It gives you something to think about on a boring day (10-year-old boy)
>
> I think TV is good because if you are bored you can wach stuff (8-year-old boy)

Having the option of watching television on a slow day is clearly valuable to these children: it is 'good' to be able to tune in to television when you are bored. Of course the voice of the dominant discourse reverberates through these comments: Why aren't these children going outside to run around and play? Why aren't they more productively filling in their spare moments, perhaps reading a book? These persistent questions, familiar to both parents and children in our western culture, are addressed in the following thoughtful comment from an 8-year-old girl:

> I reckon if you don't have anything to do it's a little bit entertaining. Cos like I mean you can read but if you kinda like don't really have a – like you've finished all the books you kinda have, it's kind of a bit of a break from walking around and stuff.

Physical activity shouldn't always be the preferred option to sitting in front of television, this young girl implies. After all, you do need a break 'from walking around and stuff'. And what better way to relax than to do something that's 'a little bit entertaining': nothing too demanding but rather a gentle way to pass the time. She tries also to deflect the other dominant discourse, that reading a book is a far more productive way to pass time than watching television, by suggesting that all the available books have already been 'finished'. She quite clearly understands the dominant culture's fixation on nurturing the child into a productive adulthood: but she nonetheless has a good try at presenting her own reality.

One thing is quite apparent from the analysis of my research and that is that children are aware of their own choices around television, they do discriminate and are without question active viewers in this respect. While they might look passive as they relax in front of the set, they have nevertheless taken an active decision about how they might pass time 'on a boring day' and 'wach stuff'. This approach to television is confirmed in Linda Sheldon's analysis (1998) of the extensive research with children conducted by the Australian Broadcasting Authority. She found that 'children were discriminating in their television viewing, [and] made active choices about programmes' (Sheldon 1998, 91). The mindless automaton, 'held in thrall' by the invading screen, appears to have little substance when listening to children's own accounts of how they engage with television – even when it is simply to pass time. While favourite shows undoubtedly provide fun and excitement and perhaps a chance to learn about the world, television is also a more mundane part of daily life, and children seek it out when they are 'bored'. It's an aspect of television that is evidently of value to their leisure hours.

This particular use of television was something pointed out to me by two 8-year-old boys. They are responding in the interview segment below to my leading, rather earnest, question:

Interviewer: Do you think TV helps you in your life in any way?

Boy 2: Yeah … [pause] … helps you to watch TV.

Interviewer: [laugh] Helps you to watch TV?

Boy 2: And it helps you to learn how to um … hmmm, what's the word? …

Boy 1: Goof off?

Boy 2: Yeah.

CHAPTER 5

The tone of their conversation was undemonstrative but the subversive humour was nonetheless clearly evident; they were, however lightly, making fun of me and my adult preoccupation, that television should in some way be productive. One of its attractions instead was that it allowed you to 'goof off' and escape the organising adult world that is focused on nurturing and improving the child. They quite cleverly demonstrated 'that it is normally in no way "special" or "unusual" for most people to watch television' (Hawkes 1973, 232). It doesn't *need* to help you with anything – except possibly to 'goof off'. This is a sentiment captured in another comment from an 8-year-old girl in my survey in answer to the question, 'What's the best thing about television?' She replied quite simply: 'It can't go anywhere'.

'Learning' from Television

The curious thing about the way children enjoy television is that it defies the dominant culture in surprisingly diverse ways. Their pleasures cross the metaphoric boundaries that are established by the rules and authority of the 'serious' scientific and educational elites in a fluid and elusive manner. And ironically it is often the entertainment value of the television programs – so disparaged in the dominant discourse – that enables this transgression.

Children, by their own account, enjoy learning from television and paradoxically this is part of the fun of it. Palmer (1986, 45) found that 'children watched TV for fun and excitement and to learn about things not usually accessible to them'. In her research with children Howard (1998, 73-4) found that they:

> pay close attention to their favourite television programmes and these have the capacity to stimulate even the very young into

thinking about such philosophical issues as the nature of social reality and questions of representation.

One 9-year-old girl in my survey gave a similar explanation of the reasons why she liked her favourite programs and what they offered her: 'they can be funny, interesting, the people'. In his exploration of the ways in which audiences engaged with Shakespeare in the 16th century and with *Big Brother* in the 21st, Hartley (2008, chap. 9) echoes these observations. He suggests that forms of entertainment, such as Shakespeare, Hollywood and television reality shows, are popular because their audiences engage with them 'for the purposes of exploring the vicissitudes of human relations as entertainment' (p. 186). When children watch their favourite programs they do appear to be 'learning' in the senses suggested by Palmer, Howard and Hartley. And while this learning might not fit into the categories dictated by school curricula, it does apparently contribute to children's lives in rich, and entertaining, ways.

In the following interview segment, the 10-year-old Chris Lilley fan mentioned above reveals the way comedy works, as Hartley (2008, 186) says, in '"universalizing" human interest'.

> Yeah ... Well to me it sorta shows like different views of different people, like it might be like just a comedy for people to enjoy but I sorta see it as well like, a comedy and sort of like what some of the stuff that happens in real life. And in *Summer Heights High* they actually had to put in the beginning of episodes, 'The characters in this episode are not based on any characters in real life' because it sorta seems like something's that so real.

Another 10-year-old girl described why she liked one of her favourite shows – an American sitcom called *Modern Family*:

CHAPTER 5

> I think it's kind of how a lot of – some TV's – well my favourite thing about it is because the show *Modern Family* you can relate to them. Yeah, like real life things happen.

She reflects on this again in a later interview:

> Yeah … like in *Modern Family*, it's a big family with all different people and they somehow just all work together and everything.

And later again she says:

> My sisters are like … identical to Hayley and Alex in *Modern Family*.

Both of these girls had been talking about how funny these two television shows were; there is no doubt the sheer enjoyment of watching these comedies had drawn them to the programs. But when asked to articulate further why they liked the shows, they both spoke about how 'real' they were, 'like real life things happen'. For the first girl, the depiction of life on the screen seemed 'so real' that she believed this had caused the producers to preface the program with a disclaimer about all characters being fictional.

Obviously both girls related to the stories and the characters; for the second girl two sisters in one of the television families reminded her of her own sisters. She took obvious delight in comparing her sisters to the two characters in the show – characters that are created with the wicked humour of the comedian's art. Both are stereotypes familiar in our culture: the teen who's already into fashion, boys and other 'adult' temptations, and the too-smart, precocious, middle child. It is apparent from their comments that both of these girls recognise and enjoy the comedy but also appreciate the way in which the show explores and reflects the realities – and quirks – of their own lives. For these girls, there is little doubt that television entertainment plays a role in both their understanding and articulation of their own culture (McKee, Collis and Hamley 2012, 2). It contributes to what they learn about life in both a valuable and enjoyable manner. The second girl is particularly captivated by how 'a big family with all different people ... just all work together and everything': perhaps a reflection of, or a dream she has for, her own family life.

That television is a rich source of learning about 'social behaviour and relationships' is something Palmer (1986, 122) also observed. Drawing on her extensive ethnographic research, she argues that the 'stories' in television:

> give children a wider sense of the world than is possible within their own neighbourhood. There seems every reason to believe that, through the stories it tells, television is one of the main sources of information about social life for children. (Palmer 1986, 143)

Or as Hartley (1999, 180) so aptly describes it, television brings 'social, geographical, environmental and demographic variety into the home'.

As discussed earlier, in the dominant discourse television is regarded largely as a waste of time, particularly for young viewers. If children can learn anything from it, they must be watching the types of programs that get the tick of approval from adults. As mentioned above, *Sesame Street* is one such program: it is seen as offering education (alphabet and numbers) cleverly embedded within the entertainment. But this narrow view of television's educational capabilities largely ignores what children themselves identify as the learning offered them by television. It is clear from children's conversations that they learn a great deal from TV and

CHAPTER 5

they often do so through their engagement in the humour and in the stories that speak to their own lives. This learning appears also to be a large part of the fun of it. It was clear from my research that children use television to inform, understand and enjoy their own lives: a finding also supported by Palmer (1986, 143) who argued that:

> children's use of both the structure and content of narratives from TV in their talk and games demonstrates their eagerness to imitate and adapt TV scenarios to their own experience.

The observation of this adaptation is a key insight into how children engage with television. It seems that they draw from the stories the elements that resonate with their own experience and, I might also suggest, the aspects that appeal to their own senses of humour.

Drawing 4: 10-year-old girl's cover sheet for story about Ja'mie

SQUARE EYES

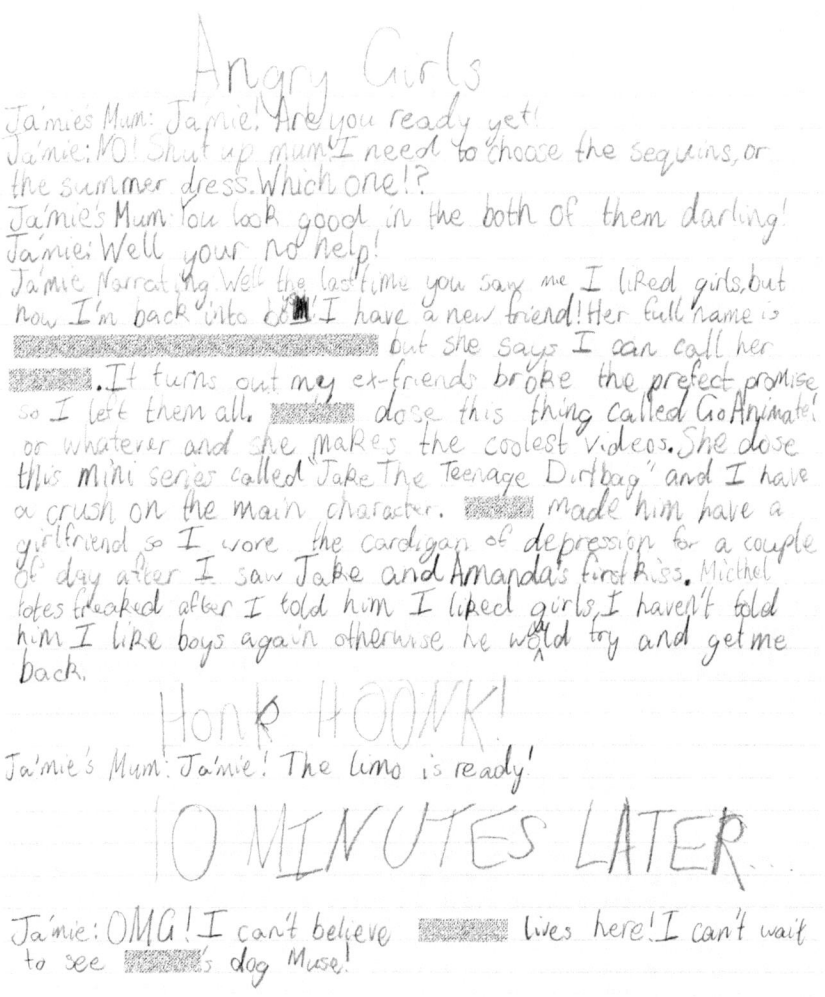

Story 2: 10-year-old girl's story about Ja'mie

The quality of this engagement was particularly evident in the story and picture created by the 10-year-old Chris Lilley fan in my research. Her story is reproduced above but it is her own account of the story in our subsequent interview that is particularly illuminating:

CHAPTER 5

Girl: Ahh, my story's like it's maybe a new series a new um Chris Lilley series called *Angry Girls* and it sort of has one of his characters Ja'mie King and I'm one of the characters in the show on the ABC and it's sort of like what people are saying and stuff, like the script and stuff.

Interviewer: So is *Angry Girls* a whole new story that you've invented?

Girl: It's a whole new story that I've sort of like invented, sort of leaving off where *Ja'mie: Private School Girl* ended.

Interviewer: Yeah. So that's fantastic. That's a really great idea. What gave you that idea?

Girl: Well it's just because I really like his comedy, like Chris Lilley's comedy series. And um … I think like one of his new ones like began around the time when I wrote this so I thought it would be cool if I sort of made like another one with Ja'mie in it. Cos *Ja'mie: Private School Girl* was supposed to be the last one but I sort of wish that there was another *Ja'mie* series so I just created another.

Interviewer: And you put yourself in there?

Girl: Mm-hmm … and I put myself in there.

Interviewer: I thought that was quite funny. I read your ending.

Girl: Yeah.

Interviewer: He gets to your place and he's, Ja'mie, or she, is really excited.

Girl: Yeah, yeah. At seeing my dog.

Interviewer: Did that make you laugh?

Girl: Yeah well I was sorta like, everybody loves my dog, so like because Ja'mie's so like poshy and stuff, like girly, girly and stuff, I'd make her like be obsessed with my dog Muse ... so ... yeah ...

This 10-year-old quite literally adapts the 'structure and content' (Palmer 1986) of Chris Lilley's television show, *Ja'mie: Private School Girl*, to create her own story where she is at the heart of the action. But this involves a sophisticated understanding of the structure and content of the shows and the girl's story is a fascinating illustration of the ways in which children learn from television. The 10-year-old has obviously grasped the fundamental building blocks of a TV show; she understands the function of a television script and the way in which the plot drives the comedy. Her story is presented largely as a scripted dialogue and she uses both a script format and Ja'mie's relationship with her mother to carry forward the plot. She has captured also the language of the original show's dialogue with a sensitive ear, recreating the mother's placating and slightly cringing tone, 'You look good in the both of them darling!' and Ja'mie's outrageously rude but characteristic reply, 'Well your no help!' The exchange resonates with the sharp satirical humour of the television show. Ja'mie's relationship with her mother, which reflects her domineering attitude in the television series, serves in this girl's story to both establish Ja'mie's character but also to develop the structure. The mother's part indicates the direction of the plot establishing that Ja'mie is preparing for an outing and then sending her on her way to her destination and towards the climax of the story with 'Ja'mie! The limo is ready!'

But it is not only the structure of the television shows that the 10-year-old draws on for her story. She also artfully weaves their content, in the form of personalities, characters and their relationships, into her own script. Her story presents a rich example of the way television stories are threaded through the lives of the viewer; and in this case the viewer literally becomes central to the action. Here is drama merging with real life and the 10-year-old's story provides an insight into how a television program has informed her own appreciation of social interactions including relationships with friends and family. Entirely literate in her grasp of the format and characters of television comedy she is able to enjoy, as Hartley (2008, 183) suggests, the 'pleasing stuff' of the show, especially the humour, but also to 'see *through* it to the conduct of human relationships within'.

It is apparent from her story that the girl has appreciated the centrality of relationships to the formation of identity. Ja'mie's narration starts off with an explicit statement of sexual preference: 'Well the last time you saw me I liked girls, but now I'm back into boys!' Ja'mie then draws on a television program herself to examine her own feelings, revealing that she has a 'crush on the main character' in the 'mini-series called "Jake The Teenage Dirtbag"'. With a flourish of self-parody, Ja'mie expresses her devastation over this character's love life choices: 'I wore the cardigan of depression for a couple of day after I saw Jake and Amanda's first kiss'. This leads her to reflect on her own relationship with her ex-boyfriend Mitchell and on the power plays involved: 'I haven't told him I like boys again otherwise he would try and get me back'.

The power struggle inherent in relationships is also raised earlier on in the 10-year-old's story with Ja'mie declaiming against her 'ex-friends'. They have transgressed the social code, which is obviously guarded closely by Ja'mie herself, and because they have broken 'the prefect promise' she has 'left them all'. In the 10-year-old's story this set-back for the old friends turns out to be a boon for the new:

she herself becomes Ja'mie's new best friend. But in the spirit of the original television show, and with a representation of Ja'mie that is true to the original character, the 10-year-old finishes with her own self-mocking twist. The girl ends her story with Ja'mie's arrival at her house but it isn't the girl that is the centre of attention in the final count, it is her dog:

> Ja'mie: OMG I can't believe M_ lives here! I can't wait to see M_'s dog Muse!

The young storyteller captures the essence of Lilley's character and his humour in this ending. Ja'mie, in her usual outrageous and self-focused fashion, disregards her passionately embraced 'new friend' of the previous scene to indulge her own pleasures. The 10-year-old girl has perceptively captured Ja'mie's personality and has also cleverly woven this into the realities of her own life as is apparent from her own explanation of the ending of her story:

> Yeah well I was sorta like, everybody loves my dog, so like because Ja'mie's all like poshy and stuff, like girly, girly stuff, I'd make her like be obsessed with my dog Muse … yeah …

Taking aspects of her own life and weaving these together with key elements of her favourite television shows, this young storyteller has imagined a world that could, just possibly, be realised. The story itself has become an exquisite reflection of her own dreams, dreams which have been inspired by Chris Lilley's comedies. These TV programs have offered her 'alternatives, hopes, wishes … the stuff of utopia' (Dyer 2002, 20).

The story within the story in this girl's creation is a fascinating reflection of the young girl's depth of interest in her favourite shows. She has been so absorbed in the comedies produced by Chris Lilley

CHAPTER 5

that she has taken an interest in their creator, watching among other videos those on the making of the programs.

Girl: I was just watching behind the scenes in *Jonah from Tonga* cos yesterday I just got it on DVD – 'Thank you Mum!' [laugh] – Anyway um so it sorta just makes … sometimes you just sit there wondering how the heck did he come up with this? But with *Ja'mie* you think, yeah, I know how he came up with this and I went on his website and he said he was inspired for *Ja'mie* by his sister.

Interviewer: Oh wow, that's interesting.

Girl: Yeah. Like I just find it crazy how he comes up with so many ideas, like people say they wouldn't just come up with their ideas saying 'How about a series with a gay drama teacher, a teenage boy from Tonga, he has like a bit of mental problems, and then I can bring in Ja'mie from the first series cos that was popular' and then end up like being one of the best of all his series.

His shows are so clever, with their outrageous characters and sharp humour, that the 10-year-old wonders how Chris Lilley could possibly come up with all the ideas for them. But while she does recognise the exaggeration that indeed provides much of the humour, at the same time she is aware of how Chris Lilley's comedies reflect 'important contemporary issues' (Hartley 2008, 183); and that they are connected to real life. As if to prove this not only to me but to herself, she proudly explains how she knows this for a fact. She has looked on the internet and found out that Chris Lilley was 'inspired for Ja'mie by his sister'.

For this young girl the enjoyment of these shows is tied closely to the ways in which they touch on her own life and interests while allowing her to dream. As Hartley (2008, 6) notes, this is one of the delights of television entertainment. Hartley argues persuasively that television allows the viewer to use:

> the imaginative resources of story, song, sight, and sound ... to think about identity, relationship, and community, in real time and space, often while our annoying family is making us dream of being somewhere else entirely. Television obliges that dream. Using its semiotic and social resources, we make ourselves up as we watch, which is why so many people have a store of shows, characters, even ads, that reminds them of how, when, and where they went about that task. (2008, 6)

With great delight this is exactly what the 10-year-old girl is doing across the many levels of her engagement with Chris Lilley's comedies. In a particularly illuminating passage of her story she reveals her own perceptions of, and dreams for, herself – and how they are closely interwoven with her favourite TV shows. These dreams are placed squarely at the heart of the story. With dramatic flair, she gives Ja'mie the role of describing, with quite obvious admiration, the 10-year-old's particular talents. Ja'mie confers status on the girl at the very beginning of this story-within-the-story by announcing that the girl is her 'new friend'. It bestows a powerful identity on the young girl – to be sought out as the friend of someone like Ja'mie.

The entire central section of this narration by Ja'mie focuses on the 10-year-old girl and it is here that she becomes herself the television producer: her dream comes true. It turns out in the story that she is the creator of a TV mini-series called *Jake The Teenage Dirtbag*: a title that quite clearly reflects the provocative humour of the Chris Lilley shows. Here, in her own story, the 10-year-old is following in the footsteps of her TV producer idol and making 'the coolest videos'. In this story, she has drawn on the TV shows themselves,

CHAPTER 5

her knowledge of how they are made and her understandings of the particular characters that she likes, to – literally – make herself up.

There is nothing passive about this young girl's engagement with these favourite television shows. Her active interest in the stories and characters has provided her with rich insights into her own and others' social and cultural lives; and she has picked up quite a flair for television script-writing in the process. It is hard to argue that this is not an imaginative and creative response to television, or that she has learnt nothing from her engagement with these programs. But above all, at the heart of this fascination with television, there is a sense of enjoyment and an unembarrassed embrace of the fun of it.

The entertainment provided by these favourite television shows is quite apparently working on many levels: not least of which is at Dyer's 'level of sensibility' (2002, 20). As Dyer points out, one of the great pleasures of entertainment is the way it provides a 'feel' of utopia. In the last section of this chapter I explore the way in which this notion illuminates further an understanding of how and why children engage with such enthusiasm in the fun of television.

The 'Feel' of Utopia

As Jenkins (1998a) suggests, the ways in which children re-fashion and adapt cultural materials – and I would suggest also, from the evidence of my research, the ways in which they redefine the established discourses on culture – are rich and varied. Children are, he observes, not outside of 'the cultural formations [and] material conditions that shape all human interactions' (1998a, 30); they demonstrate agency, and they adapt and use the 'resources provided them by the adult world as raw materials for their play activities, their jokes, their drawings, and their own stories' (p. 28).

SQUARE EYES

The imaginative but also perceptive ways in which children do this are particularly evident in the story created by an 8-year-old boy who took part in my research. In his story (see below), this young boy touches on the dominant discourse that demands children's television viewing hours be restricted for their own wellbeing. He also draws on the 'cultural materials' produced by the adult world: fairy tales and television programs – in particular an American animated television program, *Adventure Time*. Throughout his story, he clearly demonstrates his own understanding of the prevailing cultural discourses and he draws on the available materials to both inform his own way of being in the world but also to enjoy himself.

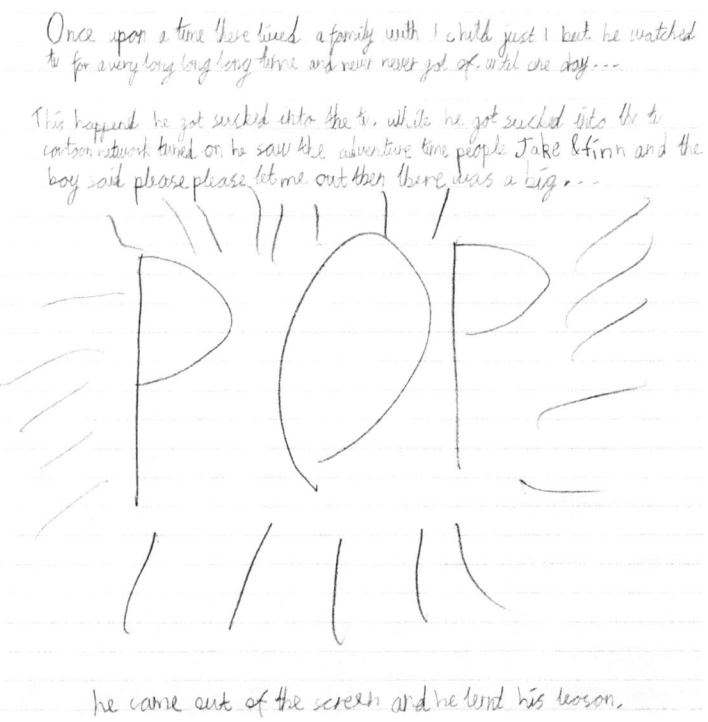

Story 3: 8-year-old boy's story of television sucking in viewer

CHAPTER 5

The 8-year-old begins with the standard opening of the fairy tale, 'Once upon a time', and then goes on to tell the story of a boy who watched too much television: 'he watched TV for a very long long long time and never never got off'. From the start, the boy acknowledges the dominant discourse but not without taking a poke at the adult-sponsored notion. A twist of irony circles through his repetitions of the key words 'long' and 'never'.

Nevertheless watching television for too long is bound to have negative consequences: such is the common-sense understanding at the heart of the dominant discourse. And that is exactly what happens in this boy's story. With a rhetorical flourish the boy continues: 'until one day … /This happend he got sucked into the tv'. The danger of watching too much television is graphically illustrated here with the story character being completely absorbed in the television – both figuratively and literally. Of course being physically sucked into the box is terrifying and the boy cries out 'please, please, let me out'. His plea is heard and with a big 'POP' the boy comes 'out of the screen'. The story ends with the echo of the voice of an admonishing parent: 'he lernt his lesson'. It's a happily-ever-after fairy tale with a moral.

This story might appear at first glance to be an imitation of a straightforward morality tale showing what happens to a child who defies adult rules. But the boy appears rather to be using this adult resource simply as the raw material of his story. The 8-year-old is in control here and he is using humour and irony to tell his own story. He is quite obviously having fun telling this tale and in the process taking an active role in the debate over the regulation of children's television viewing. He is tapping into the negative discourse but enjoying also the opportunity to have a laugh at adult concerns and to send up prevailing cultural anxieties. Adult fears for the child who is glued to the television are comically sketched when the story character is 'sucked into' the screen and then comes out with a big 'POP'. But the 8-year-old's response to the negative discourse, while not entirely accepting of the adult position, is also not simply a straightforward opposition. Even though he is making fun of adult preoccupations, he does agree with some of their concerns. This became apparent in our final interview, where the boy talked to me about his story. Here the 8-year-old is recounting the plot:

Boy: And he um … he went to the *Adventure Time* place and they kept playing there and they kept playing outside and then um he stayed there for a night because he didn't know how to get out and the next day he got sucked out by the TV portal and he learnt his lesson not to go on TV too much and to play outside like Finn and Jake.

Interviewer: Does that mean that he's not going to watch TV anymore?

Boy: No. He's just not going to watch as much like because before he watched like 24 hours every day on TV.

…

Interviewer: What do you think is a good amount of TV?

Boy: Maybe like 20 minutes and then get up and go outside and play and then watch like 50 minutes and then just not watch anymore TV.

This boy has arrived at his own interpretation of the rules and has worked out how they might be useful to him. Twenty-four hours a day of television viewing is not desirable; rather, small amounts of TV interspersed with 'play' and going 'outside' would be 'good'. Jenkins (1998a, 28) has observed that:

adult institutions and practices make 'bids' on how children will understand themselves and the world around them, yet they can never be certain how children will take up and respond to those 'bids'.

Certainly that appears to be the case with this young boy. He hasn't simply accepted the adult discourse at face value but has adapted its message to fit within his own view of life. His answer is a considered response to the discourse of regulation and shows an agency that defies the predictions of the more extreme effects researchers. His thoughtful comments counter the notion made popular by writers such as Winn (2002) that children are particularly vulnerable to the narcotic effects of the 'plug-in drug'; that they are too young or too unformed to have the capacity for self-regulation and if left to their own devices would watch television for hours at a time. The only solution according to Winn (2002, 223) is for parents to enforce the rules and 'to dredge up the strength to be strict'; that is the only way to ensure that 'television ceases to be a problem'. The implication is that children simply don't have the capacity for, and wouldn't even think about, regulating their own behaviour.

This picture of the almost feral child does not appear to be borne out in my research. Many of the children had opinions about regulating television viewing as did the boy telling this story. He is quite evidently aware of the issue and raises his own suggestions for regulation. His comments support Buckingham's (1996, 256) observations, as I discussed earlier, that:

> Children are not merely passive objects of adults' attempts at regulation – nor indeed do they uniformly resist them. On the contrary, children actively learn to regulate their own emotional responses to television.

Drawing 5: 8-year-old boy's drawing based on *Adventure Time*

But the written story and its reference to the discourse of regulation is only the beginning of this boy's creation. When we turn the page to the illustration, the story moves into the world

CHAPTER 5

of entertainment. As it turns out, the character in the story might be terrifyingly 'sucked into the tv' but he ends up in a world of fantasy and imagination: of favourite television programs and their characters. The 8-year-old's illustration shows clearly that for him television isn't defined simply by the regulations that surround it. The negative dominant discourse is not by any means the whole story and it is apparent from the boy's drawing that the 'real' world of television is far richer. The character doesn't end up in a dark hole, as might be expected as a result of defying the serious rules of correct television viewing. Instead he has popped up inside one of his creator's favourite shows, *Adventure Time*. This part of his adventure is delightfully illustrated in the picture that accompanies his written story (see drawing on left page).

This drawing gives a glimpse of a utopian world; the TV-addicted boy has ended up in *Adventure Time* and, with a smile on his face, can be seen playing with one of the main characters of the cartoon series, Finn. The two boys are playing together outside in the fresh air surrounded by luxuriantly green grass and blue lakes. The other main character of the series, Jake, the yellow magical dog, is also in the scene and is featured on the other side of a giant tree, stretching himself up to his house in the branches. It's an idyllic picture and while it does suggest a nod to another dominant discourse that surfaces in public debates about children and television – the preferability of outdoor play to passive TV viewing – there is much more to it. In this story it is the television itself that has opened up this world; a favourite show has offered 'the image of "something better" to escape into, or something we want deeply that our day-to-day lives don't provide' (Dyer 2002, 20). In this boy's story, the television set has quite literally transported the story's character to a world of outdoor play with magical friends. Paradoxically the TV has opened the window to the desired outdoor life: literally in the boy's story, but also metaphorically in that his favourite program has provided the raw materials for the creation of a hoped-for world. In such a world, it is possible to play with magical friends. This story reflects the way in which entertainment offers a glimpse of the 'alternatives, hopes, wishes' which as Dyer (2002, p. 20) suggests 'are the stuff of utopia, the sense that things could be better, that something other than what is can be imagined and maybe realized'.

But there is no hint of melancholy or loss here such as might be felt for the entirely unattainable. There is a sense that the fantasy world of his favourite television characters is woven into the fabric of daily life for this boy: it is not out of reach. This is suggested by the matter-of-fact way the boy talks about the human character in his story, demonstrating the familiar nature of his activities:

> they kept playing outside and then um he stayed there for a night because he didn't know how to get out and the next day he got sucked out by the tv portal.

Even the rather unusual exit is treated in a deadpan tone: it is nothing out of the ordinary. As for the cartoon characters in the story, they might have magical powers, but they enjoy the routine pleasures of life, such as playing outdoors.

The boy's descriptions of Finn and Jake in an earlier interview confirm his understanding of how the world of television is closely intertwined with his own. His comments illustrate the ways in which the boy's favourite television characters straddle the two worlds; the fantastical is woven into the everyday in an entirely unremarkable way. Here the 8-year-old is describing his favourite TV characters:

CHAPTER 5

> They're from Cartoon Network and they're two people, ah, one is. Jake is a dog, and he's like, he can talk to Finn, and Finn is a human. And Jake's arms can like stretch as far as he wanted. But if he stretches too long he gets really thin, like this thin [demonstrates with hand gestures], and um he can like make his fists go big and like punch the evil people and Finn is a human and he's Jake's best friend and Finn carries a sword and and Jake loves sandwiches.

The young boy starts his explanation with a description of the characters as 'two people': the implication is that they are quite ordinary and just like us – even though one is actually a dog. Of all the characteristics the 8-year-old could have noticed and shared about Jake, he alights on the fact that this magical dog loves something as commonplace as sandwiches. And it seems from his next comment that if Jake can be like humans, humans might hope to be like him:

> I would like to be Jake because like cos like if I was at the dinner table and I had to get up and get the tomato sauce [his friend laughs], if I was Jake I just could stretch and get it.

Here the fantasy plays out in the boy's imagination, not in transporting him to some magical universe, but in allowing him to avoid having to get up from the dinner table to get the tomato sauce. The way this boy talks about this favourite show illustrates what Hawkes (1973, 232) has so incisively observed about television:

> It forms part of everyday experience, meets everyday responses, and little physical separation exists between art on the television set and life in the living-room … It forms part of 'real' life.

Certainly that is the sense that comes across in this boy's story – where the TV transports the boy from his living room to the magical world of *Adventure Time* and back again – but it was also reflected in his conversations with his friend during our interviews. Not only did the favourite program inform their make-believe worlds, as illustrated by their stories, but also their social interactions. During the interviews they eagerly jumped at opportunities to recount particular scenes from *Adventure Time*, both participating in the telling, and enjoying a shared recognition of remembered scenes. As Götz et al. (2005, 105) observed in their research: 'children use the media world to foster communication with others – children and adults alike, including the researchers who interviewed them'. Quite possibly, the 8-year-old's story, written as it was in an interview session with an adult researcher in a school setting, included its reference to the dominant discourses around regulation to keep me in the picture, or to meet his perceived expectations of what I (as an adult) wanted or expected. The boy didn't, however, allow this to dictate his entire response but rather used it to create his own story; the 'bad' behaviour provided an opening to the cartoon world. This is another aspect of children's use of the media that is reflected in Götz et al.'s (2005, 99) research:

> Children are not just ... interpreting the texts in active ways, but also selectively abstracting from them various elements and features and integrating them together with ideas of their own to create new worlds of meaning.

The fantasy of *Adventure Time* obviously captured the imagination of both the boys in this interview pair and they were particularly taken by the transforming magical dog, Jake. But it was the sheer crazy humour, combined with excitement and action, which they seemed to enjoy the most. Both boys said they liked the show because it was 'funny'. The 8-year-old storyteller went on to elaborate on what this meant to him: 'they like do funny stuff. They like ... they just like play fight and all that funny stuff and like tell really weird jokes'.

CHAPTER 5

Both the boys enjoyed describing the scenes that were full of action. The 8-year-old's friend drew a picture of one of the two main characters, Finn, fighting one of the series' monsters, The Barn, which he described in our interview: 'there's these guys that want to wrestle this guy called The Barn and he's really strong and he beats everybody up'. His accompanying illustration (see below) shows Finn fighting The Barn, but when he was given the opportunity to talk more about his story, the plot grew into a far more complicated tale about Finn and Jake ending up in an argument. He was intensely absorbed in telling this story, standing up to illustrate with arm gestures how the fight played out. His friend listened avidly during these descriptions; the fights between the two friends in the cartoon seem to be of particular attraction to the boys. In the end the boy described rather breathlessly how the two cartoon friends ended up 'giving each other Chinese burns ... each other Chinese burns and spitting at each other and biting and yeah ... '. He too obviously liked the 'play' fighting 'and all the funny stuff'.

Drawing 6: 8-year-old boy's picture with The Barn (character on the left)

This 'search for excitement and fun' (Götz et al. 2005, 202) is a theme that has emerged from other researchers' work with children (see also Palmer 1986, 45) and it is quite evidently a strong drive for these two boys. Götz et al. (2005) found that this search for fun was central to the make-believe worlds of the children in their research. But what is particularly interesting about the ways in which children engage with the fun and excitement offered by television programs is how they choose certain elements, focusing on these in a way that connects with their own lives and interests. Of the numerous quirky story-lines and characters of *Adventure Time*, the two boys in my research were absorbed in the lives of the two 'people' – who might have been 'boys' – and revelled in what was to them an entertainingly fractious relationship. This active engagement with media reflects the findings of Götz et al. (2005, 109):

> Children use media stories as a springboard for their own themes and their individual narratives in which they process their experiences. In their make-believe stories with media material, they represent their perceptions of their worlds and reconstruct them in a subjectively meaningful way.

As argued in Chapter 4, this is not to suggest that the most important feature of what children 'do' with media must be to develop their own social and cultural identities; it is rather to acknowledge the complexity of their engagement with television. The stories created by these two boys, centred on a favourite show, *Adventure Time*, are interwoven with elements of their own experience and they draw on the characters and stories in ways that reflect and interact with their perceptions of their own worlds (e.g. the dog loves sandwiches, the boys go out into the fresh air to play, the thrills of 'play' fighting). But it is the search for fun that

CHAPTER 5

appears to run through the whole – that is the driving emotion that connects them to this favourite TV show and keeps bringing them back to it. As McKee et al. (2014, 6) argue, 'at the very core of why audiences consume entertainment is the satisfaction or "pleasure" that they derive from doing so'.

It appears from the analysis of my research with children that favourite television programs can prompt a whole range of pleasurable emotions, all of which might be encompassed in children's description of television as 'fun'. Here the same two 8-year-old boys talk about their particular responses to TV:

Interviewer: What do you think – like, think of the emotions when you watch television. What are the ones?

Boy 1: Happy.

Interviewer: What?

Boy 2: Happy, funny, sad and stuff like that.

Boy 1: I think like happy, sad, dramatic, annoying.

Interviewer: Annoying?

Boy 1: It's funny, ah sad. I don't know [unclear].

Interviewer: Scary or exciting?

Boy 2: Yeah, scary, yeah. Definitely.

Boy 1: Exciting.

Interviewer: Do you like scary?

Boy 2: Yeah!

Boy 1: Yes, and emotional.

Boy 2: Emotional.

This is a rich description of the range of emotions these boys feel when watching their favourite programs and gives a clear picture of the wide-ranging 'fun' of television for the two 8-year-olds. In the tumble of words, their comments certainly reflect the element of 'unruly delight' that Dyer (1992, 7) has observed is an essential element of the enjoyment of entertainment. Buckingham discovered similar responses in his research with children who watched the English soap opera serial *EastEnders* (p 200): 'they were by turns moved, deeply involved, amused, bored, mocking and irreverent'. He commented on the 'playful way in which they were able to move between these different positions' and this is an element reflected in the conversation above between the two boys in my research.

Interestingly, Boy 1's first response to my question at the start of this segment was to say that the television programs made him feel 'happy'. This was a recurrent theme in my research as is evident also from these children's comments about favourite shows:

> They are funny and make you feel good (9-year-old girl)

> Because it chse (cheers) you up when you are sad (8-year-old girl)

Dyer (1992, 7) has commented on the ways that entertainment 'works with the desires that circulate in a given society at a given time ... [and] plays a major role in the social construction of happiness'. In these two comments the pleasure the children take in their favourite shows comes in part from the expectation that it will make them happy. This is perhaps a desire circulating in our society: to escape the grind of daily life, have a laugh and 'feel good'. Dyer suggests (1992, 13) that this is part of the richness offered in our lives by entertainment:

the richness and variety of the actual forms of leisure suggest that leisure should also be seen as the creation of meaning in a world in which work and the daily round are characterized by drudgery, insistence and meaninglessness.

As Jenkins suggests, 'entertainment gratifies because it holds open the imagined possibility of satisfying spectators' actual lacks and desires' (2013, 287). This observation is closely reflected in the following comment from an 8-year-old boy (the one who loves the play fighting of Finn and The Barn): 'If I could create a TV I'd make a TV that was good for you and you could watch it whenever you wanted and you never get bored'.

Implicit in this comment is the assumption that in an ideal world the TV programs would always be fun, never boring; that the child could have as much fun as possible by being allowed to watch whenever he wanted; and that he wouldn't feel guilty about simply enjoying it because this would be 'good for you'. In other words having fun would be the 'valuable end in itself' (McKee 2008, 6). His comments touch on the dominant discourses that prevail around children and television: that television is a time-waster that offers illicit pleasure that is not 'good for you'; and that parents must police it carefully. The boy's gently reflective tone indicates that he is aware his dream is unlikely to be realised entirely but it does show that he sees television as playing a central role in providing enjoyment in life and an escape from its 'drudgery'. A world without restrictions on television would certainly be a place where the boy would expect to be happy.

One of the 10-year-old girls in my interviews carefully endeavoured to explain her feelings for her favourite program, *Seinfeld*, and how it made her happy. In an earlier interview she had described this as one of her favourite shows because 'it's like really funny all the time'.

Interestingly, she appears in the segment below not simply to be answering the question for the interviewer, but rather to be exploring for her own sake the reasons *why* this program makes her happy:

> When I watch *Seinfeld* I'll always be happy cos it's like one of the things I like enjoy doing the most. And I always watch TV when I have spare time and when I watch Seinfeld I feel happy. And I feel happy to watch a new one cos I haven't watched all of them, so that's what I really like about it.

Happiness is central to this young girl's experience of watching her favourite show. She works hard at trying to form her thoughts and articulate her feelings about this favourite, and 'happy' appears three times in her explanation. In her own hierarchy of fun, watching *Seinfeld* is at the top; it is what she enjoys 'doing the most' and is her first choice to fill any spare leisure time. That's because of the way it makes her feel. The new programs obviously provide extra delight, but the old ones too are a guarantee of happiness. She can always expect to 'feel happy' by tuning in to her favourite television show.

Maya Götz (2011) found a similar reaction to television favourites in her research with 716 German children aged 6 to 12 years old. Her research focused on children's responses to their favourite characters and on how they used these characters in developing and understanding their own identities but nonetheless her findings echo the responses of the children in my research. Götz (2011, 29) found that:

> The favourite TV character is someone who touches them in an emotionally positive way. Watching the show, spending time with the character, and having fun with her or him arouses a really good feeling.

CHAPTER 5

She pointed out that the triggers that provoked this feeling could be very different depending, for example, on the child's sense of humour. But what was the same was that children chose their favourites largely because they made them feel good – or perhaps 'happy' in the words of the 10-year-old *Seinfeld* fan.

The children here touch on something that Dyer (2002) has found to be central to our responses to and engagement with entertainment. His purpose was to define entertainment more broadly but his insights are useful in understanding children's engagement with their favourite television shows. Dyer's (2002, 3) argument is that 'entertainment's representations have been especially concerned with temporarily providing, but also in the process defining, happiness' and that 'we need constantly to have entertainment's ideas and experiences of what happiness might be and to reflect on them'. In her search for an explanation of why she likes watching her favourite program and how it makes her feel, the 10-year-old in my interview above appeared to be doing just what Dyer describes; she is reflecting on why she likes watching *Seinfeld* and what this feeling represents for her. There is no question but that it is a feeling of value and that it fills her leisure hours with joy.

CONCLUSION

But release me from my bands
With the help of your good hands.
Gentle breath of yours my sails
Must fill, or else my project fails,
Which was to please. Now I want
Spirits to enforce, art to enchant;
And my ending is despair
Unless I be relieved by prayer,
Which pierces so that it assaults
Mercy itself, and frees all faults.
As you from crimes would pardoned be,
Let your indulgence set me free.
(William Shakespeare, *The Tempest*, Act 5, scene 1, lines 327-38)

The desire to entertain and to be entertained is a powerful one. Arguably one of the greatest entertainers of all time, Shakespeare understood its centrality to human existence – and to the success of his own plays. His epilogue from *The Tempest* seeks a favourable response from each audience that it encounters – and in doing so acknowledges his purpose 'which was to please'. But in order to be pleased the audience must be able to see through 'the "pleasing stuff" of the play … to the conduct of human relationships within' (Hartley 2008, 183). The enduring appeal for more than 400 years of Shakespeare's plays attests to his ability as an entertainer to provide such insights: all of which were an integral part of the humour, the drama and the fun. Today it is apparent the audience seeks the same pleasure from the 'universality' of the popular shows on television: today's 'true heir' to Shakespeare's theatre (Hawkes 1973, 231). In the comedies of Chris Lilley, for example, the provocative humour that cleverly reveals insights into quirks of character and the wide variety of human relationships is what draws the laughter and interest of the audience. This is what marks its appeal for the 10-year-old girl in my research:

> Well to me it sorta shows like different views of different people like it might be like just a comedy for people to enjoy but I sorta see it as well, like, a comedy and sort of like what some of the stuff that happens in real life.

The relationship between the entertainer and the audience is of course essential to the success of the entertainment: to its success in providing pleasure not only to the audience but to the entertainer as well. The audience is an active player in this game of pleasure as is so clearly indicated in Shakespeare's epilogue to *The Tempest*. Through Prospero's plea, Shakespeare invites the most immediately available acknowledgment that an audience can give of its pleasure: the applause of 'your good hands'. This is a literal expression of the spectators' active engagement in the entertainment. But Shakespeare realises the audience's connection with the play goes far deeper and as a result he can demand even more from it: 'Let your indulgence set me free'. As with much of the playwright's language, the meanings of this phrase are multi-layered. He is asking for the audience's indulgence if the play is imperfect or disappointing and hopes it will 'free all faults'; he hints, with a touch of irony, that it might have divine powers and be able to grant the indulgences that can

CONCLUSION

be offered to sinners for the remission of sins; and he suggests that the audience should indulge its own pleasure through abandoning itself to the delights of his play. Through doing this the spectators will grant the playwright pleasure too and enable him to achieve his own desire: 'which was to please'. This conferral of pleasure will in turn set the entertainer free. In this one epilogue Shakespeare provides a fascinating insight into the depth and breadth of the pleasure of entertainment that acknowledges the intensity of its appeal to all of us.

Shakespeare's epilogue makes it quite clear that entertainment gives agency to the audience; there is no sense in which the audience could be regarded as passive. The spectators are the ones who can release the performers (and the playwright) 'from his bands'. It is clear that these audience members will choose their own pleasure – and will let this be known – vociferously. The audiences are plainly expected to take from the entertainment that which appeals to them. Prospero, and Puck, who begs the audience to 'Give me your hands' at the end of *A Midsummer Night's Dream*, might cajole, enchant, and manipulate the adults that come into the orbit of their plays; but in the end they have to negotiate with their audience and acknowledge its power over them. 'Gentles, do not reprehend:/If you pardon, we will mend', Puck pleads in the play's epilogue (William Shakespeare, *A Midsummer Night's Dream*, Act 5, scene 1, lines 407-8).

In seeking the indulgence of the audience, Shakespeare is aware of the endlessly varied ways the audience might respond; his task is truly enormous, to entertain such a diverse group as crowded into the theatres of his day, all of whom expected a great deal from their entertainment as is apparent from Prospero's appeals. So momentous is this task that should he fail he declares 'my ending is despair'.

Through the sardonic wit of this hyperbole, Shakespeare pokes fun at the 'life or death' importance that both he and his audience give to the pleasure of entertainment. And yet he also recognises that there is an element of truth in his words; life would be desperate without entertainment: it has an essential importance in our lives.

Part of the genius of Shakespeare lay in his ability to please his demandingly diverse audience:

> He was the supreme master of mass entertainment, as accessible to the unlettered groundlings standing in the pit as to the elite ensconced in their cushioned chairs ... he was indifferent to the rules and hostile to attempts to patrol the boundaries of artistic taste. (Greenblatt 2016)

The range of Shakespeare's audience, if not the size, could surely be compared to that tuned in to today's television: both include Greenblatt's 'unlettered groundlings' and 'the elites'. Greenblatt's comments on the playwright's paramount focus on the entertainment of his audience could also equally describe the goal of the producers of television today. In comparing the international hit reality television show, *Big Brother*, to Shakespeare's *The Taming of the Shrew*, Hartley (2008, 183) notes that both were 'full of stagy artifice – disguises, inversions, cross-dressing – and [were] not above some bawdy humor'; both sought also to provide 'modern interactive commercial entertainment'. The physical surrounds for Shakespeare's plays and today's television programs might be quite different but the central *raison d'être* of the two forms of entertainment is, as Hartley (2008, chap. 9) and Hawkes (1973, chap. 12) have noted, the same.

This drive to indulge in the pleasure of entertainment, so clearly expressed in Shakespeare's epilogues, is also fundamental to audiences' attraction to television. Their active engagement in seeking out their own pleasure is clearly evident in the analysis of my research with children. It would be surely ridiculous to suggest that today's audience was any more passive than that in Shakespeare's day simply because the level of physical comfort in watching the entertainment is different. And yet the picture of the child slumped before the screen, deliciously ensconced in a comfortable sofa, appears to lead some researchers to believe that this child has only a 'low involvement' (Comstock and Scharrer 2007, 48) in the program she is watching and that such viewing is an ultimately unsatisfying and anti-social experience (Putnam 2001, 241). To some writers this is not even the worst of it: the picture of the idle child in front of the screen so incenses Marie Winn (1985) that she rails against television's dangerous narcotic pleasures. But if you listen to children themselves talk about their attraction to television, these descriptions of a comatose child hypnotised by the screen are revealed quickly as the falsely-perceived images that they are. Children's active and often physical engagement with their favourite shows is equal to that demonstrated by spectators in The Globe as can be seen from the descriptions of the children in my research who were gripped with edge-of-the-seat anticipation in front of the screen (see Chapter 4).

Shakespeare understood how important it was to talk directly to his audience 400 years ago because he understood their passionate, and discerning, connection to their entertainment. He knew that his audiences expected much from his entertainment, just as it is clear today that children expect a great deal from their favourite television shows. Children seek out television because it provides pleasure – it is fun – and as was evident in my research there is nothing about that drive that is passive.

As did Shakespeare's plays, television entertainment too gives agency to the audience. The children in my research clearly had the capacity to discern their own pleasure, seek it out and share it with others. Something that can offer such access to pleasure surely has to be 'the funnest thing in the world' (8-year-old boy). For a 10-year-old girl the delight of television was that it 'means i can have a little world of monsters or anything'. The active use of her imagination in connection with television promises this girl her own dream world. For another child the best thing about television was that the enjoyment was shared with her mother – 'mum and I watch a lot of TV shows together and it helps us bond' – and for a further 10-year-old girl the delicious pleasure of sharing laughter at an off-the-cuff joke was clear: 'And my mum and I were falling out of our seats!'

At the end of Shakespeare's plays, the actors can literally hear from the audience; its response to the entertainment is audible in ways that the television's is not. But, as Shakespeare so clearly understood, the ways in which entertainment communicates with its audience are endless and varied, and this, I believe, is no less true of television than it was of the theatre of 16th and 17th century England. The essence of the rapport between television and its audience is perfectly captured by a 10-year-old girl in my research who said that the best thing about television was that 'it laughs with you not at you'. The connection is direct and the pleasure shared – in their own way the audience and the entertainer are as intertwined as the actor and spectators in Prospero's epilogue.

Television brings the viewer into its frame, I would suggest, through its sharing of the pleasures of entertainment. We get a clear glimpse of the way this works in the stories of the children in my research. While the spectators in Shakespeare's time shared the same space

CONCLUSION

and could literally speak to the actors, this does happen also with television, though of course in a metaphorical sense. The ways in which this occurs are delightfully revealed in two of the stories shared by the children in my research. The television is able literally to suck the viewer into its world, as we saw in the story of the 8-year-old boy who loved *Adventure Time* (see Chapter 5). At first glance this action of a disembodied screen appears slightly sinister if not malevolent. But in the drawing that accompanies the boy's story we see that on the other side of the screen there's a make-believe world of green fields and blue lakes. The boy's story is undeniably filled with pleasure; which includes not just the joy of playing with favourite cartoon characters in the fresh outdoors, but also the visceral thrill of being sucked into the devouring screen. These are all elements of the entertainment that teaches us the enjoyment of 'unruly delight' (Dyer 1992, 7).

The way in which television entertainment merges with real life around the screen (Hawkes 1973, 232), an element that gives it its power and interest, is also evident in the story of the 10-year-old girl who drew a picture of her home (see Chapter 4). In her drawing, the family cat has appeared *inside* the TV screen while the television character is walking through the front door of her house; television quite literally has merged with real life. These scenes delightfully present a picture of the ways in which television and its pleasures circulate – through and with the imagination and joys of their audiences – within the physical and imaginative surroundings of the viewer. Such a presence surely echoes the elements of participation, influence and control that were shared between the playwright, the actors and the audiences within the confines of The Globe theatre.

'Let your indulgence set me free' might be the words our children could speak to us, the adult guardians of their innocence, around the television set. Perhaps we should consider how we can indulge the pleasures that our children seek from the screen's entertainment and allow their indulgence in the fun of it. While this might be an utopian hope, beyond achievement in the real world, perhaps we could consciously attempt to set them free from the fearful negative controls that threaten to shut down the child's laughter and allow this child to enjoy what Kincaid (1998, 281) has so delightfully described as 'the full altogether of its pleasure'.

Over 400 years ago *Twelfth Night* audiences were no doubt thrilled to hear the final line of the closing song from the players who deliver the epilogue to that play: 'we'll strive to please you every day'. This might be the aim of the modern day producers of entertainment – which of course includes televisual entertainment. Given the drive to seek out the pleasures of entertainment, from both the entertainers and the audience, it seems that those who would curtail such delights are on the losing side. For children this can only be a good thing – when you consider the obvious fun they get from its cartoons, soap operas and ridiculous slapstick. A loosening of the regulations might perhaps result in the happy ending that is one of the joys of television identified by an 8-year-old girl in my research. What so delights her about her favourite program is that 'everything is good in the end'.

Why would we deny a 'feel' of this utopia (Dyer 2002, 20) to our children? Or deny the pleasures that television so obviously shares? Shouldn't there perhaps be room in our living rooms to just 'goof off' – something which was obviously precious to the 8-year-old boys in my research?

CONCLUSION

As I come to the end of this book I feel for my own part that I have succeeded just a little with one of my primary audiences, the one I felt I was bound to hear: the children who took part in my research. I heard two of the 10-year-old children talking to each other as they walked away from our interview. 'That was fun', one of them said. And the other immediately agreed.

My book has not sought to examine the content of television programs themselves: this would be a direction for further research. Rather it has sought to reflect directly on the fun that audiences (in this particular case, children) get from televisual content. Of course we have no direct evidence of what Shakespeare's audiences felt and thought of his plays; but we do have the incontrovertible evidence of his own words that to the playwright himself the pleasure of the entertainment was paramount. And I would argue this was evident in the analysis of my research with children: they watch television because it is fun.

Audiences apparently seek from television what they like and want and this means that there will be as many variations in the individual responses to programs as there are viewers. But it does seem that for children at least the desire to seek out what will provide happiness, pleasure and perhaps a 'feel' of utopia (Dyer 2002, 20) – however that manifests itself – whether through action, excitement, humour or learning – drives children to watch favourite programs. If we accept that, we might change the questions we ask about television's effect on children, and perhaps examine the ways in which we might enhance the pleasure they take in the fun of it. We might invest instead in continuing to find, as Shakespeare so effectively did, ways to please 'every day'.

SQUARE EYES

A great while ago the world begun,
with hey, ho, the wind and the rain;
But that's all one, our play is done,
And we'll strive to please you every day.
(William Shakespeare, *Twelfth Night*, Act 5, scene 1, lines 394-7)

APPENDIX

Research Details

Methods and Approaches

The methods I employed to gather my data involved three processes undertaken across a six-month period: a survey, three interviews, with one of these involving the children drawing or writing a story, and an element of participant observation. Through all these stages I sought to build a relationship with the children, using humour and an approach that allowed them to lead the conversation. The aim was to 'place the child … at the centre as "expert" on their own worlds, focusing on their own meaning-making' (Leitch 2008, 51). This approach appeared to be appreciated by a number of the children including this 8-year-old girl:

> You've made this ahh … fun and interesting, like you haven't made it like really um boring or I was going to say that but um really putting pressure on us like you're just making it go with the flow.

At the beginning of my research I spent some time standing around in the playground of the school where I conducted my research. This created an opportunity for informal chats with some of the children that I interviewed, thus enabling me to build a rapport with them in an environment outside the interview room. I was conscious that I was working in a school environment with its implications for how children might expect to behave in relationship to an adult, and I sought to present myself as an adult that was not a teacher or a parent, but someone who was interested in listening to, and learning from, their views. Some of the children were actively curious about my role and felt confident enough to inquire about it during the interviews, as is evident in this exchange with an 8-year-old girl:

Girl I've just got a question. How long have you been interviewing kids? About television?

Interviewer About this television, for this particular project I'm doing? Only since the beginning of the year when I first came.

Girl So you do different interviews with different people on different topics?

Interviewer Yeah.

In creating an informal relationship with the children I hoped to enable them to feel comfortable and confident about speaking about their views even when these might be in opposition to established discourses, particularly those reinforced in a school setting and when talking to an adult. I sought to keep in mind the context of my research and its influence, acknowledging the advice of researchers such as Barker and Weller (2003, 51):

> Although researchers attempt to place children at the centre of the research process, and can obtain some very eloquent and in depth glimpses into children's lives, researchers must also be aware of the context of the spaces in which the research is undertaken.

Even though I was not only interviewing the children but was offering an alternative in the session where they could create a story

APPENDIX

around television, I was cognisant of Buckingham's (2009b, 643) warning against assuming that inviting children to create their own drawings will release them from the influence of their surroundings and of their expectations:

> Drawing and creative story-writing are routine classroom activities, and in that context they have their own implicit rules and expectations [and are] not merely open invitations to children to express themselves.

I was conscious that it is important to recognise such constraints in order to understand their influence on the research but also in order to allow the researcher to create a more relaxed environment for the research participants. As Margaret Hagerman (2010, 95) observes, 'privileging the viewpoints and experiences of youth and distancing oneself from forms of authority in the kid's lives contribute to the establishment of rapport'.

Getting to know the children, making it clear that I was interested in what they had to say and that this research was not part of classroom instruction were important in creating a space where they felt able to express their views and even to enjoy the drawing and writing of their stories. That such an approach works in enabling children to break free of such constraints has been observed by other researchers such as Ruth Leitch (2008, 52) who writes about the value of using visual methods such as drawing in research with children:

> Children know what to do and what to expect and yet, within a research framework, the process can work somewhat differently, taking researchers into children's socio-emotional worlds outside the borders of normal classroom discourse and practice.

It is not that I expected to uncover the 'objective, universal truth of children's experiences' but rather, as Barker and Weller (2003, 52) note, 'through children centred research methods, we can offer partial glimpses that reflect in one form the complexity and diversity of children's lives'.

The quantitative method that I used in my multi-method approach was based on collecting data from a survey with children with closed questions. The qualitative methods involved collecting data from the open questions in the survey, the interviews with children, their drawings and stories, and from my own findings from participant observation.

I conducted my research with children aged 7 to 11 from one public primary school in the Australian city of Sydney. Practical reasons informed this choice in that school is an easy place to find groups of children of the same age in one place. The inner city school that I chose represented a diverse socioeconomic and ethnic population, including children from middle-class income groups and those who lived in social housing.

I began my research with a survey in which a total of 77 children took part; subsequently 20 of these self-selected to take part in the series of three interview sessions. In the survey 46% were male and 54% female. In the interviews there were 13 females and 7 males. Of these, 10 were from Year 3 (one aged 7, nine aged 8) and 10 from Year 5 (all aged 10). While it is not possible to generalise widely from such a small sample, this approach was designed to seek a range of views from the different genders, and from diverse ethnic and socioeconomic groups. I believe the choice of school supported these aims. I acknowledge that this is a relatively small sample but my aim was to gather thick and rich qualitative data, while paying attention to the need to include a diverse range of children.

APPENDIX

The reason for choosing this age group was also informed by some practical considerations. It is an age when children are still watching television as a significant source of entertainment, before this drops slightly in the teenage years according to the most recent Australian data available (Australian Communications and Media Authority 2011, 2). Although hours of television watched (on a television screen) were down slightly in 2013 on 2001 figures (33 minutes less) children are now accessing television programs through online sources (Australian Communications and Media Authority 2015b). Primary school children are also more articulate than the younger preschoolers and so the data from interviews is more easily collected and analysed.

For the first part of the mixed method approach I collected both quantitative and qualitative data from a survey of 77 children in Years 3 and 5 at the school. The closed questions were designed to collect some basic quantitative information related to rules and regulations around television at home and television viewing habits (where and when they watch and on what technology). In the design of the questionnaire I also sought some indication of how the dominant negative discourses affected children's responses; this is reflected in the placing of three slightly different questions, at different spots in the survey, that sought children's views about what they thought were the good, bad and best aspects of television. The open questions were designed to ask what they liked about television and how the stories of their favourite programs informed their lives. These questions were also designed to give me further insights into the direction my research might take throughout the interviews and this proved to be fruitful. The responses to the survey questions indicated to me that the children got significant enjoyment from their favourite programs and that the 'fun' of television was something highly valued by almost all of those who took part in the survey. This was an insight that directed me into a rich avenue of research that I pursued more closely in the interviews. The small degree of participant observation conducted during the surveys also indicated to me the significance to children of the shared enjoyment of television. I observed during the time they were at the computers that a number of the children took the opportunity when they got to the question on favourite programs to start talking to their friends (many had sat at computers next to their friends). Some got quite excited about talking about their favourite characters and this was a pattern reflected quite strongly in the later interviews. A number of the children also appeared to take their participation in this research quite seriously. These students turned occasionally to their friends and at other times to either me or the teacher for help with spelling. This reflects what Hagerman (2010, 61) found: that children 'enjoyed the experience of participating in child-centred social research [and] maintained serious attitudes toward their inclusion in social research'.

I designed an online survey for this element of my research for a number of reasons. It minimised administration and organisation on the part of the school and teachers (no paperwork to be handed out and collected) and it also was a good way of keeping the children's responses confidential as only I had access to the responses online and the responses did not include the children's names. But most importantly it was more enjoyable for the children. The children mostly enjoy their time in the computer labs at school, both because it takes them away from written school tasks and also because they are allowed spare time on the computers at the end of their lessons. They had an opportunity to do this when they had completed my

APPENDIX

survey. Children often find written questionnaires 'boring' (Barker and Weller 2003, 36) so an online survey was an attempt to mitigate this negative factor.

The survey was conducted in the first week of the school year before formal classes had been allocated and was therefore a time of greater informality in the school. I believe this helped to create a more relaxed atmosphere for the children where there was less pressure for them to conform to what they might perceive to be the expectations of the adults to respond to the survey questions in a certain manner. I introduced myself at this time in the company of a teacher and explained the aims of the research. I focused on telling them that I was interested in their own views about television and what they liked to watch.

As it turned out, the computer lab was a good place to conduct the survey as the children did appear to be more relaxed and felt able to chat to their friends as they completed the questionnaire. At some stages they quite animatedly talked about their favourite shows, obviously enjoying this opportunity to talk about television. The whole process took about one and a half hours but as the children finished the survey they were allowed to play on the computers until the school bell went and this also helped to create an atmosphere perhaps more focused on leisure and its enjoyment than prevails in the usual classroom learning environment.

At this time I also explained that I would be looking for children who would be interested in talking to me further about television and that I would be giving them consent forms to take home to their parents to sign, if they were interested in doing the interviews. The survey session thus offered an opportunity to allow the children to make a more informed decision about participating in the further interviews as they got an idea of the nature of the research and what questions were being asked. After this stage, the children were given the choice themselves about participating in the next phase of my research.

The next phase of the mixed method approach collected qualitative data from interviews with a total of 20 children. These interviews included a session where they were asked to draw a picture and/or write a story that was connected with one of their favourite television programs.

The participant observation involved noting the children's responses and interactions during the survey and the interviews, in particular the interview sessions where they drew or wrote their own story. It also involved my spending time in the playground before and after the surveys and around the time of the interviews, and when I walked to and from the classrooms with the children after collecting them for the interviews. Although this was a small part of my research data it allowed me not only to learn more about their engagement with television but also to build a rapport with the children that enabled them to feel more comfortable with me. I aimed to be a 'low-key but friendly presence' (Palmer 1986, 24) and to establish 'non-verbal communication' (Hagerman 2010, 88) with the children. Such practice is well-established:

> Hanging about is a well known research activity (Whyte 1943) and one that allows the researcher to get to know participants in more informal ways. Being there, joining in conversations and asking questions about everyday events helped to build relationships. … Trust was gained through the researcher being accepted and someone that showed interest in what they had to say. (France, Bendelow and Williams 2000, 157)

APPENDIX

Hagerman (2010, 87-8) has noted the value of participant observation, arguing that she 'was able to capture details of the interview experience that could not possibly be conveyed via the verbal statements or the children's artwork'. I followed her example and took notes after and sometimes during the interviews (when the children were engaged with their drawings or stories) and I found, as Hagerman observed, that the notes 'capture forms of nonverbal communication' (p. 88) between the researcher and the children.

For the interview process, I decided to conduct the interviews in 'friendship pairs'. This decision took into account the comfort levels of the children and the impact of group dynamics. With one friend accompanying her, a child will feel more comfortable talking to a relatively unknown adult (Flewitt 2014, 142; Mayall 2008, 112). By keeping the number down to two, I also hoped to avoid the pitfalls of groups, such as dominance by some children (Dockrell, Lewis and Lindsay 2000, 52). Interviewing in pairs can also show 'aspects of their affective relationships' (Mayall 2008, 122) and this was certainly a rich source of information for me, revealing the children's joy in sharing the fun of television. By conducting three interviews over a period of six months, I sought to build up trust with the children and thus create an opportunity for the children to feel comfortable to speak freely and openly (Lewis and Lindsay 2000, 195).

I adopted a semi-structured interview approach (Flewitt 2014, 149) where I had a set of questions at the start but during the interview I allowed the conversation to wander. By doing this I hoped to give the children space to talk about television in the ways they wanted to. I understood that my presence as a relatively unknown adult would constrain this talk in some ways but research has shown that this method allows the researcher 'somewhat to hand over the agenda to children, so that they can control the pace and direction of the conversation' (Mayall 2008, 121).

This approach was also informed by the model outlined by Lundy (2007, 922) that indicates a way of implementing Article 12 of the CRC by focusing on its four key elements:

> Space: Children must be given the opportunity to express a view; Voice: Children must be facilitated to express their views; Audience: The view must be listened to; Influence: The view must be acted upon, as appropriate.

I believe that the interview approach that I took gave the children space to speak out and an opportunity for me to show that I was listening and to explain how I would share their views to a wider audience through my research.

Using Visual Research

As noted above, the second interview in my research was based on a session where I invited the children to draw a picture or write a story related to a favourite television program. Such visual research with children has developed extensively over the past decade and contributed significantly to rich data on a wide range of issues (Thomson 2008b). It is a way of bringing children's voices 'into the project in more diverse ways' (Bragg and Buckingham 2008, 118) and the children in my research enjoyed this opportunity. As Pat Thomson (2008a, 11) observes:

> Images communicate in different ways than words. They quickly elicit aesthetic and emotional responses as well as intellectual ones (Freedman 2003) ... Furthermore, when children and

APPENDIX

young people are themselves engaged in visual research, they also seem to take pleasure in the process, suggest that they are 'getting something' out of their participation and, if they are students, compare the word-laden nature of schooling and the enjoyment gained from doing something different.

Certainly this was apparent in the responses and comments on their own drawings and stories expressed by the children in my research as I examine in Chapters 4 and 5.

In terms of the data that I hoped to collect from this process, I did not expect that the visual research would miraculously reveal previously 'uncovered' insights, psychological or otherwise. This view is supported by researchers such as Bragg (2011, 101) who challenged 'the notion that visual methods provide unmediated access to an "authentic" creative response, or indeed any kind of singular "voice"'. But as Bragg also noted, 'visual methods have rich potential and there are many sound reasons for using them in exploring less easily verbalized aspects of experience, creativity, informal knowledge and learning' (p. 101). I sought to include visual research in my multi-method approach to develop through analysis a deeper and richer picture of the ways children enjoy television and the visual research contributed to this aim. Bragg and Buckingham (2008, 121) observe of their use of visual research that 'the methods gave us access to a wider range of voices than might have been obtained through interviews alone' and I hoped to achieve the same outcome. I heeded their warning, however, that 'no data speak for themselves; we are never absolved of our responsibility to interpret' (p. 131).

My approach to enabling interpretation of the children's drawings and stories was based on the notion that I should hear from the children themselves on their own understanding of their stories to avoid the pitfalls of interpreting something wrongly. Lewis and Lindsay (2000, 193) warn that 'The more that a child's perspective is inferred indirectly, the greater the danger of misinterpreting or over interpreting what children present'. In order to facilitate this I arranged for the drawing and story-writing to happen in the second interview. During the third interview I then allowed time for them to reflect on and share with me their interpretation of their work. Leitch (2008, 53) argues that children 'need to be given the opportunity to express and explain their response in follow-up interview-type situations'. Not only does this avoid misinterpretation by adult researchers, it also allows for a fuller recognition of their right to be heard, and listened to, thus allowing children to take a more active role in the research process:

> when researchers invite children to reflect on … their own drawings, … they are genuinely interested in hearing their ideas about what is going on in the image and what meaning(s) they are making of them and to recognize and facilitate a context in which the child or young person becomes an audience to themselves. (Leitch 2008, 53)

Enabling children to contribute their views more fully and widely in terms of using means other than simply speaking is also a right recognised in another article of the CRC. Article 13 states that children's right to freedom of expression includes a right to impart information 'either orally, in writing or print, in the form of art, or through any other media of the child's choice'. This too then informed my decision to undertake visual research for my study.

This multi-method approach enabled me to collect deep and rich qualitative data from children themselves on what televisual content they watch and enjoy and how they engage with such content, which

APPENDIX

are central aims of the project. This approach also directly fulfilled the aim of the study to allow children to speak out and express themselves on an issue of importance to their lives.

BIBLIOGRAPHY

Anderson, DR 1998, 'Educational television is not an oxymoron', *Annals of the American Academy of Political and Social Science*, vol. 557, pp. 24-38.

Anderson, DR and Bryant, J 1983, *Children's Understanding of Television: Research on Attention and Comprehension*, Academic Press, New York.

Anderson, DR, Bryant, J, Murray, JP, Rich, M, Rivkin, MJ and Zillmann, D 2006, 'Brain Imaging-An Introduction to a New Approach to Studying Media Processes and Effects', *Media Psychology*, vol. 8, no. 1, pp. 1-6.

Anderson, DR, Huston, AC, Schmitt, KL, Linebarger, DL and Wright, JC 2001, 'Early childhood television viewing and adolescent behaviour: The recontact study', *Monographs of the Society for Research in Child Development*, vol. 66, no. 1, pp. 1-147.

Ang, I 1990, 'Wanted: Audiences: On the politics of empirical audience research', in E Seiter, H Borchers, G Kreutzner and E-M Warth (eds.), *Remote Control: Television, audiences, and cultural power*, Routledge, London.

Ang, I 1991, *Desperately Seeking the Audience*, Routledge, London.

Ariès, P 1973, *Centuries of Childhood*, Penguin, Harmondsworth.

Arizpe, E and Styles, M (eds) 2003, *Children Reading Pictures: Interpreting Visual Texts*, RoutledgeFalmer, London.

Arthur, L 2005, 'Popular culture: views of parents and educators', in J Marsh (ed.), *Popular culture, new media and digital literacy in early childhood*, Routledge, Abingdon, Oxon.

Australian Communications and Media Authority 2007, *Media and communications in Australian families 2007: report of the media and society research project*, Australian Communications and Media Authority, Melbourne.

Australian Communications and Media Authority 2009, *Use of Electronic Media and Communications: Early Childhood to Teenage Years*, Australian Communications and Media Authority, Melbourne.

Australian Communications and Media Authority 2011, *Digital Australians - Expectations about media content in a converging media environment: qualitative and quantitative research report*, Australian Communications and Media Authority, Melbourne.

Australian Communications and Media Authority 2015b, *Children's television viewing: research overview*, Australian Communications and Media Authority, Melbourne.

Barker, J and Weller, S 2003, '"Is it fun?" developing children centred research methods', *International Journal of Sociology and Social Policy*, vol. 23, no. 1/2, pp. 33-58.

Barker, L 2014, 'Too much screen time is harmful for children; what can parents do? ', *The Dallas Morning News*, 22 Sept, viewed 14 Sept 2015, http://www.dallasnews.com/lifestyles/health-and-fitness/health/20140922-too-much-screen-time-is-harmful-for-children-what-can-parents-do.ece

Barker, M 2001, 'The Newson report: a case study in 'common sense'', in M Barker and J Petley (eds.), *Ill Effects: The Media/Violence Debate*, 2nd edn, Routledge, London.

Barker, M and Brooks, K 1998, *Knowing Audiences: Judge Dredd, its Friends, Fans, and Foes*, University of Luton Press, Luton, U.K.

Barker, M and Petley, J 2001, *Ill Effects: The Media/Violence Debate*, 2nd edn, Routledge, London.

Barthes, R 1973, *Mythologies*, Paladin Grafton, London.

Bartsch, A 2012, 'Emotional Gratification in Entertainment Experience. Why Viewers of Movies and Television Series Find it Rewarding to Experience Emotions', *Media Psychology*, vol. 15, no. 3, pp. 267-302.

Bazalgette, C and Buckingham, D (eds) 1995, *In Front of the Children: Screen Entertainment and Young Audiences*, British Film Institute, London.

Bonner, FJ 2003, *Ordinary Television: Analyzing Popular TV*, Sage, London.

Bourdieu, P 1984, *Distinction: A Social Critique of the Judgement of Taste*, Routledge and Kegan Paul, London.

Bragg, S 2006, 'Like Shakespeare It's a Good Thing: Cultural Value in the Classroom', *Media International Australia, Incorporating Culture & Policy*, no. 120, pp. 130-141.

Bragg, S 2011, ''Now it's up to us to interpret it': youth voice and visual methods in creative learning and research', in P Thomson and J Sefton-Green (eds.), *Researching creative learning : methods and issues*, Routledge, Oxon.

Bragg, S and Buckingham, D 2008, ''Scrapbooks' as a resource in media research with young people', in P Thomson (ed.), *Doing Visual Research with Children and Young People*, Routledge, Oxon.

Bragg, S, Buckingham, D and Turnbull, S 2006, 'Media Education: Authority, Identity and Value; An Editorial Dialogue ', *Media International Australia, Incorporating Culture & Policy,*, vol. 120, pp. 76-89.

Bromley, H 2003, 'Putting yourself in the picture: a quesiton of talk', in E Arizpe and M Styles (eds.), *Children Reading Pictures: Interpreting Visual Texts*, RoutledgeFalmer, London.

Browne, R 2013, 'Screen violence changing young brains: researchers', *Sydney Morning Herald*, October 5-6, p.3.

Buckingham, D 1987, *Public secrets: EastEnders and its audience*, BFI Books, London.

Buckingham, D 1993a, *Children Talking Television: The Making of Television Literacy*, Falmer Press, Oxford.

Buckingham, D (ed.) 1993b, *Reading audiences: Young People and the Media*, Manchester University Press, Manchester.

Buckingham, D 1995, 'On the Impossibility of Children's Television: The Case of Timmy Mallet', in C Bazalgette and D Buckingham (eds.), *In Front of the Children: Screen Entertainment and Young Audiences*, British Film Institute, London.

BIBLIOGRAPHY

Buckingham, D 1996, *Moving Images: Understanding Children's Emotional Responses to Television*, Manchester University Press, Manchester.

Buckingham, D 1998a, 'Children and Television: A Critical Overview of the Research', in R Dickinson, R Harindranath and O Linné (eds.), *Approaches to Audiences: A Reader*, Arnold, London.

Buckingham, D 1998b, 'Doing Them Harm? Children's Conceptions of the Negative Effects of Television', in K Swan, C Meskill and S Demaio (eds.), *Social Learning from Broadcast Television*, Hampton Press, Cresskill, NJ.

Buckingham, D 2000, *After the Death of Childhood: Growing Up in the Age of Electronic Media*, Polity Press, Cambridge, UK.

Buckingham, D 2001a, 'Electronic child abuse? Rethinking the media's effects on children', in M Barker and J Petley (eds.), *Ill Effects: The Media/Violence Debate*, Routledge, London.

Buckingham, D 2001b, 'United Kingdom: Disney Dialectics: Debating the Politics of Children's Media Culture', in J Wasko, M Phillips and ER Meehan (eds.), *Dazzled by Disney?: The Global Disney Audiences Project*.

Buckingham, D 2002a, 'Child-centred Television?: Teletubbies and the Educational Imperative', in D Buckingham (ed.), *Small Screens: Television for Children*, Leicester University Press, London.

Buckingham, D 2008, 'Children and the media: A cultural studies approach', in K Drotner and S Livingstone (eds.), *International Handbook of Children, Media and Culture*, SAGE, London.

Buckingham, D 2009b, "'Creative' visual methods in media research: possibilities, problems and proposals', *Media, Culture & Society*, vol. 31, no. 4, pp. 633-652.

Buckingham, D and De Block, L 2007, 'Finding a global voice? Migrant children, new media and the limits of empowerment', in P Dahlgren (ed.), *Young Citizens and New Media: Learning for Democratic Participation*, Routledge, New York.

Buckingham, D and Jensen, HS 2012, 'Beyond "media panics": reconceptualising public debates about children and media', *Journal of Children and Media*, vol. 6, no. 4, pp. 413-429.

Burghardt, GM 2005, *The Genesis of Animal Play: Testing the Limits*, MIT, Cambridge, Mass.

Burns, J 2015, 'Inactive children 'become middle-aged couch potatoes'', *BBC News*, 16 March, viewed 16 March 2015, http://www.bbc.com/news/education-31876338

Bushman, BJ and Anderson, CA 2001, 'Media Violence and the American Public: Scientific Facts versus Media Misinformation', *American Psychologist*, vol. 56, no. 6, pp. 477-89.

Campbell, D 2013a, 'Peppa Pig: The wildly popular little brat leading our kids astray', *The Daily Telegraph*, 11 November, viewed 1 May 2015, http://www.dailytelegraph.com.au/news/opinion/peppa-pig-the-wildly-popular-little-brat-leading-our-kids-astray/story-fnh4jt60-1226757205661

Campbell, D 2013b, 'The ten worst kids TV characters', *Herald Sun*, 11 November, viewed 20 April 2015, http://www.heraldsun.com.au/news/opinion/the-10-worst-kids-tv-characters/story-fnh4jt62-1226763118892?nk=636a437d2d1f0bf46fad03701deed019

Carnagey, NL, Anderson, CA and Bartholow, BD 2007, 'Media violence and social neuroscience: New questions and new opportunities', *Current Directions in Psychological Science*, vol. 16, no. 4, pp. 178-182.

Carnegie, D 1937, *How to Win Friends and Influence People*, Simon and Schuster, New York.

Center on Media for Child Health 2005, 'The effects of electronic media on children ages zero to six: A history of research', Henry Kaiser Family Foundation, Menlo Park CA.

Committee on the Rights of the Child 2009, *General Comment No. 12 (2009): The right of the child to be heard*, UN/CRC/C/GC/12, United Nations, Geneva.

Committee on the Rights of the Child 2013, *General comment No. 17 (2013): The right of the child to rest, leisure, play, recreational activities, cultural life and the arts (art. 31)*, UN/CRC/C/GC/17, United Nations, Geneva.

Comstock, GA and Scharrer, E 2007, *Media and the American child*, Elsevier, Burlington, MA.

Corsaro, WA 2009, 'Peer culture', in J Qvortrup, WA Corsaro and M Honig (eds.), *The Palgrave Handbook of Childhood Studies*, Palgrave Macmillan, Basingstoke.

Corsaro, WA 2015, *The Sociology of Childhood*, 4th edn, Sage, Los Angeles.

Crockett, Z 2014, 'The Outing of Tinky Winky', *Priceonomics*, 6 October, viewed 23 October 2015, http://priceonomics.com/the-outing-of-tinky-winky/

Cupitt, M 1996, *Families and electronic entertainment*, Australian Broadcasting Authority and the Office of Film and Literature Classification, Sydney.

Davies, H, Buckingham, D and Kelley, P 2000, 'In the Worst Possible Taste: Children, Television and Cultural Value', *European Journal of Cultural Studies*, vol. 3, no. 1, pp. 5-25.

Davies, MM 1997, *Fake, Fact, and Fantasy: Children's Interpretations of Television Reality*, L. Erlbaum Associates, Mahwah, N.J.

Davies, MM 2001, *'Dear BBC': Children, Television Storytelling, and the Public Sphere*, Cambridge University Press, Cambridge.

Davies, MM 2002, 'Classics with clout: Costume drama in British and American children's television', in D Buckingham (ed.), *Small screens: television for children*, Leicester University Press, London.

Davies, MM 2004, 'Mickey and Mr Gumpy: The Global and the Universal in Children's Media', *European Journal of Cultural Studies*, vol. 7, pp. 425-40.

De Botton, A 2009, *The Pleasures and Sorrows of Work*, Hamish Hamilton, London.

Dickens, C 1981, *Great Expectations*, The Folio Society, London.

Dockrell, J, Lewis, A and Lindsay, G 2000, 'Researching children's perspectives: a psychological dimension', in A Lewis and G Lindsay (eds.), *Researching Children's Perspectives*, Open University Press, Buckingham.

Donald, J 1992, *Sentimental Education: Schooling, Popular Culture and the Regulation of Liberty*, Verso, London.

Donnelly, K 2012, 'Digital age is dumbing down our children', *The Australian*, 28 July, viewed 28 November 2014, http://www.theaustralian.com.au/national-affairs/opinion/digital-age-is-dumbing-down-our-children/story-e6frgd0x-1226436959981

BIBLIOGRAPHY

Drotner, K 2005, 'Mediatized Childhoods: Discourses, Dilemmas and Directions', in J Qvortrup (ed.), *Studies in Modern Childhood: Society, Agency, Culture*, Palgrave MacMillan, Hampshire.

Dyer, R 1992, *Only Entertainment*, Routledge, London; New York.

Dyer, R 2002, *Only Entertainment*, 2nd edn, Routledge, London.

Faulkner, J 2011, *The Importance of Being Innocent: Why We Worry about Children*, Cambridge University Press, New York.

Faulkner, K 2012, 'Is Peppa Pig making toddlers naughty? Parents despair as children copy cartoon by answering back', *Daily Mail Australia,* 9 January, viewed 18 July 2014, http://www.dailymail.co.uk/news/article-2084021/Is-Peppa-Pig-making-toddlers-naughty-Parents-despair-children-copy-cartoon-answering-back.html

Fiske, J 1989, *Television culture*, Routledge, London.

Fiske, J and Hartley, J 2003, *Reading Television*, 2nd ed.. edn, Routledge, London.

Fleer, M 2014, *Theorising Play in the Early Years*, Cambridge University Press, Melbourne.

Flewitt, R 2014, 'Interviews', in A Clark, R Flewitt, M Hammersley and M Robb (eds.), *Understanding research with children and young people*, Sage, London.

Fonseca, A 2017, 'Three reasons why television violence affects kids', *Livestrong. com,* 13 July, viewed 5 August 2017, http://www.livestrong.com/article/192272-three-reasons-why-television-violence-affects-kids/

France, A, Bendelow, G and Williams, S 2000, 'A 'risky' business: researching the health beliefs of children and young people', in A Lewis and G Lindsay (eds.), *Researching children's perspectives*, Open University Press, Buckingham.

Freedman, K 2003, *Teaching visual culture: curriculum, aesthetics, and the social life of art*, Teachers College Press, New York, NY.

Gans, H 1974, *Popular Culture and High Culture: An Analysis and Evaluation of Taste*, Basic Books, New York.

Gardner, A 2010, 'Kids' TV time linked to school woes, bad habits', *CNN Online,* 3 May, viewed 20 April 2015, http://edition.cnn.com/2010/HEALTH/05/03/kids.tv.school/

Gauntlett, D 1996, *Video Critical: Children, the Environment and Media Power*, John Libbey Media, Luton England.

Gauntlett, D 2005, *Moving Experiences: Media Effects and Beyond*, 2nd edn, John Libbey, Eastleigh.

Gauntlett, D 2007, *Creative Explorations: New Approaches to Identities and Audiences*, Routledge, London.

Gauntlett, D and Hill, A 1999, *TV Living: Television, Culture, and Everyday Life*, Routledge in association with the British Film Institute, London.

Gentile, DA (ed.) 2003, *Media Violence and Children: A Complete Guide for Parents and Professionals*, Greenwood Publishing Group, Connecticut.

Gerbner, G 1988, *Violence and Terror in the Mass Media*, Unesco, Paris, France.

Gerbner, G and Gross, L 1976, 'Living With Television: The Violence Profile', *Journal of Communication,* vol. 26, no. 2, pp. 173-199.

Gerbner, G, Holsti, OR, Krippendorff, K, Paisley, WJ and Stone, PJ (eds) 1969,

The Analysis of Communication Content: Developments in Scientific Theories and Computer Techniques, Wiley, New York.

Gillard, P 2002, 'Small Worlds: Research on Children and the Media in Australia', in T O'regan, M Balnaves and J Sternberg (eds.), *Mobilising the Audience*, Queensland University Press, St Lucia, Queensland.

Gitlin, T 1983, *Inside Prime Time*, 1st edn, Pantheon, New York.

Glenn, NM, Knight, CJ, Holt, NL and Spence, JC 2013, 'Meanings of Play among Children', *Childhood: A Global Journal of Child Research*, no. 2, pp. 185-199.

Götz, M 2006, 'What's Funny in Children's Comedy? Children judging comedy shows of German Public Broadcasters', *TelevIZIon*, vol. 19, no. E, pp. 62-66.

Götz, M 2011, 'What makes them so special? The utility value of children's favourite heroes and heroines', *TelevIZIon*, vol. 24, no. E, pp. 27-32.

Götz, M, Bulbulia, F, Fisch, S, Lemish, D, Davies, MM, Schauer, R and Homer, B 2006, 'Is that funny anywhere else? An international comparison of humour in children's programmes', *Televizion Online*, vol. 19, no. E, pp. 5.

Götz, M, Lemish, D, Aidman, A and Moon, H 2005, *Media and the Make-Believe Worlds of Children: When Harry Potter meets Pokémon in Disneyland*, Lawrence Erlbaum, Mahwah, N.J.

Gray, J 2008, *Television Entertainment*, Routledge, New York.

Greenblatt, S 2016, 'How Shakespeare lives now', *New York Review of Books*, April 21-May 11 edn, Rea S. Hederman, New York.

Gregg, M 2011, *Work's intimacy*, Polity Press, Cambridge, UK.

Hagerman, MA 2010, '"I Like Being Intervieeeeeeewed!": Kids' Perspectives on Participating in Social Research', in HB Johnson (ed.), *Children and Youth Speak for Themselves*, Emerald, Bingley, UK.

Hall, S 1986, 'Introduction', in D Morley (ed.), *Family television: cultural power and domestic leisure*, Comedia Publishing Group, London.

Hartley, J 1987a, 'Been There-Done That: On Academic Tourism', *Communication Research*, vol. 14, no. 2, pp. 251-261.

Hartley, J 1992a, *The Politics of Pictures: The Creation of the Public in the Age of Popular Media*, Routledge, London.

Hartley, J 1992b, *Tele-ology: Studies in Television*, Routledge, London; New York.

Hartley, J 1999, *Uses of Television*, Routledge, London.

Hartley, J 2003, *A Short History of Cultural Studies*, Sage, London.

Hartley, J 2008, *Television Truths*, Blackwell Publishing, Malden, MA.

Hawkes, T 1973, *Shakespeare's Talking Animals: Language and Drama in Society*, Edward Arnold, London.

Hayes, A and Jean, C 2012, 'A two-edged sword? The place of the media in a child friendly society', in W Warburton and D Braunstein (eds.), *Growing Up Fast and Furious: Reviewing the Impacts of Violent and Sexualised Media on Children*, The Federation Press, Sydney.

Henderson, E 2015, 'Watching lots of TV 'makes you stupid', say researchers Universities of California and San Francisco', *Independent*, 4 December, viewed 5 August 2016, http://www.independent.co.uk/news/science/watching-lots-of-tv-makes-you-stupid-says-american-universities-a6759026.html

BIBLIOGRAPHY

Hickman, L 2011, 'How Horrible Histories became a Huge Hit', *The Guardian*, 18 March, viewed 24 February 2015, http://www.theguardian.com/culture/2011/mar/17/horrible-histories-huge-hit

Higonnet, A 1998, *Pictures of Innocence: The History and Crisis of Ideal Childhood*, Thames and Hudson, New York.

Himmelweit, HT, Oppenheim, AN and Vince, P 1958, *Television and the Child: An Empirical Study of the Effect of Television on the Young*, Oxford University Press, London.

Hipsley, A 2011, 'Why too much TV is bad for kids', *ABC World Today*, 20 April, viewed 11 April, 2018, http://www.abc.net.au/worldtoday/content/2011/s3196728.htm

Hodge, B and Tripp, D 1986, *Children and Television: A Semiotic Approach*, Polity Press, Cambridge.

Howard, S 1998, 'Unbalanced minds?: Children thinking about television', in S Howard (ed.), *Wired-up: Young People and the Electronic Media*, UCL Press, London.

Howard, S and Roberts, S 1999, '"Teletubbies" downunder: The Australian experience', *Televizion Online*, vol. 12, no. 2, pp. 19-25.

Howard, S and Roberts, S 2002, 'Winning Hearts and Minds: television and the very young audience', *Contemporary Issues in Early Childhood*, vol. 3, no. 3, pp. 315-337.

Idato, M 2013, 'Bert and Ernie are gay? We always suspected, but...', *The Sydney Morning Herald*, 29 June, viewed 23 October 2015, http://www.smh.com.au/entertainment/tv-and-radio/bert-and-ernie-are-gay-we-always-suspected-but-20130629-2p3ft.html

Isenberg, JP and Quisenberry, N 2002, 'Play: Essential for All Children', *Childhood Education*, vol. 79, no. 1, pp. 33-39.

James, A 1998, 'Confections, Concoctions, and Conceptions', in H Jenkins (ed.), *The Children's Culture Reader*, New York University Press, New York.

James, A and James, A 2008, *Key Concepts in Childhood Studies*, SAGE, Los Angeles.

James, A, Jenks, C and Prout, A 1998, *Theorizing Childhood*, Polity Press, Cambridge, England.

Jenkins, H 1992, *Textual Poachers: Television Fans & Participatory Culture*, Routledge, New York.

Jenkins, H (ed.) 1998a, *The Children's Culture Reader*, New York University Press, New York.

Jenkins, H 1998b, 'The Sensuous Child: Benjamin Spock and the Sexual Revolution', in H Jenkins (ed.), *The Children's Culture Reader*, New York University Press, New York.

Jenkins, H 2013, *Textual poachers: television fans and participatory culture*, Updated 20th anniversary edn, Routledge, New York.

Johns, L 2012, 'On the joys of having no TV', *Daily Mail Australia*, 3 February, viewed 20 March 2015, http://www.dailymail.co.uk/debate/article-2095514/On-joys-having-TV-.html

Kincaid, JR 1998, *Erotic Innocence: The Culture of Child Molesting*, Duke University Press, Durham.

Kirkorian, HL, Wartella, EA and Anderson, DR 2008, 'Media and young children's learning', *The Future of Children,* vol. 18, no. 1, pp. 39-61.

Kleinman, Z 2013, 'Screen use is bad for brain development, scientist claims', *BBC News,* 15 May, viewed 3 June, 2016, http://www.bbc.com/news/technology-22283452

Kline, S 1995, 'The empire of play: emergent genres of product-based animations', in C Bazalgette and D Buckingham (eds.), *In Front of the Children: Screen Entertainment and Young Audiences,* British Film Institute, London.

Kline, S 1998, 'The Making of Children's Culture', in H Jenkins (ed.), *The Children's Culture Reader,* New York University, New York.

Kline, S 2005, 'Is is Time to Rethink Media Panics?', in J Qvortrup (ed.), *Studies in Modern Childhood: Society, Agency, Culture,* Palgrave MacMillan, Hampshire.

Knapton, S 2015, 'Oxford academics at war over dangers of the internet ', *The Telegraph,* 12 August, viewed 27 February 2018, http://www.telegraph.co.uk/news/science/science-news/11799022/Oxford-academics-at-war-over-dangers-of-the-internet.html

Krinsky, C (ed.) 2008, *Moral Panics over Contemporary Children and Youth,* Ashgate, Farnham.

Lansdown, G 2001, *Promoting Children's Participation in Democratic Decision-Making,* UNICEF Innocenti Research Centre, Florence.

Lealand, G and Zanker, R 2008, 'Pleasure, Excess and Self-Monitoring: The Media Worlds of New Zealand Children', *Media International Australia, Incorporating Culture & Policy,,* no. 126, pp. 43-53.

Leitch, R 2008, 'Creatively researching children's narratives through images and drawings', in P Thomson (ed.), *Doing Visual Research with Children and Young People,* Routledge, Oxon.

Lemish, D 2007, *Children and Television: A Global Perspective,* Blackwell Publishing, Malden, MA.

Levine, LW 1988, *Highbrow/Lowbrow: The Emergence of Cultural Hierarchy in America,* Harvard University Press, Cambridge, Mass.

Lewis, A and Lindsay, G (eds) 2000, *Researching children's perspectives,* Open University Press, Buckingham.

Lewis, J 1991, *The Ideological octopus: An Exploration of Television and its Audience,* Routledge, New York.

Lopez, KJ 2013, 'Innocence. Lost', *National Review Online,* 28 June, viewed 23 October 2015, http://www.nationalreview.com/corner/352318/innocence-lost-kathryn-jean-lopez

Luke, A and Luke, C 2001, 'Adolescence Lost/Childhood Regained: on Early Intervention and the Emergence of the Techno-Subject', *Journal of Early Childhood Research,* vol. 1, no. 1, pp. 91-120.

Lumby, C 1999, *Gotcha: life in a tabloid world,* Allen & Unwin, St Leonards, N.S.W.

Lumby, C and Funnell, N 2011, 'Between heat and light: The opportunity in moral panics', *Crime Media Culture,* vol. 7, no. 3, pp. 277-291.

Lundy, L 2007, "'Voice' Is Not Enough: Conceptualising Article 12 of the United

BIBLIOGRAPHY

Nations Convention on the Rights of the Child', *British Educational Research Journal,* vol. 33, no. 6, pp. 927-942.

Machell, B 2017, 'Screen junkies: kids addicted to technology', *The Australian,* 8 April, viewed 4 August 2017, http://www.theaustralian.com.au/life/weekend-australian-magazine/screen-junkies-kids-addicted-to-technology/news-story/0fd36c72590239abd98d94cc84847b76

Maher, I 2016, 'Kids addicted to screens? Here's how to unplug them', *Australian Financial Review,* viewed 31 August 2016, http://www.afr.com/technology/kids-addicted-to-screens-heres-how-to-unplug-them-20160821-gqxuth#ixzz4IrJ1J321

Markham, P 2015, 'Children addicted to television at age of two', *Daily Mail Australia,* 14 Sept, viewed 14 Sept 2015, http://www.dailymail.co.uk/news/article-96452/Children-addicted-television-age-two.html

Marsh, J 2004, 'The Techno-Literary Practices of Young Children', *Journal of Early Childhood Research,* vol. 2, no. 1.

Marsh, J 2005, 'Ritual, performance and identity construction: young children's engagement with popular cultural and media texts', in J Marsh (ed.), *Popular culture, new media and digital literacy in early childhood*, Routledge, Abingdon, Oxon.

Mayall, B 2008, 'Conversations with children: working with generational issues', in P Christensen and A James (eds.), *Research with children: perspectives and practices*, Routledge, Oxon.

McCain, R 2003, 'Neil Postman: Sceptical American critic of the internet, television and the information age', The Guardian, 4 November, viewed 23 April 2015, http://www.theguardian.com/news/2003/nov/04/guardianobituaries.usa

McKee, A 2008, 'Looking for fun in Cultural Science', *Cultural Science,* vol. 1, no. 2, pp. 1-12.

McKee, A, Collis, C and Hamley, B (eds) 2012, *Entertainment Industries: Entertainment as a Cultural System*, Routledge, Oxford.

McKee, A, Collis, C, Nitins, T, Ryan, M, Harrington, S, Duncan, B, Carter, J, Luck, E, Neale, L, Butler, D and Bachstrom, M 2014, 'Defining entertainment: an approach', *Creative Industries Journal,* 6 Oct 2014, http://dx.doi.org/10.1080/17510694.2014.962932

McNamara, J 2015, 'The Golden Age of Television', *ABR Online,* no. 370, April.

Meire, J 2007a, 'Qualitative Research on Children's Play: A Review of Recent Literature', *ICCP Brno Conference*, Brno.

Meire, J 2007b, 'Qualitative Research on Children's Play: A Review of Recent Literature', in T Jambor and J Van Gils (eds.), *Several Perspectives on Children's Play*, Garant, Antwerp.

Mentzer, R 2014, "'Thomas the Tank Engine' and other awful shows', *wausaudailyherald.com,* 26 November, viewed 26 January 2015, http://www.wausaudailyherald.com/story/opinion/2014/07/23/thomas-tank-engine-terrible-shows/13008905/

Messenger Davies, M 2010, *Children, Media and Culture*, Open University Press, Maidenhead, UK.

Murdock, G 2001, 'Reservoirs of dogma: an archaeology of popular anxieties', in M Barker and J Petley (eds.), *Ill Effects: The Media/Violence Debate*, 2nd edn, Routledge, Oxford.

Murray, J 1969, *The Box in the Corner*, Georgian House, Melbourne.

Murray, JP 2012, 'Children and media violence: Behavioural and neurological effects of viewing violence', in W Warburton and D Braunstein (eds.), *Growing Up Fast and Furious: Reviewing the Impacts of Violent and Sexualised Media on Children*, The Federation Press, Sydney.

News agencies 2014, 'Watching three hours of TV won't harm children but any longer could lead to bullying, study says', *The Telegraph*, 14 February, viewed 16 February 2015, http://www.telegraph.co.uk/health/children_shealth/10638574/Watching-three-hours-of-TV-wont-harm-children-but-any-longer-could-lead-to-bullying-study-says.html

Nussbaum, E 2014, 'Castles in the air', *The New Yorker*, 21 April, viewed 13 November 2014, http://www.newyorker.com/magazine/2014/04/21/castles-in-the-air

Oliver, R 1998, 'The Teletubby takeover', *The Sydney Morning Herald*, 9 February, viewed 29 November 2013, http://newsstore.smh.com.au/apps/viewDocument.ac?page=1&sy=smh&kw=Andrew+and+Medhurst+and+Teletubbies&pb=smh&dt=selectRange&dr=entire&so=relevance&sf=text&sf=headline&rc=10&rm=200&sp=nrm&clsPage=1&docID=news980209_0944_8997

Palmer, P 1986, *The Lively Audience: A Study of Children around the TV Set*, Allen & Unwin, Sydney.

Parnell, K 2016, 'The 10 kids' TV shows more painful than childbirth', *The Daily Telegraph*, 10 January, viewed 10 May 2016, http://www.dailytelegraph.com.au/rendezview/10-kids-tv-shows-obviously-created-to-torment-parents/news-story/8207021d1fc928206cf069ce6afe5219

Pearson, G 1983, *Hooligan: A History of Respectable Fears*, Macmillan, London.

Petley, J 2001, 'Us and them', in M Barker and J Petley (eds.), *Ill Effects: The Media/Violence Debate*, 2nd edn, Routledge, London.

Piaget, J 1964, *The Child's Conception of the World*, Routledge and Kegan Paul, London.

Plato 1948, *The Republic*, AD Lindsay, J.M. Dent & Sons Ltd, London.

Postman, N 1985, *The disappearance of childhood: how TV is changing children's lives*, W.H. Allen & Co., London.

Postman, N 2006, *Amusing Ourselves to Death: Public Discourse in the Age of Show Business*, 20th anniversary edn, Penguin, New York.

Prout, A 2000, 'Children's participation: control and self-realisation in British late modernity', *Children & Society*, vol. 14, no. 4, pp. 304-315.

Prout, A 2005, *The Future of Childhood: Towards the Interdisciplinary Study of Children*, RoutledgeFalmer, London.

Putnam, RD 2001, *Bowling Alone: The Collapse and Revival of American Community*, Simon & Schuster Paperbacks, New York.

Radway, JA 1991, *Reading the romance: women, patriarchy and popular literature*, University of North Carolina Press, Chapel Hill.

BIBLIOGRAPHY

Rich, M 2014, 'Foreword', in DA Gentile (ed.), *Media violence and children: a complete guide for parents and professionals*, 2nd edn, Praeger, California.

Richards, C 1995, 'Room to Dance: Girls' Play and 'The Little Mermaid'', in C Bazalgette and D Buckingham (eds.), *In Front of the Children: Screen Entertainment and Young Audiences*, British Film Institute, London.

Riley, NS 2017, 'Kids TV shows push cultural limits – but they're damaging kids', *New York Post*, 19 March, viewed 4 August 2017,

Rivett, G 2014, 'Neuroscientist Susan Greenfield warns young brains being re-wired by digital technology', *ABC News*, 20 November, viewed 31 August 2016, http://www.abc.net.au/news/2014-11-20/neuroscientist-warns-young-brains-being-reshaped-by-technology/5906140

Roberts, S and Howard, S 2005, 'Watching Teletubbies: Television and its very young audience', in J Marsh (ed.), *Popular Culture, New Media and Digital Literacy in Early Childhood*, Routledge, Abingdon, Oxon.

Robinson, M 1997, *Children Reading Print and Television*, Falmer Press, London.

Robinson, M and Turnbull, B 2005, 'Verónica: an asset model of becoming literate', in J Marsh (ed.), *Popular culture, new media and digital literacy in early childhood*, Routledge, Abingdon, Oxon.

Rosin, H 1999, 'A 'Tubby' Ache For Jerry Falwell', *The Washington Post*, 11 February, viewed 23 October 2015, http://www.washingtonpost.com/wp-srv/style/tv/features/falwellteletubbies.htm

Rousseau, JJ 1969, *Émile*, B Foxley, (Trans.), J. M. Dent & Sons Ltd, London.

Salomon, G 1984, 'Television Is "Easy" and Print Is "Tough": The Differential Investment of Mental Effort in Learning as a Function of Perceptions and Attributions', *Journal of Educational Psychology*, vol. 76, no. 4, pp. 647-58.

Sanghavi, D 2012, 'Are TV and Video Games Making Kids Fat?', *Slate*, 13 April, viewed 6 August 2017, http://www.slate.com/articles/health_and_science/medical_examiner/2012/04/are_video_games_making_kids_fat_screen_time_and_childhood_obesity_.html

Sefton-Green, J 1993, 'Untidy, depressing and violent: a boy's own story', in D Buckingham (ed.), *Reading audiences: young people and the media*, Manchester University Press, Manchester.

Seiter, E 1998, 'Children's Desires/Mothers' Dilemmas: The Social Contexts of Consumption', in H Jenkins (ed.), *The Children's Culture Reader*, New York University Press, New York.

Seiter, E 1999a, 'Power Rangers at Preschool: Negotiating Media in Child Care Settings', in M Kinder (ed.), *Kids' Media Culture*, Duke University Press, Durham.

Seiter, E 1999b, *Television and New Media Audiences*, Clarendon Press, Oxford.

Sheldon, L 1998, 'The Middle Years: children and television - cool or just plain boring?', in S Howard (ed.), *Wired-Up: Young People and the Electronic Media*, UCL Press, London.

Sheldon, L and Loncar, M 1996, *Kids Talk TV: 'super wickid' or 'dum'*, Australian Broadcasting Authority, Sydney.

Solberg, A 1990, 'Negotiating Childhood: Changing Constructions of Age for Norwegian Children', in A James and A Prout (eds.), *Constructing and Reconstructing Childhood: Contemporary Issues in the Sociological Study of Childhood*, The Falmer Press, London.

Spigel, L 1998, 'Seducing the Innocent: Childhood and Television in Postwar America', in H Jenkins (ed.), *The Children's Culture Reader*, New York University Press, New York.

Spohr, M 2015, '19 Incredibly Annoying Characters On Kids' TV Shows', *BuzzFeed*, 3 March, viewed 10 May 2015, https://www.buzzfeed.com/mikespohr/the-definitive-ranking-of-the-most-annoying-characters-on-ki?utm_term=.djy3eVq3E#.eqm2VNq21

Steiner, GA 1963, *The people look at television: a study of audience attitudes*, Knopf, New York.

Sutton-Smith, B 1997, *The Ambiguity of Play*, Harvard University Press, Cambridge, Mass.

Sutton-Smith, B 2008, 'Play Theory: A Personal Journey and New thoughts', *American Journal of Play*, vol. 1, no. 1, pp. 82-125.

Thompson, K 1998, *Moral panics*, Routledge, London.

Thomson, P 2008a, 'Children and young people: voices in visual research', in P Thomson (ed.), *Doing Visual Research with Children and Young People*, Routledge, Oxon.

Thomson, P (ed.) 2008b, *Doing Visual Research with Children and Young People*, Routledge, Oxon.

Turnbull, S 2001, 'Once more with feeling: talking about the media violence debate in Australia', in M Barker and J Petley (eds.), *Ill Effects: The Media/Violence Debate*, 2nd edn, Routledge, Oxford.

Valkenburg, PM and Calvert, SL 2012, 'Media and the Child's Developing Imagination', in DG Singer and JL Singer (eds.), *Handbook of Children and the Media*, SAGE, California.

Valkenburg, PM and Van Der Voort, THA 1994, 'Influence of TV on Daydreaming and Creative Imagination: A Review of Research', *Psychological Bulletin*, vol. 116, no. 2, pp. 316-339.

Vom Orde, H 2008, 'Children, television and emotions', *Media Psychology*, vol. 1, no. 2, pp. 97-116.

Vonow, B 2012, 'More children need glasses from hours glued to TV', *Courier Mail*, 12 March, viewed 15 March 2015, http://www.couriermail.com.au/lifestyle/parenting/more-children-need-glasses-from-hours-glued-to-tv/story-e6frer7o-1226296367941?nk=970172d7ea167b92c76c9fc28813a335

Walkerdine, V 1989, 'Video replay: families, films and fantasy', in V Burgin, J Donald and C Kaplan (eds.), *Formations of fantasy*, Routledge, London.

Warburton, W and Braunstein, D (eds) 2012, *Growing Up Fast and Furious: Reviewing the Impacts of Violent and Sexualised Media on Children*, The Federation Press, Sydney.

Willett, R 2015, 'Children's Media-referenced Games: The Lived Culture of Consumer Texts on a School Playground', *Children & Society*, vol. 29, no. 5, pp. 410-420.

BIBLIOGRAPHY

Williams, R 1989, 'Drama in a dramatised society', in A O'connor (ed.), *Raymond Williams on television: selected writings*, Routledge, New York.

Winn, M 1985, *The Plug-in Drug*, Viking Press, New York.

Wober, M and Gunter, B 1982, 'Television and personal threat: fact or artifact? A British survey', *British Journal of Social Psychology*, vol. 21, no. 3, pp. 239-247.

Wolfenstein, M 1998, 'Fun Morality: An Analysis of Recent American Child-Training Literature', in H Jenkins (ed.), *The Children's Culture Reader*, New York University Press, New York.

Yapp, R 2014, 'Children who watch too much TV may have 'damaged brain structures'', *Daily Mail Australia*, 11 January, viewed 27 November 2014, http://www.dailymail.co.uk/health/article-2537240/Children-watch-TV-damaged-brain-structures.html#ixzz3KE0IoArY

Zipes, J 2013, *Happily ever after: Fairy tales, children, and the culture industry*, Taylor and Francis, Hoboken.

INDEX

ABC Kids, 123
ABC3, 165
action, 21, 24, 25, 109, 123, 124, 136, 143-6, 149, 178-9, 244-5, 258-9, 275
adult secrets, 14, 46, 57, 65-72, 108, 117, 136, 137, 195, 197, 205, 216-7
adventure, 143, 255
Adventure Time, 116, 122, 250-60, 273
Amazing World of Gumball, The, 230
Amusing Ourselves to Death, 35, 40
Anderson, Daniel, 182
Anderson, DR and Bryant, J, 200
Anderson, DR et al., 16, 107
Ang, Ien, 29, 202
Angry Boys, 206
Angry Girls, 243
Ariès, Philippe, 47
    concept of family, 67
    education and pleasure, 48, 60
    modern culture of childhood, 43-46
    obsession with childhood, 67
Arizpe, E and Styles, M, 37
Arthur, Leonie, 62, 63
audiences, 23, 26, 29-30, 32, 202
    and TV, 15-19, 96, 150-1, 179
    and entertainment, 233, 238, 261, 268-9, 275
    as experts on TV, 30-1
    children as, 109, 232
    parents and children as, 200, 203
    passive and indifferent, 27-9
    research with, 32, 41, 202-3
Australian Broadcasting Authority, 236
Australian Broadcasting Corporation (ABC), 128, 130, 243
Australian Communications and Media Authority (ACMA), 14, 65, 66, 114, 207, 281
Australian Financial Review, The, ix

Australian Senate Committee report (1978), 33
Australian, The, 128
Bachelor, The, 103
Bad Education, 116
Bandura, Albert, 36
Barker, J and Weller, S, 278, 279, 283
Barker, Leslie, 1
Barker, M and Brooks, K, 32, 41, 98, 107, 136, 143, 146, 150, 152, 211, 232
    fandom and practices of pleasure, 109-110
Barker, M and Petley, J, 3, 29, 32, 40, 127
Barker, J and Weller, S, 278, 279-80, 283
Barker, Martin, 9, 10, 11, 211
Barthes, Roland, 10, 34, 72
Bartsch, Anne, 96-7
Batman, 107
Bazalgette, C and Buckingham, D, 42, 94, 127
BBC News, 128
Bell, Vaughan, 128
Big Bang Theory, The, 105
Big Brother, 35, 47, 103, 105, 238, 270
Bishop, Dorothy, 128
Block, The, 105
Blue Peter, 133
Bonner, Frances, 98, 107
Bourdieu, Pierre, 56, 59, 63
Bowling Alone, 233
Boy Scouts, 51
Bragg, S and Buckingham, D, 286, 287
Bragg, S, Buckingham, D and Turnbull, S, 60
Bragg, Sara, 59, 220, 287
brain, TV's effects on, 1, 16, 20, 27, 121, 126-9, 131, 185

Breaking Bad, 103
bro'Town, 199
Bromley, Helen, 37
Browne, Rachel, 1, 127
Bryant, Martin, 9, 14
Buckingham, D and De Block, L, 33
Buckingham, D and Jensen, HS, 12
Buckingham, David, xi, 2, 24, 26, 51, 60, 61, 64, 71, 76, 112, 131, 163, 187, 197, 198, 203, 279
   children, TV and emotions, 15, 32, 64, 77, 93-4, 101-2, 123, 129, 253
   children, TV and social relations, 97, 113, 136, 164-6, 176, 177, 180-1, 220-1
   listening to children, 13, 33, 38, 78, 117
   moral panics, 9-12
   negative effects of TV, 4-5, 7-8, 16-8, 20, 21, 40, 75, 211
   parents regulating TV, 65, 68, 118-9, 199, 207-8, 212, 223-4, 226
   taste in TV, 220
   TV, pleasure and education, 120, 132, 205, 262
Bulger, James, 9-11, 14
Burghardt, Gordon, 80, 82
Burns, Judith, 131
Bushman, BJ and Anderson, CA, 8, 12
Campbell, David, 14, 56, 61, 62
Carnagey, NL, Anderson, CA and Bartholow, BD, 16
Carnegie, Dale, 52
Cartoon Network, 257
cartoons, 23-6, 56, 61, 71, 107, 225, 230, 274
Center on Media for Child Health, 106
Centuries of Childhood, 44
Child's Play 3, 9
childhood, 119, 182
   and education, 47-9, 58-9, 64, 120
   controlling pleasures of, 44-6, 66-71, 77, 80, 137
   history of, 43-52, 67
   innocence of, 11, 44-5, 47, 49, 57, 63, 73-4, 93
   regulation of leisure in, 51, 82, 86-7
   sexualisation of, 67-8, 72-5, 135-6
   western notion of, 14, 42, 63
Children Reading Pictures, 37
Children Reading Print and Television, 37
Children Talking Television, 220
comics, 4
computers, 1, 209, 212, 282-3
Comstock, GA and Scharrer, E, 8, 17, 106-7, 200
   children, violence and TV, 25-6
   passive TV audience, 27-30, 34, 152, 228, 271
Corsaro, William, 88, 186, 221
creativity, 15, 31, 33-42
Crockett, Zachary, 72
Cupitt, Margaret, 114, 207-8
Daily Mail Australia, 33, 61, 127
Daily Telegraph, The, 61
Davies, H, Buckingham, D and Kelley, P, 78, 202, 227
   children's taste in TV, 7, 56-7
   children, TV and humour, 42, 83, 89, 111, 122, 218, 221, 225
Davies, Máire, 51
   on education and TV, 47, 60, 61, 107
   on TV and fun, 85, 94, 103, 133
   on TV as a threat, 89
   research with children, 89, 117, 120, 122, 132
   social use of TV, 111, 123, 232
De Botton, Alain, 52, 53
De Certeau, Michel, 77
Deary, Terry, 223
Dickens, Charles, 82, 137
Disney, 9, 102
Disney Channel, 99
Dockrell, J, Lewis, A and Lindsay, G, 285
Donald, James, 48-50, 55, 58-9, 77-8
Donnelly, Kevin, 128
Dora the Explorer, 107
drama, 35, 57, 60, 105, 138, 146, 151, 232, 245, 268
Drotner, Kirsten, 98-9, 105, 106, 183, 192
Dyer, Richard, xi
   on entertainment, 100-102, 233

INDEX

entertainment and happiness, 214, 265
entertainment and sensibility, 129, 249
feel of utopia, 154, 162, 196, 229, 246, 255-6, 274-5
unruly delight, 193, 203, 262-3, 273
EastEnders, 205, 262
education and television, 47, 51, 55-6, 58-64, 70-1, 89, 106-7, 116, 118-21, 185-6, 200, 240
Émile, 45-6
Endemol, 105
entertainment, 69, 71, 99, 231-3, 238, 240
    academic research into, xvii, 90, 95, 98, 100, 102, 109
    and adult secrets, 70, 224
    and education, 47, 51, 58, 213
    and happiness and utopia, xvi, 101, 196, 256, 263, 265
    and pleasure, unruly delight and sensibility, 101, 129, 162, 203, 249, 261, 262
    and TV, xv, 105, 107, 179, 208
    business investment in, 101
    negative effects of, 4, 6, 11, 35, 39, 102, 137, 213, 215
eyes, TV effects on, 121, 126, 127, 129, 130
family, 49, 76, 79, 161-3, 179, 229, 238-240, 245
    and conflict around TV, 119, 207-8, 212-7
    Ariès concept of, 67
    public sphere invading private, 68
    sharing TV viewing, 89, 97, 151-2, 155, 159, 198, 202
fandom, 41, 107-10, 143
fantasy, 23-4, 39-41, 147, 149, 229, 255-8
Faulkner, Joanne, 78-9
    children as media experts, 66
    on innocence of childhood, 11, 66-8
    sexualisation of the child, 73-5
Faulkner, Katherine, 61
Fiske, J and Hartley, J, 26

Fiske, John, 225
Flaubert, Gustave, 137
Fleer, Marilyn, 83
Flewitt, Rosie, 285
Fonseca, Adam, 3
France, J, Bendelow, G and Williams, S, 284
Friends, 116
Game of Thrones, 103
Gardner, Amanda, 131, 197
Gauntlett, D and Hill, A, 54
Gauntlett, David, 13, 23, 28, 32, 33
    attitudes to popular culture, 4, 6
    children and TV, 36-8, 40
    on media effects, 16, 18-9, 22
    on moral panics, 11
    violence on TV, 25-6
Gentile, Douglas, 8, 127
Gerbner, G et al., 8
Gerbner, G and Gross, L, 23, 26, 31, 137, 138
    TV's hypnotic effect, 234
Gerbner, George, 1, 8,
    on cartoons, 61
    on media effects, 16, 26, 28, 30,
    on violence and TV, 22-23, 106, 127
Giles, Fiona, xi
Gillard, Patricia, 183, 198
Girl Scouts, 51
Gitlin, Todd, 107
Glenn, NM et al., 84, 85
Globe, The, 271, 273
Gomez, Selena, 167
Götz, M et al. (2005), 13, 33, 38
    children, TV and imagination, 40-1
    children, TV and social relations, 177, 180, 258
    fun, threat and excitement, 103, 147-9, 179, 260
    make-believe worlds, 111, 147, 170
Götz, M et al. (2006), 42, 89, 103
Götz, Maya, 264
Gray, Jonathan, 107, 213, 215, 216
Great Expectations, 82
Greenblatt, Stephen, 270
Greenfield, Susan, 128
Gregg, Melissa, 52-3

Hagerman, Margaret, 279, 282, 284, 285
Hall, Stuart, 152
happiness, 68, 88, 135-6, 162, 196, 214, 262-5
Hartley, John, xi, 3, 16
   cultural hierarchies, 6-7, 17, 31, 36, 38, 103
   desire/fear divide over TV, 14-5, 30
   guilt and TV, 55, 214-5
   on Shakespeare, 47, 102, 105, 238, 270
   TV reflecting life, 105-6, 231, 238, 240, 245, 247-8, 267
   TV's appeal, 31, 47, 104-5, 181-2, 233
   TV's private pleasures, 97-8, 107-8, 112, 152, 192
   TV's tactile power, 139-40
Havisham, Miss, 82, 89
Hawkes, Terence, xi, 139, 270
   on TV and reading, 147
   TV and society, 105, 138
   TV, theatre and audiences, 47, 136, 146, 150-1, 155, 163, 179, 211, 232-3, 268
   TV as part of life, 237, 257, 273
   TV's universality, 146, 158, 164
Hayes, A and Jean, C, 19
Henderson, Emma, 2
Herald Sun, 56
Hickman, Leo, 223
Higonnet, Anne, 45, 67, 74, 78
Himmelweit, H, Oppenheim, AN and Vince, P, 16, 19-21
Hipsley, Anna, 130
Hodge, B and Tripp, D, 16, 21, 23, 75-6
   on cartoons, 24
   on children's imaginations, 33
   on TV and education, 59, 64, 114
Hollywood, 5, 7, 99, 238
Horrible Histories, 192, 200, 203, 217, 222-4
How to Win Friends and Influence People, 52
Howard, S and Roberts, S, 62, 78
   on *Teletubbies*, 42, 61, 88, 142

pleasure of TV for toddlers, 72, 88, 94, 142-4, 149
Howard, Sue, 29, 237-8
humour, 42, 83, 89, 111, 122, 218-233
   and children's bad taste, 196, 201, 218, 220-1, 225-7
   and children, parents and TV, 185, 192, 197-208
Ice Age, 172
Idato, Michael, 70
imagination, xv, 15, 31, 33-42, 147, 158, 255, 257-8, 272, 273
   and play, 80, 88
Incredibles, The, 160-1, 163
Independent, 2
Inside Prime Time, 107
Isenberg, JP and Quisenberry, N, 81
internet, 65, 66, 128, 247,
Ja'mie: Private School Girl, 206, 241-8
James, A and James, A, 88
James, A, Jenks, C and Prout, A, 82-3, 87, 103, 104
James, Allison, 83
Jenkins, Henry, 7, 224, 249, 252-3
   on childhood, 46, 49
   on entertainment, 263
   on fandom, 32, 41, 108-10, 158
Johns, Lindsay, 33
Jonah from Tonga, 206, 247
Judge Dredd, 109
Keeping Up with the Kardashians, 103
Kids' Media Culture, 177
Kincaid, James, 87
   on children and happiness, 68, 88, 136, 274
   sexualisation of the child, 73, 136
Kinder, Marsha, 177
Kirkorian, HL, Wartella, EA and Anderson, DR, 182
Kleinman, Zoe, 128
Kline, Stephen, 12, 38, 50, 81
Knapton, Sarah, 128
Krinsky, Charles, 11
Lansdown, Gerison, 190
Lealand, G and Zanker, R, 60, 76, 77, 114, 184, 192, 198-9, 221
learning from television, 105-6, 109,

INDEX

120, 123, 181, 193, 232, 237-249, 275
Leavisites, 58
Leitch, Ruth, 277, 279, 288
Lemish, Dafna, 38
Lesser, Harvey, 36
Levine, Lawrence, 102
Lewis, A and Lindsay, G, 285, 288
Lewis, Justin, 97
Life With Boys, 227, 228
Lilley, Chris, 206-7, 208, 217, 238, 242-4, 246-8, 268
Lion King, The, 9
Lopez, Kathryn, 70
Luke, A and Luke C, 66
Lumby, C and Funnell, N, 12-3
Lumby, Catharine, xi, 68-9
Lundy, Laura, 286
Machell, Ben, 1
Macquarie University, xi
Magic Mountain, xiii
Maher, Irene, ix, 2
make-believe, 147, 149, 170, 179, 258, 260, 273
Markham, Peter, 2
Marsh, Jackie, 62, 66, 181
Mayall, Berry, 285, 286
McCain, Robert, 39
McKee, A et al., 100, 101, 125, 261
McKee, A, Collis, C and Hamley, B, 100, 240
McKee, Alan, xi,
    on fun and entertainment, 99-100, 182, 263
McNamara, James, 35, 56, 103
Meire, Johan, 85, 88, 89, 176
Mentzer, Robert, 56, 198, 227
Midsummer Night's Dream, A, 269
Miss Havisham, 82, 89
Mister Rogers' Neighborhood, 106-7
Modern Family, 238-9
Monsters Inc, 156-7
moral panics, 9-13, 24, 211
Moving Images, 94-5
Mr Bean, 225
Muppets, 70
Murdock, Graham, 4, 7, 11, 17-8
Murray, John, 2

Murray, John P, 20
musicals, 101
My Kitchen Rules, 105, 151
myths, 10, 34, 72-80, 85, 87, 211
narrative, 25, 35-37, 51, 62-3, 147, 156, 164, 241, 260
National Review Online, 70
Neighbours, 133
New York Post, The, ix
New Yorker, The, 69-70, 117
Nickelodeon, 99
novels, 4,
Nussbaum, Emily, 117
Octonauts, The, 218-9
obesity, 3, 5, 87
Oliver, Robin, 72
opera, 102
Oxford University, 128
Palmer, Patricia, xi, 153, 234, 244
    on children learning from TV, 111, 120, 229, 237-8, 241
    children, TV and fun, 85, 89, 94, 103, 111, 122
    children, TV and social relations, 164, 171, 177, 240
    children's TV favourites, 129-30, 132
    physical excitement and TV, 141
    research with children, 2, 184, 260, 284
parents, x- xvi, 8-9
    denigrating children's taste in TV, 55-7, 197-8, 226-7
    regulating TV for children, 13-4, 65-6, 68, 73, 75-9, 114, 118-9, 185, 207-8, 212-3, 223-4
    enjoying TV with children, 192, 195, 197-207
Parents Magazine, 57, 198
Parnell, Kerry, 198
passivity, 14, 27-9, 33-4, 51, 54, 141, 142
Peppa Pig, 14, 61-2, 63
Petley, Julian, 4-6, 131
physical engagement with TV, 136, 140-50, 271
Piaget, Jean, 82
Plato, 4

play, 24-5, 39-41, 45, 50, 52, 54, 80-91, 103, 140, 146
   and TV, 177-182, 252, 255-6
pleasure, 46, 215
   and childhood, 46-9
   and fandom, 107, 108-110
   and play, 86, 90
   children and TV, xv, xviii, 2, 8, 13, 21, 41-2, 76, 79-80, 93-6, 122-3, 125, 132
   fear of children's pleasure, 14, 36, 42-3, 55, 61-3, 106, 118-9, 135
   in entertainment, 100-2
   parents control over children's TV pleasures, ix, x, xiv, 65-73, 77, 117
   protecting children from, 44-7, 58-9
   versus education and work, 50-5, 60, 64, 116
Plug-in Drug, The, 1, 34, 39, 141
popular culture, 32, 47, 53, 77-8, 184, 192, 199
   academic research into, 108
   and bad taste, 55, 59
   and education, 58-65, 78, 79, 114, 116, 120
   effects on the 'other' of, 5-6
   historic attitudes to, 3-7, 55, 102-3
   negative views of, 6-7, 31, 38, 42, 55, 59, 69, 76, 89, 93
Port Arthur, 9
Postman, Neil, 34-5, 38, 39, 107, 137-8, 147, 182
Potter, Harry, 123
Prout, Alan, 48, 79, 104
Przybylski, Andrew, 128
Putnam, Robert, 233, 271
Radway, Janice, 54
reading and television, 33-41, 147, 213, 233, 235
Reith, John, 58
Rich, Michael, 107
Richards, Chris, 140-1, 152, 154-5, 199
Riley, Naomi, ix
Rivett, Gary, 128
Roberts, S and Howard, S, 78
Robinson, M and Turnbull, B, 62
Robinson, Muriel, 37, 62-3

Rocky, 192, 209, 212, 213
Rocky 6, 209, 212
Rosin, Hanna, 72
Rousseau, Jean-Jacques, 45-6
Salomon, Gavriel, 34, 35, 38, 39
Sam & Cat, 230, 231
Scream, 123
Sefton-Green, Julian, 181
Seinfeld, 185-6, 192, 204-6, 208, 217, 263-5
Seiter, Ellen, 51, 59, 60, 61, 64, 66, 104, 114, 117, 190, 223, 225-6
Sentimental Education, 48
Sesame Street, xiv, xvii, xviii, 51, 61, 69-71, 106, 133, 240
Sesame Workshop, 70
sexualisation of the child, 72-5, 135
Shakespeare, William, 47, 102, 103, 105, 185, 238, 267-72, 275-6
Sheldon, L and Loncar, M, 85, 221, 223
Sheldon, Linda, 234, 236
SheZow, 216
Silver Brumby, The, 157
Simpsons, The, 111, 232
Singer, Jerome, 36
smartphones, 1, 2, 65
soap opera, 106, 205, 262
Solberg, Anne, 104
Sound of Music, The, 9
Spigel, Lynn, 7, 51, 57, 67, 68, 82, 198, 224
Spohr, Mike, 198, 226
Star Trek, 198
Star Wars Lego, 143
Star Wars: The Clone Wars, 143
Steiner, Gary, 54-5
Summer Heights High, 206, 238
Superman, 107
Sutton-Smith, Brian, 81, 88, 90
Sydney Morning Herald, The, 127
Sydney University, 130
tablets, electronic, 1, 2
Taming of the Shrew, 47, 105, 270
taste, xvii
   and popular culture, 6-7, 55-9
   as arbiter of social distinction, 56, 59, 220, 226-7

INDEX

and Shakespeare, 270
children's taste in TV, 7, 55-7, 196, 201, 218, 220, 226-7
Tattoo Nightmares, 204, 208
technology, 1, 51, 52, 128, 138, 281
Telegraph, The, 128
Teletubbies, xiii, xiv, xvii, 42, 51, 61, 71, 88, 142
Tempest, The, 267-8
theatre, 5, 102, 136, 138, 146, 151, 268, 269, 272, 273
Theorizing Childhood, 104
Thompson, Kenneth, 10-11
Thompson, Robert, 14
Thomson, Pat, 286-7
Tom and Jerry, 23-4
Turgenev, Ivan, 137
Turnbull, Sue, xi, 9
Twelfth Night, 274, 276
United Kingdom,
and child poverty, 48
education and popular culture, 64
historical attitudes to popular media, 4
television, xiii, 42, 61, 117, 142, 200, 203, 205, 218
United Nations Committee on the Rights of the Child, 86, 182
United Nations Convention on the Rights of the Child (CRC), 86, 182, 286, 288
United States, 15, 64
Constitution's Fifth Amendment, 69
criticism of American television, x, 23-4, 59, 99, 102
cultural hierarchies in, 102
movies, 123, 156, 172,
Supreme Court, 69
television, 61, 105, 109, 111, 117, 143, 144, 167, 178, 185, 231, 238, 250
uses and gratifications theory, 96-7
Uses of Television, The, 104
utopia, 101, 154, 162, 196, 214, 246, 249, 255-6, 274-5
Valkenburg, P and Calvert, S, 34
Valkenburg, P and Van der Voort, T, 39

Venables, Jon, 14
violence on television, 14-26, 126-7
and cartoons, 23-4, 26, 71
and changing behaviour debate, 12-4, 106
changing brains, 127-8
damaging effects of, 2-4, 30, 210, 212
regulating children's viewing of, 66-8, 117
Vom Orde, Heike, 96
Vonow, Brittany, 130
Walkerdine, Valerie, 117
Warburton, W and Braunstein, D, 12, 16, 127
We Can Be Heroes, 201
Westinghouse television, 137
Willett, Rebekah, xi, 95-6, 180
Williams, Raymond, 138-140
Winn, Marie, 1, 34-5, 38-9, 107, 141, 142, 152, 182, 253, 271
Wizards of Waverly Place, 167
Wober, M and Gunter, B, 22
Wolfenstein, Martha, 7, 67
Woods, Anne, 71
Work's Intimacy, 52
World's Craziest Fools, 209-10, 226
Yapp, Robin, 127, 131
YooHoo & Friends, 166-9, 171-3, 177, 181, 190-1, 227
You've Been Framed, 225
Young Justice, 144-5, 178, 216
Zipes, Jack, 35-6